MODERNISM AT MID-CENTURY

Edited by Robert Bruegmann

Modernism at Mid-Century

THE ARCHITECTURE OF THE UNITED STATES AIR FORCE ACADEMY

The University of Chicago Press
Chicago and London

Library of Congress Cataloging-in-Publication Data

Modernism at mid-century : the architecture of the United States Air Force Academy / edited by Robert Bruegmann.

p. cm.

Includes bibliographical references.

1. United States Air Force Academy--Buildings. 2. Skidmore, Owings & Merrill--Criticism and interpretation. 3. Architecture, Modern--20th century--Colorado--Colorado Springs. 4. Colorado Springs (Colo.)--Buildings, structures, etc. I. Bruegmann, Robert.

NA6610.C66U546 1994

727' .3' 0978856--dc20 94-21222

The University of Chicago Press, Chicago 60637

The University of Chicago Press, Ltd., London

Printed in the United States of America

03 02 01 00 99 98 97 96 95 94 1 2 3 4 5

ISBN: 0-226-07693-8 (cloth)

0-226-07694-6 (paper)

Front and back matter captions

Page 1: view of Dining Hall. Photograph by Hedrich-Blessing, 1959. Courtesy of Chicago Historical society. Page 2: view of Chapel ceiling under construction. Photograph by Skidmore, Owings & Merrill, c.1961. Page 3: view of Chapel ceiling as completed. Photograph by Elizabeth Gill Lui, 1986. All of the Lui photographs in this book were taken as part of a commission by the USAFA Association of Graduates. Frontispiece (page 4): view of Chapel. Photograph by Elizabeth Gill Lui, 1986. Page 10: view of Academy. Photograph by Hedrich-Blessing, 1986. Page 13: final rendered site plan of Cadet Area. Drawing by Skidmore, Owings & Merrill, c.1954-55. Page 200: view of "Give Me Men Ramp." Photograph by Elizabeth Gill Lui, 1986.

MODERNISM AT MID-CENTURY

Designed by Lorraine Wild/ReVerb

Composed by Chris Haaga in Meta type, Bodoni type, Memphis type, and Futura type.

Printed by Donahue Printing, Los Angeles, CA on 80# Patina Matte.

Bound by Roswell Book Bindery in Gane's Army Weave Dixie canvas.

∞ The paper used in this publication meets the minimum requirements of the American National Standard for Information Sciences—Permanence of Paper for Printed Library Materials, ANSI Z39.48-1984.

CONTENTS

CONTRIBUTORS

Robert Bruegmann is professor of architectural history at the University of Illinois at Chicago. He has written extensively about modern architecture, urbanism, and landscape and has contributed criticism to the journal *Inland Architect*.

Jory Johnson is a landscape architect on the faculty of the University of Illinois at Urbana-Champaign. He has written criticism of contemporary landscape design and is the author, with Felice Frankel, of the book *Modern Landscape Architecture: Redefining the Garden*, published in 1991.

Robert Nauman is an art historian who teaches at the University of Colorado, Denver, and is finishing a doctorate at the University of New Mexico, Albuquerque.

Sheri Olson has architecture degrees from the University of Arizona and Columbia University. She practices architecture in New York with the firm of Klinkon Olson Architects and has taught at the University of Texas at Austin and at Ball State University.

James Russell has a Master's degree in architecture from Columbia University. He has practiced architecture in Philadelphia and New York and is currently a managing senior editor at *Architectural Record* magazine in New York.

Kristen Schaffer is an architectural historian and an assistant professor in the School of Architecture at Syracuse University. She has worked on master planning and space programming at Cannon Design, Inc., in Buffalo and has written the introduction to the reprint of the *Plan of Chicago* published by the Princeton Architecture Press in 1993.

ACKNOWLEDGMENTS

The authors of this volume would like to thank the many individuals who provided invaluable help during the preparation of the book. The first individual on this list must be Bradley Hosmer, Lt. Gen. USAF, Superintendent of the Academy from 1991 through 1994, who had the idea to create this book, and who assured cooperation from the Air Force during its preparation. Also from the Academy, we would like to thank: Archivist Duane Reed, who was unfailingly helpful with our searches for material in the Academy's Special Collections; Association of Graduates Executive Vice President Richard Coppock, who gave advice and encouragement; and Architect Duane Boyle who, charged with overseeing the preparation of the book from the Academy's side, made it a personal crusade. From the firm of Skidmore, Owings & Merrill, which was entrusted with overseeing contractual arrangements for the book and securing illustrations, the following should be mentioned: Marilyn Taylor, partner in charge, who provided us with encouragement but allowed us a free hand; Michael Keselica in New York, who saw through the delicate negotiations that made the book possible; Mary Konsoulis in Washington, who was instrumental in shaping the appearance of the book; Pat Gorman, Michelle Grunau, and John Ravitch in Chicago, all of whom helped track down the images we needed. From the University of Chicago Press we would like to thank Karen Wilson, Senior Editor, who was willing to take a gamble on an unorthodox book with too little time and too many participants, and John McCudden, whose deft hand performed essential corrections on the text. Designer Lorraine Wild brought a genuine interest in the topic and remarkable visual acuity to the project. Other individuals who provided help include, from the National Park Service Air Force Project: Kirk Cordell in Atlanta; from the United States Navy: Louis Wall, Coordinator of Cultural Resources for the West Coast Region; from the National Archives, Rocky Mountain Region: Eileen Bolger; at MIT Archivist Helen Samuels; Col. Stephen F. Noonan (Ret.), formerly of the Air Force Construction Agency, who recalled his work during the construction of the Academy; Sarah Ksiazek, who shared with us her research on Louis Kahn, architecture, and American society in the 1950s; Fred Merrill, who lent a scrapbook compiled by his father, Edward Merrill; John Burchard, who allowed us to reproduce the conversation between his father and Walter Netsch; Kevin Roche, who provided information on Eero Saarinen; and Rod Dresser of the Taliesin Foundation. Also helpful were former SOM employees Gertrude Lempp Kerbis, Louis Rocah, Stanley Allan, Jack Hartray, Roger Margerum, Ken Naslund, Mitsuru Otsuji, Ralph Youngren, Albert Lockett, and Jack Train, all of whom shared their recollections with us. For their help in securing images, we would like to thank William Garnett; Balthazar Korab; Julius Shulman; Mary Davis of the Pikes Peak Library District; Sheila Maselli of ESTO; Jack Hedrich, Mike Houlahan and Kathleen Economon of Hedrich-Blessing; and Larry Viskochil and Eileen Flanagan of the Chicago Historical Society. We would also like to thank Fannia Weingartner, who did a heroic job of substantive editing of the book; Dan Kiley, who delighted us with his recollections; and last, but not least, Walter Netsch, who was always ready with information and advice. Finally, as editor, I would like especially to thank the essayists in this volume, Kristen Schaffer, Jory Johnson, Sheri Olson, Robert Nauman, and James Russell, who were obliged to struggle with vast amounts of material, bureaucratic snafus, and impossible deadlines to make this book possible and who did so with uncommon patience and good grace.

Robert Bruegmann

Introduction

A line of cadets marching precisely along the marble strips on the Court of Honor, the spires of the Chapel glinting against the spectacular natural backdrop of the Front Range. For millions of Americans these images instantly conjure up the United States Air Force Academy at Colorado Springs, one of the most conspicuous and familiar of American landmarks.

But, as so often happens with familiar images, the relationship between the image and the institution that it evokes is complex and shifting. In the case of the Air Force Academy the apparently unambiguous, hard-edged architectural forms of the buildings set into play reactions that are far from clear. While for many visitors, for example, the marble lines in the terrazzo pavement echo beautifully the controlled precision required of an Air Force pilot or officer, for others they suggest the rigidity of military bureaucracies. Likewise, while some individuals see in the Chapel spires the soaring lines of a Gothic cathedral rendered in twentieth-century materials, others see instead a row of upended fighter planes poised for attack. As the essays in this book demonstrate, these reactions are not new. They have been part of the history of the Academy from the very beginning.

As these essays also make clear, the task of designing the Academy was a long and complicated one. In addition to the issues involved in every architectural commission—issues relating to the fit between function and form, symbolic content and aesthetic ideals—the designers found themselves caught up in the currents of two turbulent historical situations. The first was the struggle by architects who thought of themselves as progressive or "Modern" to gain ascendancy in American architectural practice. The Academy commission represented one of the largest and most conspicuous opportunities in postwar America, and for many observers the finished buildings provided conclusive evidence that the "battle of Modernism" had been won.

The other situation involved the role of the American military in the postwar years. Although the United States had emerged from World War II as the strongest military power in the world, the specter of the atom bomb and the escalation of the Cold War combined to sabotage any sense of real national security. This, in turn, meant that the military continued to play a large and very visible role in American life. Because many of the most sensitive military installations were of necessity shielded from view behind high fences, buried under mountains, or hidden in the vast deserts of the West, the burden of representing the military to the public fell increasingly on institutions that the public could see. Notable among these were the Pentagon in Washington and the three major service academies at West Point, Annapolis, and Colorado Springs. Because the Air Force as a separate service was a new, postwar creation and because the design of its Academy was conceived at the height of the Cold War, the buildings at Colorado Springs came to carry a disproportionate share of this symbolic burden.

Given the extraordinarily conspicuous role the Academy design played both in the turbulent currents of postwar American history and in the history of modern architecture, one might expect that the complex would loom large in historical and architectural writing. After an initial burst of publicity when the Academy opened, however, its architectural design has hardly been mentioned in books on modern architecture or American history. As the Epilogue suggests, the reasons for this silence are complex. They have to do, at least in part, with the rise and fall of avant-garde positions in architecture and with a pervasive antimilitary sentiment that has characterized much of academia in the years since the Vietnam War.

The contributors to this book did not attempt to resolve all of the thorny issues that still swirl around the design of the Academy. It is probably too important a site and too recent a design for us to see it with any kind of historical perspective. What they did attempt to do, first of all, was to look at as much of the available information on the design of the Academy as they could locate. They found a prodigious mass of material, including hundreds of linear feet of documents, thousands of drawings, photographs scattered in archives in Colorado Springs, Denver, Chicago, Washington, and elsewhere, and a considerable store of memories preserved by individuals who had participated in the design process. Using these materials, the essayists have sketched in the broad outlines of the story from the selection of the architects in 1954 to the opening of the Chapel in 1962, and have explored in more detail a few interesting events and themes connected with this story.

As I read over these essays, it is obvious how many other topics remain to be explored. There is very little in the book about the buildings outside the cadet area, for example, despite the fact that some of these, notably the heating plants, are among the most handsome at the Academy. Similarly, it would have been interesting to know more about the history of pedagogy at West Point and the impact of this experience on the design of the Colorado Springs complex. A great deal of additional research needs to be done on the materials and technologies used at the Academy and on how they related to advanced practice at the time. We hope that others will be able to look further into these and additional topics.

Part 1 of this book contains an essay by architectural historian Kristen Schaffer that provides an overview of the planning and design of the first phase of the Academy. Accompanying her narrative is a series of short photo essays by various authors that provide additional perspectives on key actors and events. The main narrative is followed, in Part 2, by a series of analytical essays. The first, for which I am responsible, discusses the architectural decisions made at the Academy from a sociological and political perspective. Following this, landscape architect Jory Johnson meditates on the history of the site and the landscape designs for the new institution. This, in turn, is followed by an essay by art historian Robert Nauman on the way that architects Skidmore, Owings & Merrill used renderers and architectural photographers to present their ideas to Congress and the general public. Architect and journalist James Russell puts into historical perspective some of the new architectural technologies explored at the Academy. Then, in the first of two essays, architect and critic Sheri Olson turns from architecture to design on a smaller scale, looking into the designs for furnishings and uniforms. In the second essay she delves into the history of the Chapel and the controversies that it generated. Finally, in Part 3, comes a collection of interviews and recollections. This section includes a conversation between SOM designer Walter Netsch and historian John Burchard conducted shortly after the Academy was first occupied, some recollections by another SOM architect, Gordon Bunshaft, taped about 1982, and an interview with General Bradley Hosmer, a 1959 graduate of the Academy and its superintendent from 1991 to 1994.

To illustrate their essays, the authors have selected a few of the extraordinary visual artifacts produced during the period of design and construction at the Academy. Included are splendid photographs of the site by the famous American photographer Ansel Adams, air views by William Garnett, design drawings by SOM, construction photographs by the Colorado Springs firm of Stewart's, and photographs of completed buildings by such well-known architectural photographers as Hedrich-Blessing and Balthazar Korab. The book also contains striking recent photography by Colorado artist Elizabeth Gill Lui.

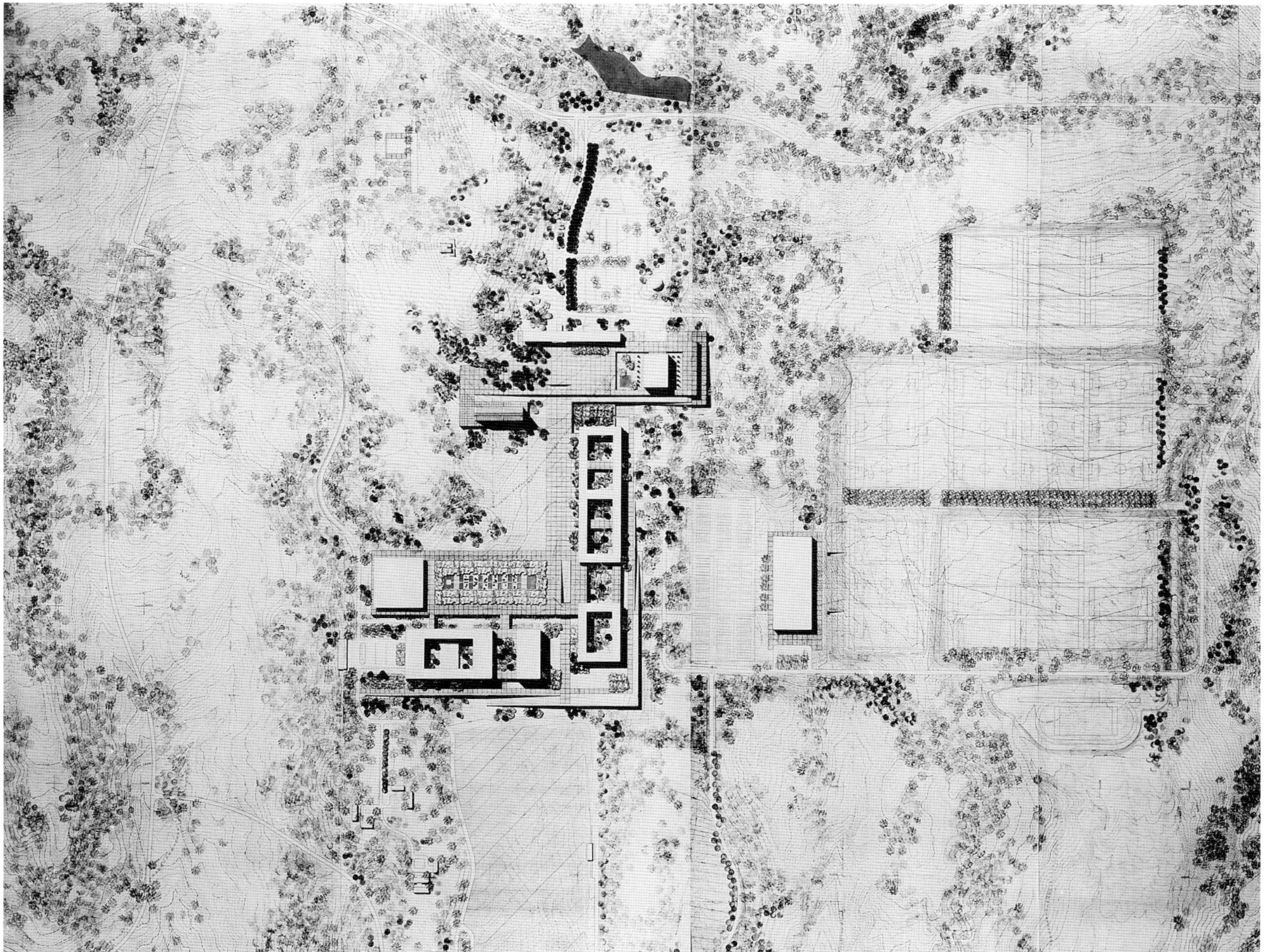

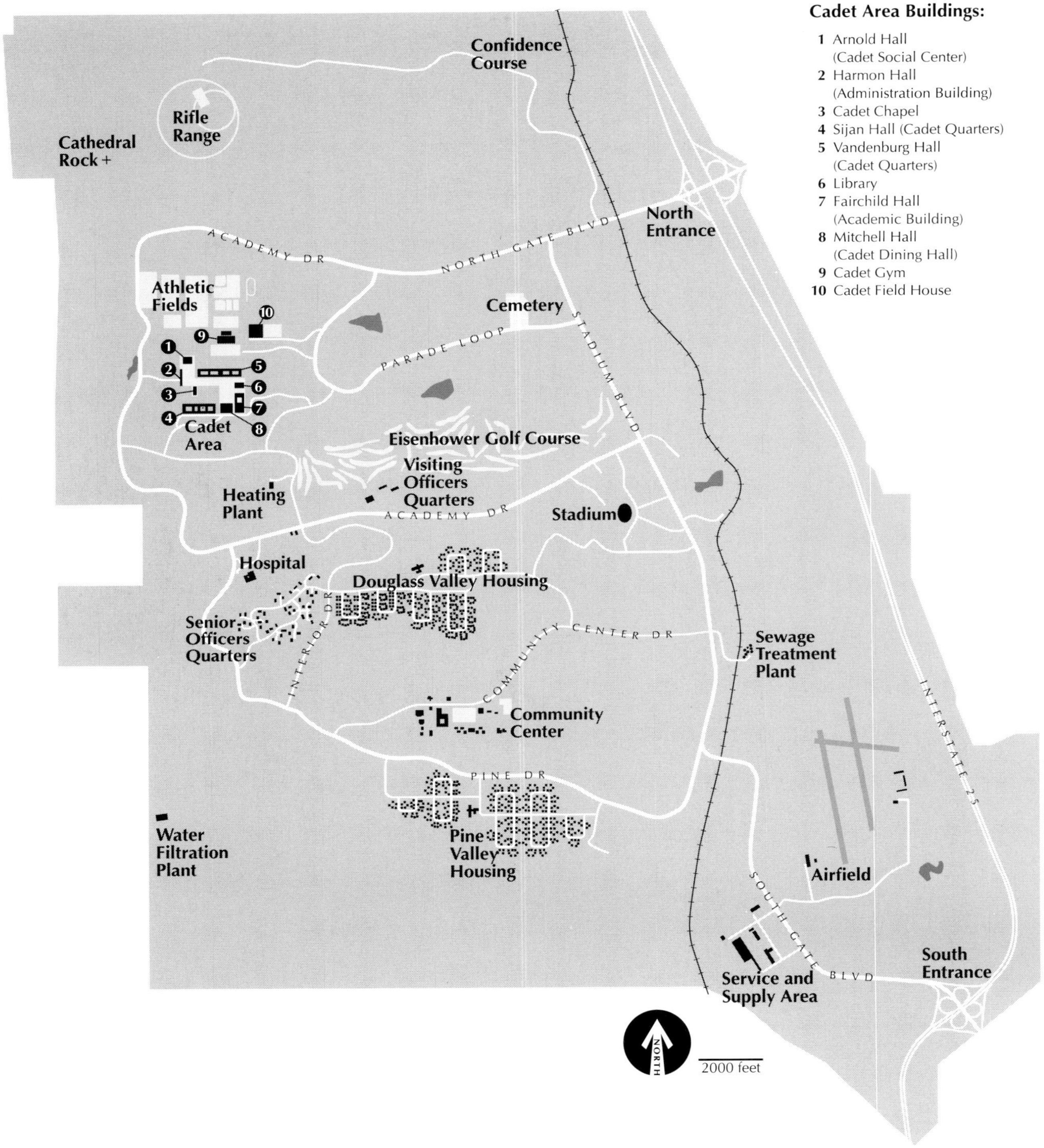

1. Site plan of Academy, 1984. Redrawn by Dennis McClendon, 1994, from data on USGS maps, Air Force diagrams.

PART 1

DESIGNING AND BUILDING THE ACADEMY

Kristen Schaffer

Creating a National Monument: Planning and Designing the Academy

The site of the United States Air Force Academy is dramatically beautiful, in the way Western landscapes often are—tough, large-scaled, with awe-inspiring vistas. The Academy complex spreads out along the foothills of the Rampart Range, where the plain rises into ridges, then soars abruptly into the hills and mountains that guard the western edge of the site. The site itself is hilly and uneven, with relatively little flat terrain, its elevation changing by over 1,600 feet from the highest to lowest point. From the air, the Academy looks like a community set in a national park, with its most important complex of buildings, the Cadet Area, prominently located on the highest ridge (fig. 2).[1] The scale of these buildings is deceptive, and their size is hard to gauge because of the gigantic verticals of the mountains against which they are seen. The buildings, with the notable exception of the Chapel, are rectilinear, and sit on terraces formed by the reshaping and expansion of the ridge into an artificial mesa.[2]

The Academy Chapel is a gleaming, faceted structure, made of seventeen bays of aluminum-clad tetrahedrons separated by strips of colored glass (fig. 3). The Chapel is vertical, triangular, with a broken profile so unlike the horizontal rectilinear structures of the rest of the Cadet Area. The upward movement of the tetrahedrons, the sweep and shining skin of their forms trigger an association with modern aircraft and flight. They suggest skyward motion, especially when seen against the backdrop of the mountains. Yet even the rectilinear buildings of the Cadet Area are anything but static. Take Vandenberg Hall, for instance, the original Cadet Quarters and the building that defines the northern edge of the mesa. From inside the Cadet Area on the paved courtyard known as the Terrazzo, Vandenberg Hall is but three stories high. Looking eastward down its entire length, one finds that its long, low proportions and great horizontal dimension create a sense of rapid movement. With increasing momentum, the eye rushes along the facade of the building, moving faster and faster eastward until the pavement falls away, while the eye continues, out over the parade ground below and, ultimately, off the end of the mesa and eastward into the distance. This is not a representation of the forms associated

2. Aerial view of Academy. Air Force photo c. 1984. The buildings of the Academy sit on the ridges and in the valleys at the junction of the Rockies and the Great Plains. U.S. Air Force Academy Library, Special Collections Branch.

3. View of Cadet Area from Academic Building looking west toward (from left in background) Chapel, Administration Building, Cadet Social Hall, with Cadet Quarters in right foreground. Hedrich-Blessing photograph, 1984. The Cadet Area buildings form the backdrop for the daily rituals of the Academy.

4. View of Academic Building from Cadet Dormitory with Dining Hall in background. Hedrich-Blessing photograph, 1984. A great retaining wall borders the Terrazzo Level. Bridges connect it and the Academic Building.

3

with flight, but an evocation of its sensation. Visually propelled by the long line of the building, our gaze flies off the edge, into the space beyond. Here on the Terrazzo, with the insistent presence of sky and space, one feels poised for flight. This is not a place for the fainthearted or the easily dizzied. On sunny days the expanse is exhilarating: on windy, snowy ones, even in the discomfort, there is a sense of triumph.

Looking at the Academy today, with its starkly beautiful site and clean modern design, one sees nothing that betrays the national controversies, painstaking preparations, and lengthy discussions that preceded its construction (fig. 4). The following account presents some of the crucial issues and developments that marked the realization of the plan for a separate academy for the United States Air Force.

The Need for an Academy The need to establish an air service academy equivalent to the Army's West Point and the Navy's Annapolis was recognized very early in the history of powered flight. The first specific arguments in favor of an air academy were advanced following World War I:

> **As the Military and Naval Academies are the backbone of the Army and Navy, so must the Aeronautical Academy be the backbone of the Air Service. No service can flourish without some such institution to inculcate into its embryonic officers love of country, proper conception of duty, and highest regard for honor.**[3]

Advocates of an air academy were not just concerned about the training of pilots, or the training of officers. They wanted the education of career officers, the future leaders of the air service, to attain a level equal to that of West Point and

4

Annapolis graduates. This need was recognized by such air-power advocates as Generals Henry H. Arnold and William Mitchell. However, their efforts and those of others were unsuccessful until the post-World War II era.[4]

When President Harry S Truman, on 26 July 1947, signed the act creating a separate Air Force co-equal with the Army and the Navy, it became clear that arrangements would have to be made to provide the new branch of the armed forces with career officers.[5] At first, the other academies met this need, but the Air Force desired to match their distinguished educational institutions with one of its own.[6] In 1945, 1947, and again in 1949, bills introduced in Congress nominated Randolph Field near San Antonio, Texas, as the site of the future Academy. Randolph, dedicated in 1930, had become the Air Corps Training Center and gained the nickname "West Point of the Air" (fig. 48). Other bills proposed other sites but were not acted upon.[7]

In 1947 and 1948, the efforts to establish an air academy opened up a discussion of the curriculum at all the service academies.[8] One study proposed a "composite" education, in which the armed services would utilize civilian institutions for the first two years of study and military academies for the last three.[9] This proposal, and the issue of whether flight training should be included as part of the air academy's curriculum, caused much controversy. Boards and task forces were formed to study these issues, and no two completely agreed.[10] In 1949, however, three events contributed significantly to the creation of an Air Force Academy.

In March 1949, Secretary of Defense James Forrestal appointed Dwight D. Eisenhower, then President of Columbia University, to serve as vice chair under Robert E. Stearns, President of the University of Colorado, for the newly formed Service Academy Board. Its charge was to review and assess the existing methods of training officers in the armed forces, and "to recommend a general system of education for the three services." The Board urged the establishment of an Air Force Academy "without delay," as a four-year program equal to that of West Point and Annapolis.[11] Eisenhower was a strong supporter of this recommendation, and would continue in his support when he became president in 1953.

In November 1949, Secretary of the Air Force Thomas K. Finletter appointed the Site Selection Board, and charged that it recommend a site by the following November.[12] With the assistance of the U.S. Army Chief of Engineers, the Air Force Office of the Directorate of Installations, and the Chicago architectural firm of Holabird & Root & Burgee, the Board analyzed 354 sites, and narrowed them down to 8 for further study by the architectural firm.[13]

Among the top choices were Randolph Air Force Base and the Colorado Springs site that would ultimately become home to the Academy (fig. 5).[14] Colonel A. E. Boudreau had noticed the latter site while driving from Colorado Springs to Denver, and thought it came closer to satisfying the criteria for physical beauty than either of the two sites that had been proposed by the city of Colorado Springs. The Board agreed that this site was indeed "most suitable," and a recommendation to this effect was transmitted to the Secretary in a sealed envelope in June 1951. In the absence of legislation authorizing creation of the Academy, the envelope remained sealed.[15]

And in December 1949, General Hoyt S. Vandenberg, Air Force Chief of Staff, appointed Lieutenant General Hubert R. Harmon head of the Office of Special Assistant for Air Force Matters, which was created to handle "all planning for the future Air Force academy including site, facilities, equipment, building, curriculum, etc."[16] Harmon would dedicate the remainder of his life to the service of the Academy, and would become its first Superintendent. Thus, by the end of 1949, important support for the Academy had been garnered, its future site had been identified and a leader had been chosen to realize the Academy.

Early Architectural Considerations While some Air Force officials concerned themselves with securing legislation, developing the curriculum, and locating a site, others turned their attention to facility planning and consideration of architectural form. For instance, in 1948 when establishment of the Academy at Randolph Air Force Base seemed likely, planners

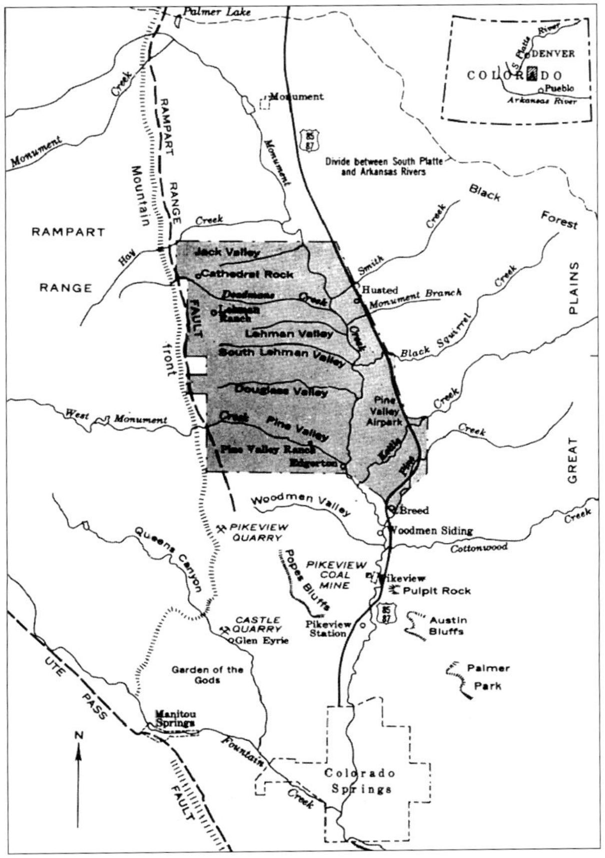

5. Location map showing Academy property in relation to Colorado Springs. From *Quest*. In the 1950s the Academy site was located well beyond Colorado Springs. Today the growing city encroaches rapidly. U.S Air Force Academy Library, Special Collections Branch.

expressed their intention to "harmonize" the architectural design of new structures with the style of the existing buildings. Upon closer scrutiny, however, it became clear that the Randolph site was inadequate. The expansion could add only 2,000 acres, bringing the total to 4,500 acres, far below West Point's 15,063 acres, the proposed standard for the Air Force Academy.[17]

A brief statement of January 1949, entitled "Suggested Architectural Treatment for the Air Force Academy," sought to define an appropriate architectural expression and style for the Academy. It expressed concern about excessive cost should the Academy choose "an ornate type of architecture which would call for various embellishments." However, there was even more concern that the buildings might "have a too modern architectural appearance," one that would soon make them look dated. In a rather curiously phrased recommendation, the paper urged that the "styling of architecture probably best suited would incorporate functional planning. However, the exterior architectural appearance of the buildings would be pleasing by virtue of ingenious handling of mass, choice of materials, and the correct proportions and orientation of fenestration." The awkwardness of the phrasing, and the apparent uncertainty in the use of architectural terminology, indicated a lack of experience in talking about architectural forms, styles, and concepts. Finally, the statement clearly indicated the desired result: the buildings should have "a dignified and institutional character in keeping with the magnitude of the project."[18]

Harmon, in a set of recommendations on the appearance of the Academy, suggested that if the Academy departed from the "classic traditions of West Point," it might be designed in the modern style represented by architect Edward Durrell Stone's Hotel El Panama (fig. 55). Harmon described it as the most delightful modern building he had seen, and

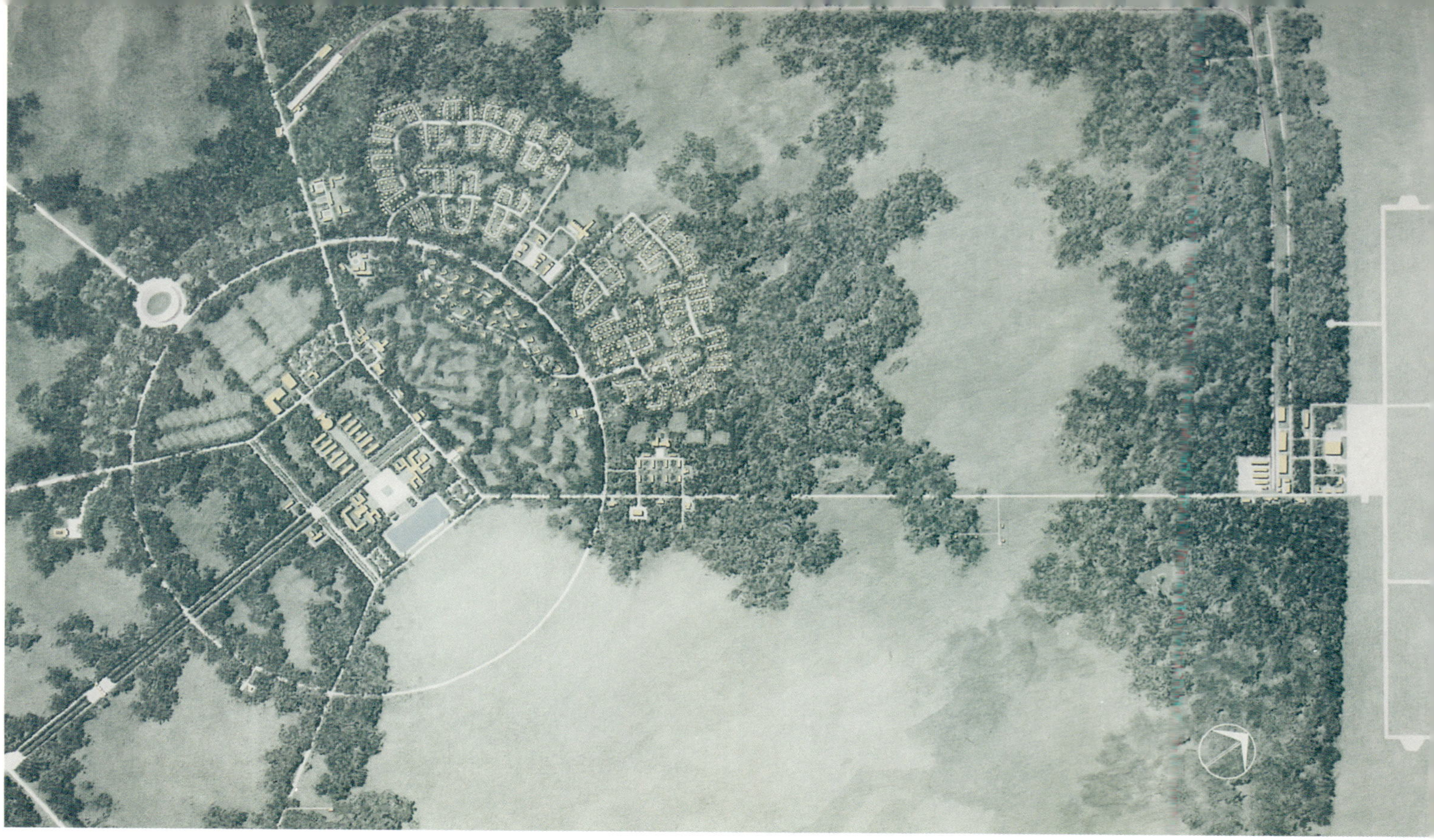

others agreed.[19] Thus, from an early date, Air Force planners were considering modern architecture for the Academy.[20]

The first architectural plans for the Academy date back to 1947 and 1948, when Secretary of the Air Force W. Stuart Symington asked Ellery Husted, a New York architect, to provide some sketches for an air academy.[21] In 1952 rumors surfaced that the Pentagon had developed designs, and early that year Harmon admitted to having "spoken informally" with the internationally known architect Eero Saarinen about such matters but knew of no plans.[22] Then, in 1953, Secretary of the Air Force Harold E. Talbott called Husted back to prepare preliminary sketches, determine an "ideal layout" for a hypothetical site, and construct a small scale-model, as well as estimate needs and costs.[23] For this project, his firm, Gugler, Kimball and Husted of New York, associated itself with Harbeson, Hough, Livingston and Larson of Philadelphia.[24]

After discussions about programmatic requirements, the Air Force planners and the Husted team identified the academic or Cadet Area, housing, and the airfield as the three major components of the project. These key areas required separation and screening from one another but connection by a perimeter road.[25] Harmon believed that the need for a grand architectural concept and adequate provision for expansion dictated a more compact cadet area with the gymnasium, "barracks," and the classroom building in close proximity. This tight clustering of facilities would allow both objectives of good functional relationships and aesthetic monumentality.[26] When the associated architects submitted their report in February 1954, their site plan showed a circular arrangement of major buildings, curiously similar to the circular layout of Randolph Air Force Base (fig. 6). Drawings for individual buildings showed a circular cadet Dining Hall, Cadet Quarters with a toilet and shower room between every other dormitory room, and a large cadet chapel (for Protestants) with an adjacent small chapel (possibly for Jewish services) and a separate Roman Catholic chapel.[27]

The Air Force planners knew that they were embarking upon a project for which they had neither collective nor

6. Plan, Project for U.S. Air Force Academy at a hypothetical site. Gugler, Kimball and Husted with Harbeson, Hough, Livingston and Larson, architects, 1954. These architects proposed a scheme in which the major buildings would surround an open-ended quadrangle. U.S. Air Force Academy special collections Branch.

individual experience. Because, apparently, there was "no one in the Air Force who [had] made a study of American campuses and school plants," they proposed that key officers involved in the planning and design of the Air Force Academy should travel to Mexico City to study the new University of Mexico complex then under construction.[28] The University of Mexico was the most extensive grouping of modern university buildings then under construction and was viewed as a national monument in that country. It was also roughly the size projected for the Academy complex (fig. 54).[29]

The officers returned from Mexico impressed with what they had seen. Although the layout of the complex was based on a conventional quadrangular plan, this basic scheme had been freely manipulated to achieve a functional arrangement. The predominant materials were brick, concrete, and especially glass, with few surfaces that would require repainting.[30] The observers remarked on the structural frame which allowed the exterior walls to be made of any material desired because they were not being used for support. And they also commented on the fact that most of the buildings were on pilotis (a French term for piles or pillars), noting that "only a few buildings have anything on the ground floors" other than the structural supports.

> **This gives the effect of the building sitting on stilts or suspended in the air. One standing at ground level gets a virtually uninterrupted view in all directions. The impression of floating, of flying, thus created by the peculiar construction may have possibilities in the architecture of an Air Academy.**[31]

In their trip to Mexico, these Air Force observers experienced firsthand the planning, design, and construction principles of Modern architecture. An asymmetrical arrangement of buildings within a rectangular plan, the raising of buildings on pilotis, and the extensive use of glass were all characteristics of the Modern style. The studies, inquiries, and comments by Air Force personnel suggest that they were willing to explore Modern architecture, and especially to recognize its symbolic potential for the Academy. The officers also reported that from their conversations with the participants in the Mexico City project they had learned the value of teamwork and of involving the future users in the planning and design process.[32]

Harmon did not undertake the Mexico City trip but continued to oversee the planning of the Academy. He hoped that "the site selected could be as magnificent as . . . West Point."[33] And he maintained his preference for fewer, larger structures. He responded favorably to a report that the Naval Academy administration was pleased with the arrangement of having all students in one barracks.[34] In light of the eventual solution, his views on the subject are pertinent:

> **One large barracks is bound to result in a number of rooms which, because of light, ventilation, or both, are undesirable. On the other hand, it contributes to grandeur in the architectural concept. I, myself, like the idea of [an]**

7. View of the site looking west toward Rampart Range. Photograph by Ansel Adams. April 1955.
Skidmore, Owings & Merrill commissioned Adams to take a series of photographs to be used in the Colorado Springs exhibition.

enclosed area or areas, i.e., one or two large buildings each in the form of [a] quadrangle with a large open 'patio' in the middle.[35]

Harmon then referred specifically to the Great Quadrangle of Christ Church, the largest quadrangle at Oxford University. Here one can see a thoughtful and productive assessment of an architectural concept without regard to style. Such an appreciation of precedent is useful in communicating particular ideas to architects.

Passage of the Bill President Truman, it should be recalled, signed the legislation that created a separate Air Force, but it was up to President Eisenhower to support and sign legislation creating a separate Air Force Academy. When the newly elected President was asked at a press conference in March 1953 whether there ought to be a separate Air Force Academy, Eisenhower "indicated that he thought the matter was all settled."[36] Yet even with this absolute support by the President, the bill was not heard until January 1954,[37] and at times the pace of legislative progress was discouraging. At one point, Harmon recommended that the Academy simply be established at Randolph Field, in order to put an end to the political manueverings over the site, as many senators still wanted to secure the Academy for their home state.[38] Fortunately, this did not happen, and an "Act to provide for the establishment of a United States Air Force Academy and for other purposes" was finally signed on 1 April 1954.[39]

Planning studies and cost estimates provided essential information to the Congress. It was in the context of the Air Force's preparation for the passage of legislation that Talbott had engaged the Husted firm to provide a cost estimate and ideal plans for a hypothetical site.[40] Over the years of planning, estimates for the Academy varied. In 1949 the cost of the Academy had been estimated at $171 million, based on national average costs at a hypothetical site. Later estimates, which generally gave construction (not total project) costs, ranged from $148 to $165 million.[41] One estimate, made at some time between 1952 and 1954, put the cost at $165,772,299. This included an airfield and stadium, as well as architectural and engineering fees, with equipment and installation estimated at $7,770,190.[42] The cost estimates made by the Husted group in December 1953 gave a construction cost of $123,590,908, apparently excluding architectural and engineering fees and a 10 percent contingency.[43] When the Senate Committee on Armed Services began hearings on the Academy bill in February 1954, the estimated cost of the Academy was presented as approximately $145 million on "any typical . . . site within the continental United States," with about $25 million needed for site preparation.[44]

The legislation creating a separate Air Force Academy specified that the total cost was not to exceed $126 million, that a maximum of $26 million could be appropriated before 1 January 1955, and that only $1,000,000 could be expended on temporary facilities.[45] This project ceiling of $126 million would prove to a be a problem, one that should have been evident at the time, given that construction estimates already exceeded that amount.

The act also mandated that the Secretary establish a five-member commission to advise on the location of the permanent site.[46] If the commission could not provide a unanimous choice, it was to provide a list of three sites, from which the Secretary would have to choose.

A Second Site Selection Commission Five days after the bill to establish an Air Force Academy was approved, Talbott appointed a Site Selection Commission. Among those appointed to serve was American aviation hero Brigadier General Charles A. Lindbergh, USAF (retired).[47] The Commission immediately set to work evaluating the sites, making use of the reports and surveys considered by the previous Board.[48] A total of 582 sites was submitted, including 325 submitted to the previous board. Of the total, 354 were rejected outright and 67 were studied further, 34 of which were visited and 33 inspected from the air. The sites visited included Maxwell Air Force Base, Alabama; Randolph Air Force Base, Texas; Lake

Geneva, Wisconsin; Alton, Illinois; and the Colorado Springs, Colorado, site favored by the previous board.[49] The Commission looked for sufficient acreage; topography suitable for the Academy's needs combined with scenic beauty appropriate to a national monument; a community with cultural institutions; a climate with four seasons; sufficient water supply; available utilities; proximity to transportation lines; reasonable cost; and suitability for flight training.[50] It gave particular attention to the criteria of natural beauty and the potential of the site to provide an appropriate setting for this future national monument.[51] Lindbergh believed that "the Commission should recommend a site which was adequate for the creation of an Air Force tradition just as West Point has served in that respect for the Army and Annapolis for the Navy." Lindbergh believed "the Colorado Springs site . . . filled the requirement very well" (fig. 7).[52]

When the Commission could not reach a unanimous agreement because it could judge no site superior in all respects, it recommended three sites in its 3 June 1954 report—Lake Geneva, Alton, and Colorado Springs—without assigning priority.[53] Talbott visited the three sites and at the end of June announced that the Air Force Academy would be permanently located at Colorado Springs, and that the interim Academy would be located at Lowry Air Force Base in Denver.[54]

The location of the Air Force Academy at Colorado Springs surely must have pleased President Eisenhower, as he had a great fondness for Colorado.[55] Mamie Doud Eisenhower's family had a home in Denver, and the Lowry headquarters building had become the "summer White House."[56] There has been some speculation that the Colorado Springs site was chosen with the President in mind, although there is no apparent evidence of his involvement. Yet later he would admit that he had been "very anxious that the Academy be in the state I love so much."[57]

Architect Selection The Air Force announced its intention to hire an architect soon after the Air Force Academy bill was signed into law in April 1954. Much work already had been done in preparation for this event.[58] In fact, as early as May 1950, the Air Force had sought advice from Leopold Arnaud, Dean of Architecture at Columbia University, about a possible national competition for the selection of the architect. Arnaud agreed to "submit a tentative plan outlining how the competition should be held, the time required and the estimated cost."[59]

In March 1954, the Project Office for the Air Force Academy was established within the Directorate of Installations, and a Deputy Director of Installations was appointed to oversee the project.[60] The Project Office would sort through the applications of architectural and engineering firms and provide the Secretary with a short list of firms with suitable experience in long-term planning, design, and construction supervision. The Secretary would then establish a board "to select a representative combine of such firms to develop both the master planning and the long-range engineering for the Academy."[61] Harmon had concerns about the process, however, thinking it unwise to "marry" firms into such a joint venture. He was worried about the likelihood of an unwieldy organization and recommended that the Air Force select an already associated group. He wanted the Air Force to be able to contract with one firm which would be responsible for the performance of the entire group.[62] Harmon also had concerns about assembling an advisory board for the Secretary that would include civilian architects, and preferred one composed solely of high-ranking military officers. Fortunately, Harmon's opinion did not prevail, for the architects of the Academy would later say that the consultant architects gave them the sounding board they needed.[63]

In April, the American Institute of Architects was notified that "a committee of Air Force officers" would review qualifications and make a selection.[64] Discreet inquiries into the architect selection process, however, were being made well before 1954. As early as 1949 William Adams Delano, of Delano and Aldrich, had written to Cornelius V. Whitney, Assistant Secretary for Air, to enquire about the project,[65] and even before the Academy was officially created the well-known industrial design firm of Raymond Loewy and Associates had reportedly offered to do for free the preliminary

Skidmore, Owings & Merrill:
EARLY HISTORY

8. SOM partners at a partners' meeting in Chicago office, 1953. From left: John O. Merrill, Nathaniel A. Owings, Louis Skidmore. SOM Archives, New York.

"SOM bears its name almost as a trademark. It is like a brand name," noted a 1950 bulletin of the Museum of Modern Art in describing a recent exhibit of the firm's work.[1] Skidmore, Owings & Merrill became known for Modern design produced by a team of professionals. While the firm's contributions to the development of architectural design cannot be ignored, it was probably the way Skidmore, Owings & Merrill practiced architecture that was the greatest factor in its selection for the Air Force Academy project.

Romance between Louis Skidmore and Eloise Owings, the sister of Nathaniel Owings, provided the impetus for the founding of the firm. The couple had met in 1928 while she was studying fashion in Paris and he was traveling on a fellowship. While in Europe, Skidmore had tracked down key commissioners of the upcoming 1933–34 World's Fair in Chicago. Through these contacts, he secured a position as Assistant General Manager in Charge of Design and Construction for the fair. Although largely an administrative rather than a design position, this was a considerable coup for Skidmore, since there was not much work for architects during the Great Depression. Shortly after they were introduced by Eloise, Owings joined Skidmore as development supervisor for the fair. Besides providing the first opportunity for their collaboration, the fair gave the two men valuable experience with working in lightweight, mass-produced materials on a complex project with a demanding schedule. They also developed business contacts that were to be valuable years later. In many ways the fair was excellent preparation for the projects in Skidmore and Owings's future.

In 1937, a year after formalizing their partnership, Skidmore left Chicago to set up the partnership's second office in New York. The firm had received a commission in New York with the stipulation that a partner be in residence to oversee the work. For Skidmore and Owings this offered an ideal opportunity to secure for each architect a space of his own. Work on the 1939 New York's World Fair generated additional commissions for the burgeoning office. But more important, with offices in the Midwest and on the East Coast, the concept of decentralization had become a part of the firm's philosophy. Multiple offices were not unknown in the architectural profession at the time, but Skidmore, Owings & Merrill was certainly the largest to be decentralized.

Skidmore and Owings invited architect-engineer John O. Merrill to join them in 1939 as a limited partner (fig. 8). Merrill was a significant addition to the growing practice; including an engineer within the firm facilitated the structural innovations for which Skidmore, Owings & Merrill would become well known and also allowed the firm to offer more services to its clients. As Skidmore later noted: "Up until the War most U.S. architects were trained to work only on small plots: they left the problem of coping with large scale projects—industrial plants, airfields—to the engineers. We felt that if the architect wasn't to limit himself to domestic housing he would have to win back his role as the creator and coordinator of big projects."[2] Perhaps he exaggerated a little to make his point—most large firms at the time had in-house engineering services—but his statement demonstrates the early emphasis Skidmore, Owings & Merrill placed on marketing a diversity of services to clients. These services included master planning, engineering, and construction supervision, as well as design. The package-deal approach had great appeal to the large corporations that made up the majority of Skidmore, Owings & Merrill's clients.

World War II brought the firm its first major commission and established a lasting government connection that would prove profitable in the future. The unusual nature of this project was apparent from the beginning, when two men strolled into the New York office in 1942 and casually stated they needed a town, and fast. The town was Oak Ridge, Tennessee, part of the super-secret Manhattan project, whose purpose was to produce plutonium for the atomic bomb. The government needed all the elements for a town of 30,000 people, including housing; commercial, religious, and municipal buildings; and roads and utility systems, all to be completed by 1945.[3] Working completely in the dark as to the project's purpose, and literally in the mud, Skidmore, Owings & Merrill put together a team of 450 architects, engineers, and surveyors to do on-site design.[4] The methods devised to cope with the extreme urgency of the project laid the organizational foundation for the firm. The crushing schedule, diverse services required, and difficult working conditions provided invaluable experiences. The project also established the firm's expertise at master planning on a large scale. When the war ended, the firm was retained to develop a master plan to turn Oak Ridge into a permanent city.

Skidmore, Owings & Merrill was well positioned to profit from the postwar building boom. Young architects swarmed to the office to work for the "firm with the future."[5] From 1947 to 1958, Skidmore, Owings & Merrill's staff doubled, from 480 to 1,000.[6] Driving this expansion was the large volume of work; in 1947 the firm had completed projects with construction costs totaling over $28 million; by 1957 this figure had reached more than $177 million.[7] A 1958 article in *Fortune* magazine estimated that Skidmore, Owings & Merrill's earnings were $1.5 million for 1957 alone.[8] Sharing the wealth, and bringing their own special talents to the firm, were four partners added in 1949: J. Walter Severinghaus, a housing specialist; Robert W. Cutler, a hospital expert; William S. Brown, a prefabricated housing expert; and Gordon Bunshaft, a designer, who brought to Skidmore, Owings & Merrill a style for which the firm would become famous.

9. View of Lever House. Photograph by Ezra Stoller, © Esto, c. 1952. Lever House set the standard for hundreds of steel and glass commercial structures in postwar America.

By 1952 Skidmore, Owings & Merrill had completed several large projects, but the most significant of these, and the one that made its reputation, was Lever House in Manhattan. One of its innovative features was a street-level plaza, made possible by raising up the first floor of the building on columns. Lever House exemplified the new character of high-rise office towers in the U.S., with unobstructed floors, artificial lighting, and air-conditioning. Its green-glass and stainless-steel tower set perpendicular to the street offered a striking image among the brick walls of Park Avenue (fig. 9). The development of the curtain wall on Lever House made a significant contribution to the acceptance of modern architecture as the corporate architecture of the 1950s. Other prominent Skidmore, Owings & Merrill projects that preceded the Air Force Academy included the U.S. Naval Postgraduate Technical School in Monterey, California (1952–55), designed by Walter Netsch, Jr.; the Inland Steel Building in Chicago (1954–58), designed by Netsch and Bruce Graham; and the Manufacturers Trust Company in New York (1954), designed by Bunshaft. In addition to the firm's experience, in-house talent, and organizational abilities, the partner's personal and professional contacts made Skidmore, Owings & Merrill a formidable competitor for the Air Force Academy commission.

—*Sheri Olson*

Notes

1. "Skidmore, Owings & Merrill," *Museum of Modern Art Bulletin* 18, 1 (Fall 1950): 7.
2. "The Architects from 'Skid's Row'," *Fortune*, January 1958, 210.
3. Ibid.
4. Henry-Russell Hitchcock, introduction to *The Architecture of Skidmore, Owings & Merrill*, by Ernst Danz (New York: Fredrick A. Praeger, 1963), 8.
5. "The Architects from 'Skid's Row'," 212.
6. Ibid., 138.
7. Ibid.
8. Ibid.

architectural designs.[66] Other firms, such as Welton Becket's, used political contacts in an effort to get the job, directing correspondence to the Assistant to the President, the Assistant to the Assistant to the President, the Air Force Aide to the President, the Air Force Director of Legislative Liaison, and the Secretary of the Air Force.[67]

The Air Force Academy was one of the largest, most important postwar architectural projects, and architects, contractors, and building material suppliers from all parts of the country were clamoring for it. When the project was announced, the Air Force was soon inundated with letters from members of Congress on behalf of interested constituents. Senator Sam J. Ervin wrote to the Secretary to say that he thought North Carolina granite would make an excellent building material. Senator John F. Kennedy wrote on behalf of a Massachusetts granite concern. Senator Russell B. Long asked for the consideration of a Baton Rouge firm that had missed the submission deadline. Senator Lyndon B. Johnson recommended a firm from Lubbock, Texas. And Senator Everett M. Dirksen forwarded a letter from a member of a rather large joint-venture association.[68]

From architects, the Air Force received more than 300 applications which it sifted down to 261, representing 70 individual and 191 joint-venture submissions.[69] Firms were expected to present evidence of their experience and abilities, and the selection process was "based upon the quality and extent" of the architects' past performance in comparable projects. Particular attention was paid to previous work on Air Force installations.[70]

Like other prospective firms, Skidmore, Owings & Merrill (SOM) submitted a response to the Air Force's questionnaire on qualifications, experience, capabilities, key personnel, and representative work, and supplemented its response with supporting materials and the firm's brochure, highlighting its experience. The firm touted its reputation for designing and administering large-scale projects, and substantiated its claim with examples of its experience. In the 1940s and early 1950s, SOM had handled a number of large-scale government projects, including the Atomic Energy Commission's $60 million "Atom City" in Oak Ridge, Tennessee, and a number of overseas projects for the Armed Services. A more recent government project was the U.S. Naval Postgraduate School in Monterey, California, which, in its programming and early planning phases, had provided the firm with the kind of experience useful for the Academy project.[71]

SOM's submission was in joint venture with Moran, Proctor, Mueser and Rutledge, consulting engineers who specialized in site selection, foundations, structural and soils engineering, and with Syska and Hennessy, engineers known for mechanical and electrical design services, power plant and sewage disposal design. Clearly, SOM was the dominant partner, requiring only specialized engineering assistance. The firm identified its role in the joint venture as "overall coordination and administration of the complete project." It would provide "master and site planning, [and] all architectural and engineering services" except those provided by its consultants. The application stressed the fact that the three companies had worked together before, although not in joint venture. Nathaniel Owings, in his cover letter to the Secretary of the Air Force, indicated the firm's "willingness to associate with additional firms" if this would be advantageous.[72] SOM offered the Air Force a range of experience that was hard to match, and the assurance that it could handle such a large project smoothly. Since at this time the firm had offices in Chicago, New York, San Francisco, and Portland, Oregon, it was experienced in coordination.

The Selection Board culled from the large number of applicants a short list of the firms whose representatives would be interviewed, including SOM, Kittyhawk Associates, Eero Saarinen, Harrison and Abramovitz, Pietro Belluschi, and Pereira and Luckman.[73] The finalist firms each had the opportunity to view the site. Owings decided that, given the variety of terrain and the complex nature of the program, SOM should not submit a sketch design for the final interview so that the project would "not be encumbered by a priori attitudes." Instead, SOM presented a work progress chart, from master planning and design through the construction phase. This took the form of a "fifteen foot long six foot high

10. Organization chart, Skidmore, Owings & Merrill, 1954. This chart was created to show lines of authority on the immense Academy construction job. From *SOM News,* June 15, 1956. SOM Archives, Chicago.

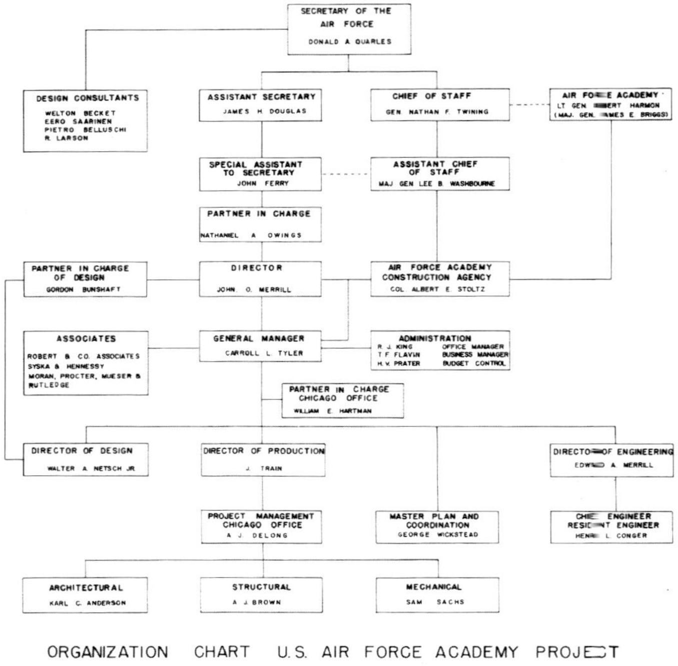

folding screen" showing the firm's intention with regard to research, programming, scheduling, and design.[74] SOM presented itself as interested in the process of design and capable of managing the complexities of the project. This strategy apparently worked, for after the interviews the field narrowed to SOM, Kittyhawk Associates, and Pereira and Luckman of Los Angeles. Pereira and Luckman was then eliminated because it was designing air bases in Spain. This left Kittyhawk Associates and SOM.[75]

SOM's ultimate competitor was an unlikely and possibly unwieldy joint venture put together by architect Richard Hawley Cutting, of Cutting and Associates of Cleveland.[76] Perhaps to increase the joint venture's chance of winning, or to give it an identity, Cutting convinced Frank Lloyd Wright, then in his eighties but still America's best-known architect, to head the group. This backfired when Wright effectively withdrew from the competition by refusing to go to Washington to make the required personal presentation to the Secretary and Selection Board. Since the "world knows what I can do in architecture," Wright announced, "I will not volunteer to plead my case." Because Cutting knew that the American Legion had threatened to reveal Wright's "anti-militaristic activities and associations," he did not press him to go to Washington.[77] Thus, by the final round of the competition, Kittyhawk Associates was without its head.

Skidmore, Owings & Merrill was awarded the contract on 23 July 1954. To their joint venture was added the Atlanta engineering firm of Robert and Co.—experts in water supply, sewerage and irrigation—formerly associated with the Kittyhawk group.[78] At the same time, Talbott appointed three architects as his consultants: Wallace K. Harrison of New York and Eero Saarinen of Detroit, both contenders in the competition, and Welton Becket. Harrison soon resigned and was replaced by Pietro Belluschi, Dean of the School of Architecture and Planning at the Massachusetts Institute of Technology. Some time later, Roy F. Larson of Harbeson, Hough, Livingston and Larson was added to the group.[79]

A number of stories have been advanced as to why SOM was awarded the commission. One suggests that at the interview Owings, understanding how eager the Air Force was to graduate the first Academy class from the new campus, promised to make this possible. Owings himself credits the social connection of Talbott's wife to Eloise Skidmore, and

The Architectural Consultants

Of the architects appointed to an advisory board by the Secretary of the Air, the best known were Pietro Belluschi, Welton Becket and Eero Saarinen.

Pietro Belluschi Belluschi, Dean of Architecture and Planning at MIT, had already had a long, successful career. His design for the Equitable Building (1948) in Portland, Oregon, was elegant and precedent-setting (fig. 11). It was one of the first office buildings to be sheathed in aluminum, to be sealed and air-conditioned, to employ double-glazed windowpanes, and to incorporate a traveling window-washing crane.[1]

Belluschi first gained national attention in 1931 with his design for the Portland Art Museum and was well known throughout the Northwest for a series of outstanding churches, houses, and shopping centers.[2] When he accepted the position as dean in 1951, Skidmore, Owings & Merrill acquired his thriving Portland office.[3] Belluschi stated that design should be derived from functional demands and then be implemented without reference to prevailing aesthetic norms. This corresponded closely to statements by partners at Skidmore, Owings & Merrill. Thus both his ideological position and his practical professional experience put him in a position to be helpful to SOM in his role as architectural and technical adviser on the Air Force Academy project.[4]

Welton Becket Previous to his experience with the Air Force Academy, Becket, with partner Walter Wurdeman, had built a large architecture-engineering practice in California based on a variety of building types. His first big commission was the streamlined Pan Pacific Auditorium (1941), The partners then turned to the design of "English" cottages and half-timbered mansions for Hollywood stars. During World War II, the partners parlayed their experience into government contracts to design housing for the military in California. In the period of prosperity after the war, Becket developed the "total design" concept, hiring sufficient in-house experts to address all the requirements of large building projects from preliminary research and site selection to traffic surveys and economic analysis.[5] In this regard the firm was very similar to Skidmore, Owings & Merrill. When Wurdeman died unexpectedly in 1949, Becket bought out his partner's heirs and established Welton Becket and Associates.

At the time that this firm was pursuing the Academy project, it had already completed numerous projects across the country and overseas including the Beverly Hilton in Beverly Hills (1952) (fig. 12), Capitol Records tower (shaped like a stack of records) in Los Angeles (1954), the western headquarters of the Prudential Insurance Company in Los Angeles (1947), and forty projects as master planners for UCLA.[6] Becket saw the latter as ideal qualifications for securing the Air Force Acad-

12

11

11. Equitable Building, Portland, Oregon. Photograph by Roger Sturtevant, 1948. As an architectural consultant to the Air Force Academy, Pietro Belluschi brought to the job the professional experience gained from his precedent-setting Equitable Building (1948) as well as the prestige of his position as dean of MIT's School of Architecture and Planning.

12. Beverly Hilton Hotel, Beverly Hills, California. Photograph by Julius Shulman, 1952. During his testimony before Congress on the Air Force Academy, Frank Lloyd Wright singled out Welton Becket's Beverly Hilton (1952) as evidence of the inadequacies of the architectural consultants.

emy commission. His associate Jack B. Beardwood contacted his old acquaintances in Washington, D.C., in an attempt to ensure that the firm's application "not be buried in some lower echelon drawer."[7] Although disappointed at not being named architects for the Academy, Beardwood gladly accepted a consultant's position for Becket, noting "that although we get none of the meat and potatoes we at least get a sprig of the prestige parsley."[8]

Eero Saarinen Eero Saarinen was the architectural consultant who was probably the most familiar with the issues that faced Skidmore, Owings & Merrill as architects for the Air Force Academy. At the time, Saarinen's experience included the winning entry in the St. Louis Jefferson Memorial Competition (1947–48, built 1959–64), the Kresge Auditorium and Chapel at MIT (1953–56), and the General Motors Technical Center in Warren, Michigan (1948–56).[9] The Jefferson Memorial design established Saarinen as an architect in his own right, distinct from his famous father, Eliel, who had become well known as an architect in Finland and had founded the Cranbrook Academy of Art in Michigan in the 1920s. Eero Saarinen's winning entry in the St. Louis competition, better known as the Gateway Arch, was a spectacular project that tackled head-on the question of how Modern architecture could produce monuments. His design for the Kresge Chapel attempted to break with the orthogonal geometry of modern architecture, just as Walter Netsch's chapel design for the Academy would do several years later. The $20 million GM Technical Center was Saarinen's first major built work and the largest commission awarded to a modernist architect up to that time.[10]

The Technical Center's immense scope and scale were similar to those of the later Skidmore, Owings & Merrill design for the Academy, as was the machine aesthetic vocabulary Saarinen employed for the project (fig. 13). His master plan placed a number of low, rectangular buildings, around a large central lake in a manner resembling Mies van der Rohe's plan for the Illinois Institute of Technology (1940).[11] The Center also produced several technological firsts, including prefabricated wall panels of laminate and porcelain, luminous ceilings of modular plastic pans, and the neoprene gasket weather seal.[12] On this project Saarinen demonstrated his ability to work well with large corporations and institutional clients. Together with SOM, Saarinen determined the trends that loomed large in the corporate American architecture of the postwar decades.

—*Sheri Olson*

Notes

1. Walter L. Creese, "The Equitable Revisited," *Architectural Forum* (June 1968): 43.
2. Jo Stubblebine, ed., *The Northwest Architecture of Pietro Belluschi* (F. W. Dodge Corporation: New York 1953), 7.
3. "Pietro Belluschi:The 1972 Gold Medalist," *Architectural Record* (April 1972): 119–26.
4. The introduction to Meredith L. Clausen's *Spiritual Space: The Religious Architecture of Pietro Belluschi* (University of Washington Press: Seattle, 1992) contains an account of his career.
5. Adolf K. Placzek, ed., *Encyclopedia of Architects* (Macmillan: New York, 1982), vol. 1, 161.
6. William Dudley Hunt, Jr., *Total Design: Architecture of Welton Becket and Associates* (New York: McGraw-Hill, 1972), 12, 13.
7. Jack B. Beardwood, Los Angeles, to Charles Willis, Washington, D.C., 29 March 1954, USAFA, RG 120, Ser. 17.
8. Kristen Schaffer brought this information to my attention. Beardwood to Willis, 27 July 1954, USAFA, RG 120, Ser. 17.
9. On Saarinen, see Aline Saarinen, ed., *Eero Saarinen on His Work,* 1962.
10. Rupert Spade, *Eero Saarinen* (New York: Simon and Schuster, 1971), 11.
11. Wolfgang Pehnt, ed., *Encyclopedia of Modern Architecture* (New York: Henry Abrams, 1964), 247.
12. Spade, *Saarinen,* 13.

13. GM Tech Center. Photograph by Ezra Stoller, © ESTO, 1958. The General Motors Technical Center in Warren, Michigan (1948–56) was Eero Saarinen's first major work and was similar to the Air Force Academy in scale and scope.

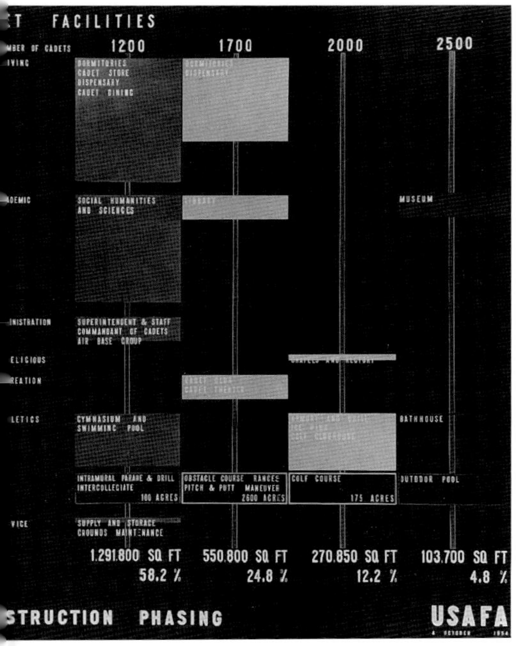

14. Work chart, Skidmore, Owings & Merrill, 1954. Prepared to show the flow of work, this chart projected the construction schedule for all buildings at the Cadet Area during various phases of construction. SOM Archives, Chicago.

the volunteer work his partner Louis Skidmore had done for her New York Women's Hospital Board. Another version speculates that a contributing factor was a recommendation from Frazar Wilde, head of Connecticut General Life Insurance, for whom SOM had designed the corporate headquarters. Wilde, a friend of Talbott's, was said to have been enthusiastic about his experience with SOM.[80] The more likely reason was that no other firm had had as much experience with so many large-scale projects as SOM, nor did many have the political acumen, social connections, and business polish of the SOM partners.

Organization and Programming After years of delay, congressional politics, and military indecision, now that the dream was about to become a reality, great pressure was exerted on SOM to quickly produce a master plan, followed by design and construction drawings. The firm began to plan the Academy almost immediately after winning the competition.[81]

SOM assembled a design and production team, headed by Owings, that would see the project through to completion. At the upper levels were partner John O. Merrill, Director; Carroll L. Tyler, General Manager; and Gordon Bunshaft, Partner in Charge of Design. Walter Netsch, as Director of Design, and Jack Train, as Director of Production, would have the most intense and sustained interaction with the project. Flexible design teams were then formed under Netsch to work on the various components: a team for the cadet area, with smaller groups working on the major buildings, and teams for housing, service and supply, the community area, the officers cluster, and the airfield.[82]

To control the project within the Air Force, headquarters established the Air Force Academy Construction Agency (AFACA) and gave it complete responsibility for the construction of the Academy. Installations would prepare the facility requirements and AFACA would issue the "Design Directives" to the architects.[83] These criteria could be refined, altered, corrected, and improved throughout the design process, and the program requirements could change continuously.[84] Even though the design criteria would come to SOM through Installations and AFACA, the SOM team would report and make their presentation to the Office of the Secretary, through John Ferry, Special Assistant to the Secretary, and James H. Douglas, Assistant Secretary. These layers of bureaucracy tended to insulate the architect from the real client and user, that is, the Academy represented by Harmon. Harmon's own place in the organization chart is somewhat peripheral, with a "dotted line" relationship to the Chief of Staff, under whom was Installations (fig. 10).[85]

In the fall of 1954, the architects and client met for a series of programming sessions. Netsch, who had had experience in the programming and design of the U.S. Naval Postgraduate School, went to Washington to work on the initial program with the Academy planners (fig. 14). The architects challenged some of the recommendations and conclusions of the Air Force planners. Netsch later said that the "architect ought to challenge the client at every point if only to force him to sharpen his understanding of what he really wants." He added, however, that "the architect will not always be right in his challenges and should not be so stubborn as to never admit he was wrong." For instance, the architects did

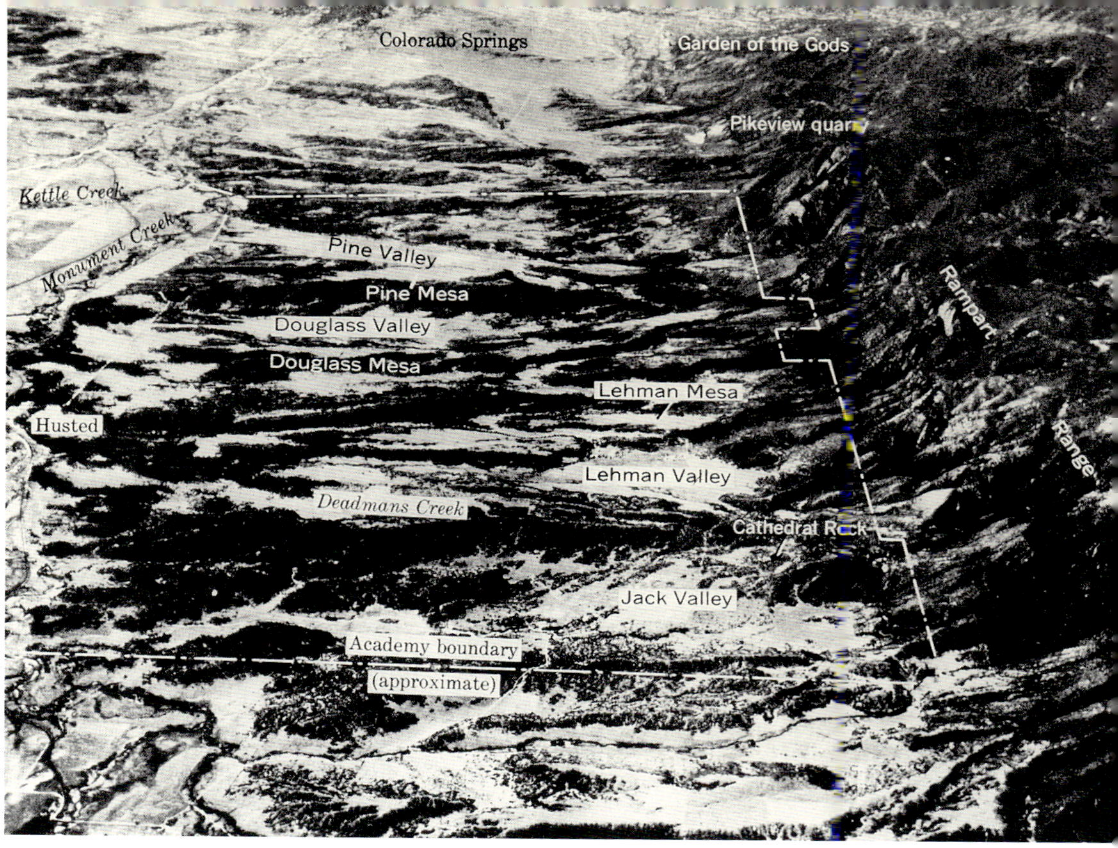

15. Academy site. Over this aerial view looking south, the boundaries of Air Force property have been indicated and the major features identified, c. 1954. From *Quest.* U.S. Air Force Academy Library, Special Collections Branch.

not understand the importance of assembling the entire cadet wing at mealtimes and the need for "direct visual and aural contact," since the orders for the day were given at that time. As a result, they had proposed a series of more intimately scaled dining rooms. The architects admitted that this would have been a mistake on their part, since here the client really knew best.[86]

There was also some disagreement between SOM and Air Force planners over the Academy's educational philosophy, one that depended heavily on rote learning. Air Force planners had required that sufficient blackboard space be provided in each classroom so that the entire class could work at the board simultaneously. Planners also wanted to be able to completely control the lighting in each classroom, dictating the elimination of classroom windows. Since they knew that other educators disapproved of these kinds of methods, the architects wished to "protect" the client by anticipating design modifications if the teaching methods changed. And in an effort to provide the opportunity for individuality in the cadet's quarters, the architects argued against having the quarters be like "a caserne or barracks." SOM wanted to create a dormitory environment more like that of the civilian college campus. They had to be sure, however, to satisfy the Air Force's instructions that the quarters be designed to enhance the identity of each squadron, keeping each squadron together as a recognizable unit and not divided by floors or courtyards. The architects also had wanted to locate toilet rooms between every other cadet room, as was being done in civilian campus design. However, the Air Force officers trained at West Point wished to duplicate the "ritual" of the cadets having to run down flights of stairs to the gang toilets in the basement. As a compromise it was decided to group toilets at the corners of each floor of the Cadet Quarters.[87]

The Site, the Architect, and the Master Plan The site designated for the Academy had been chosen for its dramatic beauty rather than for adaptability to the specific and complex needs of the institution.[88] It would exert a strong influence on the design of the campus, and greatly challenge the architects.

16. Designers working at SOM on Academy model. Photograph c. 1955, reproduced from SOM, Fortieth Aniversary book. The Air Force Academy commission was seen as an opportunity of a lifetime by the SOM architects assigned to work on it. In this photograph Walter Netsch (right) helps position trees on the model in the Chicago office.

Skidmore, Owings & Merrill: THE PROJECT TEAM

At the time Skidmore, Owings & Merrill was commissioned to design the Air Force Academy, the firm had regional offices in San Francisco and Portland, Oregon, as well as in Chicago and New York. The national and decentralized character of the firm allowed each office to draw on the specialties, facilities, and personnel of other offices while operating autonomously. The elected position of coordinating partner was developed to facilitate communication among the offices. As coordinating partner during the Academy project, J. Walter Severinghaus managed policy and personnel practices, and prepared the agenda for the annual partnership meetings to keep all four offices on the same track.[1]

To combat the bureaucratic tendencies inherent in a large organization, and to stimulate the exchange of ideas among regional offices, personnel were often switched from one office to another. Partnership groups were considered fluid, so that the experience and availability of personnel could be balanced among the offices. Skidmore, Owings & Merrill believed that this helped unify the firm's production and standardize its organization in a manner that paralleled the way the building industry was being standardized at the time.

Projects were organized the same way in all of Skidmore, Owings & Merrill's regional offices. The managing partner for each project oversaw five functioning groups: project management, design, production, construction, and administration.[2] The design group's tasks included programming, architectural and interior design, and materials and methods research. Programming, the process of determining the functional and spatial requirements of a client, was perceived as a crucial step: "the more thorough it is, the easier the rest of the process will be."[3] Through sketches, models, and discussions the design of the project evolved. The production group's responsibilities included the hundreds of detailed drawings and specifications needed to describe the building fully to a contractor. The construction group observed the building of the project and administered the construction contracts. The administrative group consisted of nontechnical personnel who dealt with office procedures, records, and accounting. Working together, this team of professionals took a project from design sketches to finished product in an efficient and organized manner.

At the height of the Air Force Academy project, Skidmore, Owings & Merrill employed 900 architects, engineers, designers, city planners, landscape specialists, and estimators.[4] The firm was headed by 14 general partners, 18 associate partners, and 44 participating associates.[5] New partners had to be unanimously elected and were selected from the echelons of associate partners and participating associates. Partners were not allowed to sell their shares to anyone outside the firm.[6] On the Academy team there were five general partners to handle the design and management of the project: Nathaniel A. Owings, the head of the San Francisco office, was responsible for maintaining the liaison with the Air Force; John O. Merrill, a senior partner in Chicago, was the partner-in-charge of the project; from the Chicago office, William E. Hartmann acted as chief administrator and coordinated all phases, including site planning, working drawings, and construction observation; Gordon Bunshaft, design partner in New York, acted as design consultant on the Academy; as project designer, Walter A. Netsch, Jr., who became a partner in 1955, headed the design team in Chicago.[7] The actual design work was further divided into four major components under Netsch: Stanislaw Gladych, master planning; Ralph Youngren, the academic area; John Hoops, service and supply; and Carl Kohler, housing. In the 280-person Denver field office, Carroll L. Tyler was general manager in charge of the Academy operation, assisted by director of engineering Edward A. Merrill (John O. Merrill's brother) and chief architect Albert Lockett.[8] Production manager Jack Train handled the complicated contractual arrangements necessary for a project of this size.[9]

In Chicago the project team consisted of young, enthusiastic architects who realized that the Air Force Academy was "the biggest opportunity available for an architect at that time" (fig. 16).[10] The project schedule was intensely demanding especially since Netsch, who was affectionately referred to as "the original motivator" by team member Roger Margerum, always wanted to look at a design concept in two or three different ways.[11] This meant extensive overtime and personal sacrifice. The project team also included architectural technology researchers led by Robertson Ward. Technological innovations played a significant role in the success of Skidmore, Owings & Merrill's projects at a time when many building systems were first being developed.

At the time of the Air Force Academy project, Skidmore, Owings & Merrill's work was one of the most fully developed examples of architecture produced by teamwork. The firm was part of the new attitude toward architectural practice developed by Walter Gropius, who asserted that teamwork would produce "good 'anonymous' architecture rather than . . . flashy 'stunt' design."[12] This philosophy also appealed to the corporate client, who preferred to deal with an architect who performed like a rational businessman rather than a temperamental artist. The uniqueness of the teamwork approach was acknowledged in the 1950 exhibition of Skidmore, Owings & Merrill's work at the Museum of Modern Art in New York: the first exhibit of a firm rather than of an individual architect.[13] The exhibit noted that Skidmore, Owings & Merrill team members "work together animated by two disciplines which they all share—the discipline of modern architecture and the discipline of American organizational methods."[14] But not everyone was enthusiastic about the teamwork approach. Some designers within the firm felt that it was imposed on them as a means to prevent them from receiving credit. Critics believed it produced an intolerable anonymous quality in Skidmore, Owings & Merrill's work and questioned if teamwork could replace the force of individual genius in architecture.

—*Sheri Olson*

Notes

1. "$2 Billion Worth of Design by Conference," *Business Week*, 4 December 1954, 103.
2. William E. Hartmann, "S.O.M. Organization," *Bauen & Wohnen* (April 1957), 115.
3. "$2 Billion," 104.
4. "Academy Challenge to Architectural Firm," *Colorado Gazette Telegraph*, 31 August 1958, 11.
5. Ibid.
6. "The Architects from 'Skid's Row'," *Fortune*, January 1958, 212.
7. Walter A. Netsch, Jr., was born in Chicago in 1920, and received a Bachelor of Architecture from MIT in 1943. After three years in the Army Corps of Engineers, Netsch worked as a designer with Morgan Yost, Chicago. In 1947, he joined Skidmore, Owings & Merrill in San Francisco, and while with that office spent a few years in Japan and Okinawa designing air bases for the military during the Korean War. He designed (with Pietro Belluschi) St. Trinity Lutheran Church in Walnut Creek (completed 1956), and the Greyhound Bus maintenance facility in San Francisco (1953). Walter Netsch arrived at Skidmore, Owings & Merrill's Chicago office in 1954 shortly before the competition for the Academy.
8. "The Architects from Skid's Row," 138.
9. Interview with Jack Train, SOM construction manager, December 1992, by Kristen Schaffer.
10. John F. Hartray, during interview of architects who had worked at SOM on the Air Force Academy project. Present were team members Mitsuru Otsuji, Stanley Allan, John F. Hartray, Louis Rocah, Gertrude Lempp Kerbis, and Roger Margerum; interview by Sheri Olson, 17 June 1993. Transcript at the USAFA Archives.
11. Ibid.
12. Sigfried Giedion, *Walter Gropius: Work And Teamwork*, New York: Reinhold, 1954), 15.
13. "Skidmore, Owings & Merrill," *Museum of Modern Art Bulletin* 18, 1 (Fall 1950): 5.
14. Ibid.

Situated some six miles beyond what was then the built-up area of Colorado Springs, the site lay below the Rampart Range that formed its western boundary. Containing almost 27 square miles of variable terrain, the dominant characteristic of the site was a series of ridges extending eastward from the mountains like the fingers of a hand. The eastern part of the site was somewhat flatter, with the only large aggregation of level terrain occurring in its southeastern corner. Running north-south through the site on this eastern section, were Monument Creek, U.S. Highway 85 and 87, which linked Colorado Springs and Denver, the Denver & Rio Grande Western Railroad and the Atchison, Topeka & Santa Fe Railway. Between the ridges were valleys, each with its own creek. Near the northern edge of the site was Jack Valley, south of which a narrow ridge overlooked Cathedral Rock, a landmark in the northwestern corner of the site. To the south was Lehman Valley, and then, continuing southward, Lehman Ridge (known as Lehman Mesa), South Lehman Valley, Douglass Ridge, Douglass Valley, Pine Ridge, and Pine Valley. Thus the site was a series of undulating land formations, rising and falling as one moved north and south across it. The valleys were open to the east, as the ridges came down out of the foothills onto the eastern plain (fig. 15).

The architects had not been involved in the selection of the site, yet they had the unusual opportunity to determine its boundaries. The choice of the western edge was fairly obvious— the Rampart Range and the boundaries of Pike National Forest. Land already federally owned or controlled would provide excellent protection against any encroachment. The northern and southern boundaries were not so clearly defined. Here, boundaries were designated over the brows of hills so that conflicting land-use on adjacent properties would not be visible. The determination of the eastern boundary was trickier. It was desirable to include land east of the highway to avoid "non-conforming or blighting development" along the highway and to provide floodplain protection.[89]

The architects soon realized that the site was much hillier than it looked against the steep slope of the mountains, and found that much of the land was not easily usable. SOM started with geodetic and aerial topographic surveys, and consultations with meteorologists. The architects visited the site numerous times, viewing it from a helicopter, wandering over it by jeep, and tracing it out by foot. Onto the difficult site they had to fit, in addition to the classrooms, dormitories, libraries, dining halls, gymnasiums and playing fields typical of a college campus, numerous other facilities, including, for example, an airfield, service and supply functions, and housing and amenities for Air Force personnel. In developing a master plan for the Academy, SOM had to be concerned with the relationship of all these parts to one other, as well as the "intangible condition" that this national project would be subject to public scrutiny and outside influence.[90]

The airfield was one of the first facilities to be sited, since its extreme requirements could be satisfied only in the limited area of level terrain. Fortunately, one runway would afford 93 percent wind coverage, but only if the small landing strip that existed on the site were shifted slightly. Yet even this required the relocation of the highway and the Atchison, Topeka & Santa Fe Railway line, as well as the reconfiguration of Kettle Creek, a tributary of Monument Creek. At the same time, the engineers identified the hundred-year floodplain that would be kept clear of buildings.[91] With the location of the airfield determined, SOM then sited the other facilities in relation to the airfield so that the inevitable noises would not disturb the educational and residential areas. This resulted in a triangular arrangement among the parts, with the cadet area being located in the northwestern, the residential community in the southwestern, and the airfield in the southeastern corners. This, in turn, led to the creation of the road system, which had both an internal network of roads and an external one, which served as the arterial for the inner network and as a conduit for the public.[92]

The siting of the cadet academic area, which would symbolize the Academy to the public, was an issue of utmost importance. SOM explored a number of possibilities including one in Douglass Valley, hidden away like Shangri-la; one

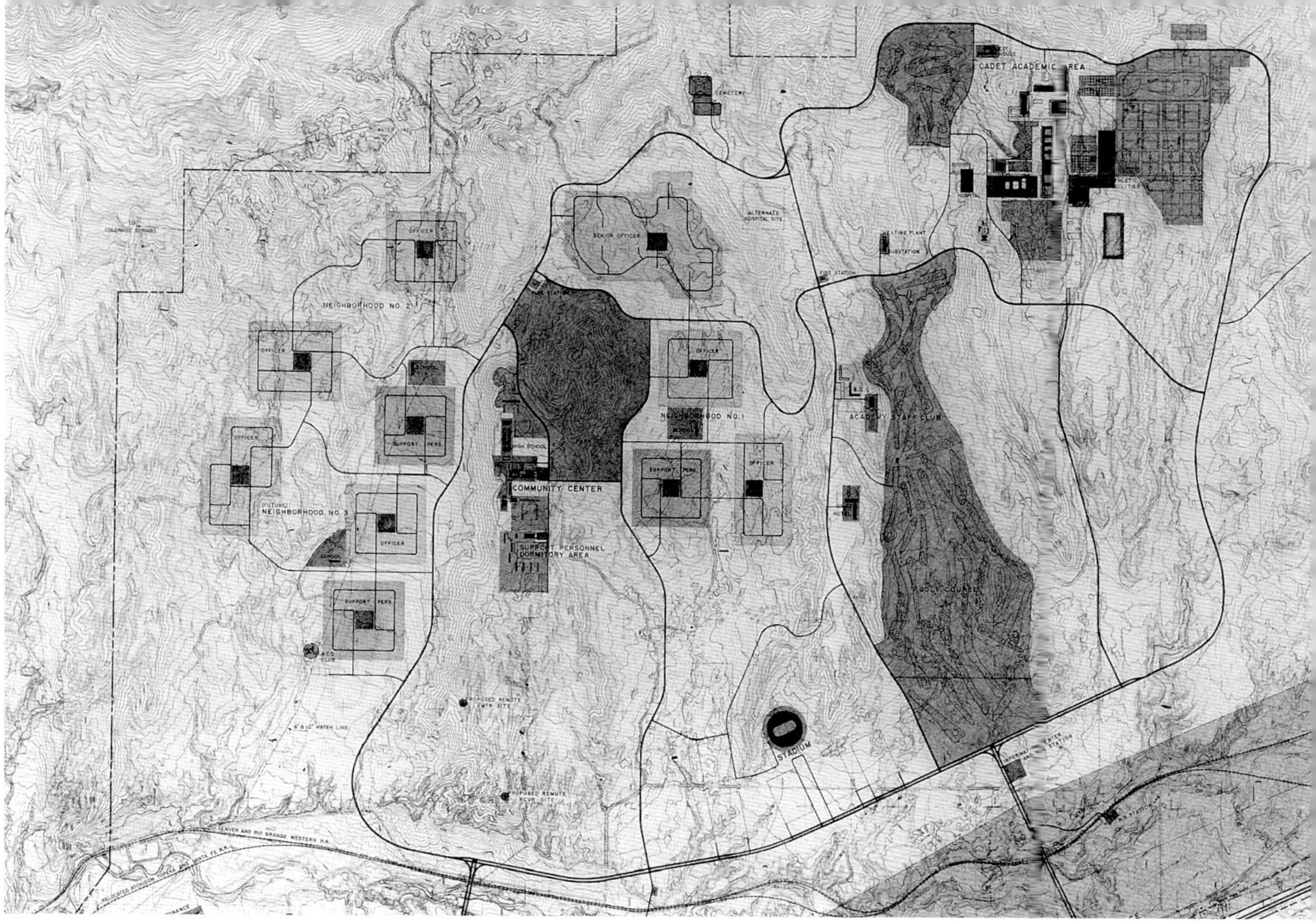

17

on Lehman Mesa, where the Cadet Area is now located; one on the narrow ridge overlooking Cathedral Rock; one near the highway; and a rather "grandiose" scheme, spanning and "damming up" one of the valleys. Proponents of the highway scheme wanted to locate the Cadet Area there as a kind of "advertisement" for the Academy, but when the officials stood near the highway and looked toward the site, they were convinced that the Cadet Area would look much better "closely related to the mountains." Clearly, aesthetic as well as functional considerations shaped the layout of the Academy on the site. Thinking that the mesa location might be overdramatic, Harmon wanted to build the Cadet Area in one of the valleys. He was concerned also about the ability to expand the Cadet Area if it were located on a narrow mesa.[93] Three of the schemes—for Douglass Valley, Lehman Mesa, and the ridge overlooking Cathedral Rock—received further attention.

The architects considered Lehman Mesa the obvious choice because it was the highest elevation on the site, had a large area of relatively even terrain, and was directly adjacent to a level area suitable for playing fields. Lehman Mesa also seemed to best satisfy the less tangible requirements of the Air Force, the mandate to create a national monument, to establish in a few short years a sense of place potent enough to contain the seeds of a tradition. Lehman Mesa offered great potential because, as a point of transition between the mountains and the plain, it had a special feel. It presented an expansive view east over the plain.[94] And, with the buildings set so close to the mountains, the grandeur of the mountains could be felt. This was the site finally chosen.

The Secretary, consultants, and architects quickly agreed upon the scale and concept of the buildings for the Cadet Area, and an L-shaped configuration was adopted. From then on, the master planning process went fairly smoothly. Abstract principles and planning criteria did not raise difficult objections. "At this point we had no cornices for the critics to hang their objections on," one of the architects stated, and the consultants were helpful.[95] Following countless meetings on site boundaries and real estate, zoning, subsurface water supply, utilities, weather and soils and geology data, and railroad and highway relocation, preliminary presentations were made in February 1955, and the Secretary reviewed preliminary building designs in March. A partial and preliminary plan report was submitted in April. The architects, meanwhile, had continued programming studies and conferences with members of the Air Force in January and February 1955. Through March, SOM was "engaged in intensive preparation of overall design features,"[96] using flow diagrams of cadet movement to convince Air Force officials. "Flow, function and architecture" were seen by the architects as being so closely allied that "the approval of one automatically settled the design of the rest."[97]

The master plan was presented on 1 June 1955 (fig. 17).[98] The arrangement of facilities from the southern to the northern part of the site was marked by a gradual transition from accessible to restricted areas. Thus the facilities requiring the most contact with the civilian world were located on the southern part of the site, closest to Colorado Springs. The housing was distributed in Pine and Douglass Valleys, with the community center located on Pine Ridge in between the two (fig. 18).[99] The community center included support personnel dormitories, a dining hall and service club, as well as the commissary, community chapel, library, theater, gymnasium and swimming pool, and concessions. The high school was originally located here too. The bachelor officer quarters, visiting officers quarters, and officers mess were located on Douglass Ridge, between the residential sector and the Academic Area. The stadium was sited just east of Douglass Ridge, where it sloped down to the plain.

18

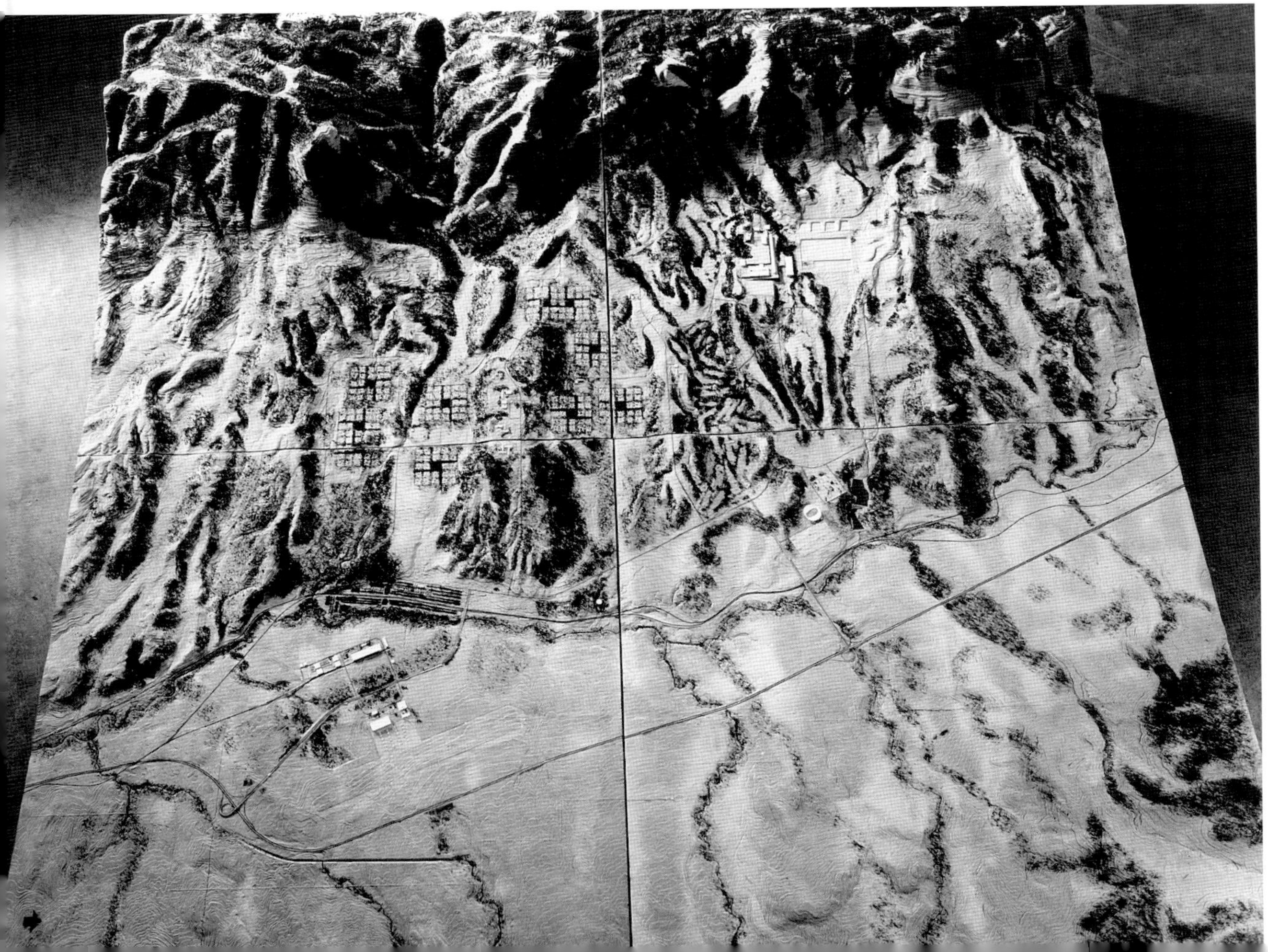

17. Site plan from SOM master plan, 1955. In this site plan the Pine Valley and Douglas Valley housing areas with the community center between them are on the left. The Cadet Area is to the right. At the bottom of the image are the railroad and a piece of the highway to Denver and Colorado Springs. SOM Archives, Chicago.

18. Site model. Photograph by Ezra Stoller, © Esto 1955. This model was made for the Colorado Springs Arts Center exhibition.

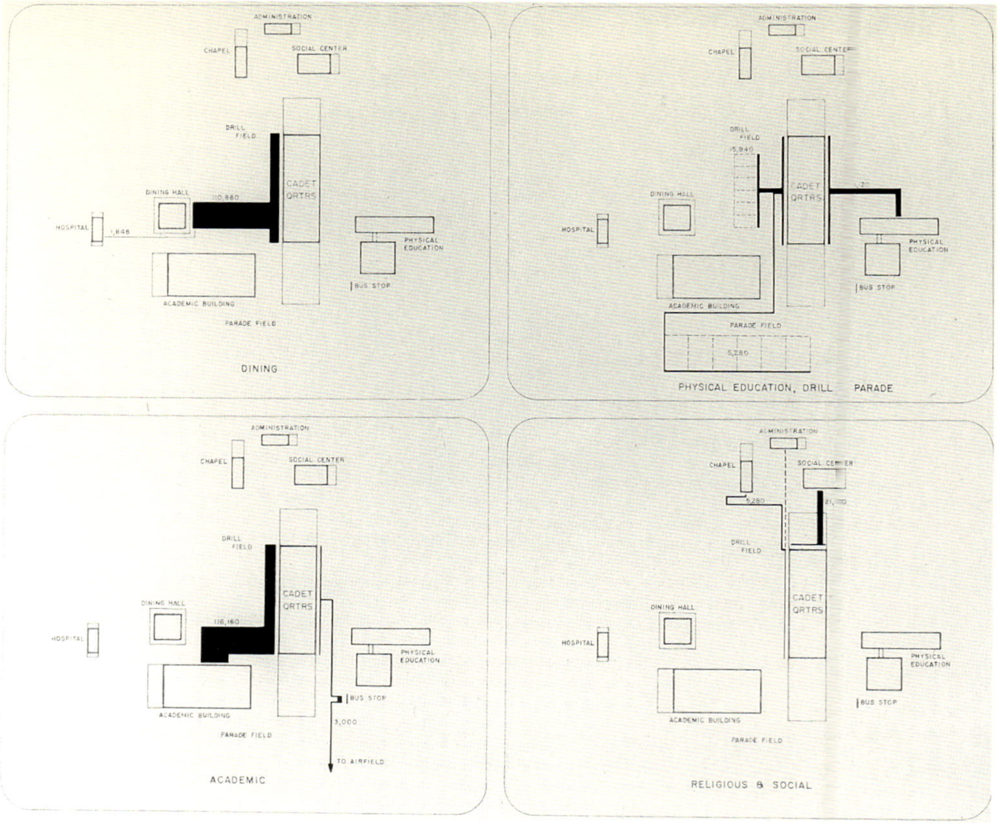

19. Cadet flow diagrams from the SOM Master Plan, 1955. These diagrams were used to study the relationships between the buildings and to ensure adequate circulation for the cadets, whose strict daily schedule allowed no time for wasted steps. SOM Archives, Chicago.

For the Lehman Mesa Cadet (or Academic) Area, the architects offered two slightly different schemes. In both the 19
superintendent's house overlooked the parade and drill field to the east. The hospital was to be located just to the south of the academic area; a museum to the west; and athletic playing fields directly to the north in adjacent upper Lehman Valley. Further to the north were the maneuver areas and firing ranges. The master plan also included a survey of existing structures on the site—mostly ranch houses, barns, and outbuildings—and indicated that some might be retained for temporary use.

The master plan was based on an estimated population of 2,640 cadets, 1,493 military work personnel, and a civilian workforce of 2,333.[100] The plan of the cadet area was based on the anticipated volume of circulation by the cadets and the terrain of the site (fig. 19). The L-shaped configuration already agreed upon formed the basis of the cadet area plan. Cadets differ from other college students in the restricted realm of their movements and in the extreme demands on their time. Proximity is therefore of great importance. The Cadet Quarters constituted the long bar of the L, and was located on the northern edge of the mesa. It determined the location of all the other facilities. The architects nestled the Quarters into the mesa in order to use the change of grade to advantage in the building's section. Thus the architects developed their planning solution—that is, the location of the building—at the same time they established the design idea that allowed the planning scheme to work. The bulk of the building's mass would be visible from outside the Cadet Area, but would be largely hidden from the pedestrian Terrazzo Level. The Academic Building formed the shorter base of the L, at the east end of the mesa, and similarly accommodated the change of level in its section. This location, adjacent to the Cadet Quarters, was determined by the expected high volume of cadet movement between the two buildings. Both buildings contained interior courtyards. Next to the Academic Building, the Dining Hall was sited atop the southeastern

21

20

20. Model of Cadet Area at Colorado Springs Art Center. Photograph by Ezra Stoller, © Esto, 1955. In this view looking southeast the Chapel is shown as a folded plate concrete design. From the Chapel clockwise, the Administration Building, the Cadet Social Center, the Cadet Dormitory, the Academic Building, and the Dining Hall. Stoller No. 55 Q: 2.

21. View of Chapel from the Cadet Social Center. Gouache rendering by George Rudolph, 1955, for the Colorado Springs Art Center exhibition. The Cadet Social Center in this view is almost entirely glazed. The Chapel is shown as a concrete plate structure. SOM Archives, Chicago.

corner of the mesa, opposite the Cadet Quarters to satisfy proximity requirements. The location of the Dining Hall also created a sense of enclosure and provided a long approach for the ceremonial formation and march of cadets into mess.

Separated from the Cadet Area by its higher level, and located at the western end of the site, was the Court of Honor, where the public would interact with the cadets. Here were located the Administration Building and the cadet Social Center. Sited at the northwest corner of the academic area, the Social Center closed the Court of Honor on the north; the Administration Building formed the western boundary. Sitting on its own high podium to the south, and oriented in the master plan on an east-west axis, the Cadet Chapel marked the south edge of the court. Outside the Court to the northwest was the original location for the Academy museum and, in one scheme, the planetarium as well. At lower levels, the physical education buildings and athletic fields were located to the north of the mesa, and the parade ground to the east. Thus the Cadet Quarters served as the center of all cadet activities. All other cadet facilities were located within a ten-minute walk.

Once the major site plan decisions were approved, and the L-shaped configuration of the Cadet Area was accepted, SOM was directed to ready their work for public presentation even though the master plan was not yet completed. The architects, in addition to the master plan, had been working on the designs of the individual buildings, developing their proportions, choosing materials, and determining the character of the facades. By April 1955, these initial designs were far enough along that the Secretary designated May 13–15 for a public exhibition. The presentation should be "as extensive and forceful as necessary to fully inform members of Congress, the news media and the public about the Air Force Academy and its architecture," the Secretary was advised, but not so "elaborate and expensive that Appropriations Committee Members might successfully take exception to it."[101]

The Exhibition and Its Fallout SOM had just six weeks to ready its work for exhibition at the Colorado Springs Fine Arts Center. To aid in presenting the initial designs and plans in models, drawings, and photographs, SOM engaged internationally known and respected consultants: Herbert Bayer, exhibition design; George Rudolph, perspective rendering; Ansel Adams, land photography; William Garnett, aerial photography; and the Richard Rush Studio and Theodore Conrad, models (figs. 20-21, 74-79).[102]

Secretary Talbott invited all forty members of the House Armed Services Committee and fourteen members of the Senate Armed Services Committee; the nineteen members of the Senate Appropriations Committee and fifteen members of the Department of Defense Subcommittee of the House Committee on Appropriations; as well as the two Colorado senators and four representatives. Also invited were members of the Air Force such as Superintendent Harmon, General Nathan F. Twining, Chief of Staff, and Colonel Albert E. Stoltz, Director of AFACA.[103] The Air Force arranged tours of the exhibit, first for members of Congress, and later for the press, followed by a tour of the site.

After the presentation, Talbott called the exhibition "magnificent," complimented the architects on their "enthusiasm and drive," and indicated his approval of the overall planning concept, the disposition of buildings, and the use of the site. His only reservation focused on the extensive, almost exclusive, use of glass as the exterior cladding material in the Cadet Area. He suggested revisions, and urged SOM to make better use of the consultants.[104]

Initially, members of Congress who viewed the exhibit seemed to accept the buildings and overall plan with the exception of the Cadet Chapel. Representative Dewey Short, Chair of the House Armed Services Committee, wrote to Talbott that he enjoyed "looking over the plans and models very much, and considering the complexities of such a vast new institution, the designs are wonderful. It was a marvelous conception of what the Academy should be." He too had reservations about the Chapel, but these were rather moderate. He hoped the Chapel could be "much higher," and its "design . . . altered so that it will be a real spire of spiritual inspiration."[105] Others, like Senator John Stennis, evinced a clear predisposition against the proposed design. He "was disappointed in the modernistic and futurist type of architecture," as he thought "the traditional and conventional type of structures . . . would create more of an atmosphere of learning." His comments on the Chapel were more severe. He characterized it as "a cruel twist to the whole subject of religion and spiritual instruction," and hoped that the design of the Chapel would be "entirely abandoned."[106] Others expressed concerns over the materials to be used—glass, steel, and aluminum—but nothing in the initial reaction to the presentation suggested the storm of protest that was soon to erupt.

The negative response was spearheaded by special-interest groups. Reacting to the model, manufacturers of masonry construction materials predictably took great exception to the minimal use of marble, limestone, travertine, and granite, and the complete absence of brick. Opposition coalesced when these groups conveyed their displeasure to their representatives in Congress while the latter were considering appropriations for the Academy. Construction on the Academy began on 1 July 1955, when the contracts for the roads were let, but if it were to be ready in time for the Air Force to graduate its first class from the new campus in June 1959, road, utility, and site work would have to begin immediately. Yet, as of 1955, Congress had appropriated only $15 of the $126 million authorized.[107]

Representative John E. Fogarty (D-R.I.) led the assault on the SOM design, declaring that it was "not American in conception and is unworthy of the traditions of this nation." Before his election to Congress, he had been president of the Rhode Island Bricklayers Union, Local 1, which covered the entire state. Fogarty was particularly offended by the Chapel, admitting that the reason was the lack of brickwork, but continuing that he thought glass and metals to be "alien to American monumental design—even European." The *San Francisco Chronicle* expressed regret that the Air Force was subjected to this criticism, "criticism that had little validity outside the curious doctrine which holds that election to Congress automatically transforms the electee into an infallible authority on every art, technology and method of doing business."[108]

Strange Alliances:
FRANK LLOYD WRIGHT AND CONGRESS

22. Frank Lloyd Wright pointing out his vision of escalators and waterfalls during a visit to the site of the future Air Force Academy. Photograph by Ed Welter for *Free Press,* spring 1955. In this photograph are, from left, an unknown figure, Wright, William Thayer Tutt, and Charles Leeming Tutt Jr. The Tutts played a key role in obtaining the Academy for Colorado Springs. Wright's scathing review of Skidmore, Owings & Merrill's design before Congress in 1955 threatened to hold up funding for the project and ignited a major architectural debate.

The most highly publicized architectural debate surrounding the Academy project occurred during the 1955 congressional appropriation hearings. At the center of the debate was Frank Lloyd Wright's testimony before Congress on Skidmore, Owings & Merrill's preliminary designs.

Economic motives, rather than aesthetics, played a large, if carefully concealed, role in the orchestrated attack on the designs for the Academy. The new Allied Masonry Council, which represented the interests of labor, contractors, and producers of brick, stone, and tile, was understandably dissatisfied with the glass and steel vocabulary employed in the preliminary sketches. Not only were its members upset about not getting a bigger share of the construction budget, but they were also concerned about the design's potential for establishing new trends for the future. Aware of the political nature of the project, the Allied Masonry Council hired a successful Washington lobbyist, Douglas Whitlock, to promote its interests before Congress.

Representative John E. Fogarty (D-R.I.), a member of the full Appropriations Committee and the past president of the Rhode Island Bricklayers Union, led the attack. For the *Congressional Record* Fogarty provided lengthy disquisitions on the advantages of brick walls; and attacked the Skidmore, Owings & Merrill design as a "monument to experimental materials."[1] Whether Fogarty's motivations were economic or partisan—several of the more outspoken critics of the Academy were Democrats—it is apparent from his testimony that he genuinely despised Modern architecture and believed it to be un-American.[2] It was Fogarty who suggested that Wright be invited to testify as an expert witness before the House subcommittee hearings on funding for the project.[3] Wright had already dubbed Skidmore, Owings & Merrill's design a "factory for birdmen" after being sent sketches by a newspaper that then widely publicized his derogatory remarks.[4]

Wright was more than willing to come to Washington to testify against his old nemesis, the International Style, especially if someone else was willing to pick up the tab. His opinion was further biased by his unsuccessful pursuit of the Air Force commission as a member of the Kittyhawk Associates team put together by Cleveland architect Richard Hawley Cutting. Upon learning that Wright was among the competitors for the Academy, the National Americanism Commission of the American Legion prepared a scandal sheet on Wright with the intention of making it public. At the time, the commission was headed by former FBI agent Lee Pennington, who had assembled the agency's thick file on Wright's allegedly subversive activities. Although never a card-carrying Communist—in fact the Wisconsin chapter of the Communist Party accused him of slurring it—Wright was a pacifist and in lectures, articles, and on national television had made antimilitary comments.[5] It is difficult to understand how Wright reconciled his antimilitary attitudes with his desire to design a major commission for the Air Force.

Had Wright known of the Legion's intentions he might have chosen to stand up to its bullying.[6] After all, it would not have been the first, or the worst, public scandal he had faced. But in July 1954, before the Legion could make its smears public, Wright withdrew because he refused, as a matter of principle, to compete for the job with other architects.[7] In a telegram to Cutting, Wright declared, "The world knows what I can do in architecture. If officials of the air force have missed this, I can do no more than feel sorry for what both have lost."[8]

Wright was presented with a perfect opportunity for revenge. On 7 July 1955, at the age of eighty-eight, he made a dramatic appearance, with his flowing white hair and Western hat, to testify behind closed doors before the House Appropriations Subcommittee. An earlier witness had testified as "Mr. Average Man;" Wright was clearly "Mr. Architect."[9] After deriding Skidmore, Owings & Merrill's scheme for its lack of soul, Wright eagerly described his own vision for the project (fig. 22).[10] The chapel would be sited on top of the mountain as a crowning feature, with the rest of the Academy located along a central axis rising up to it. Escalators would bring the cadets up and down as needed. Wright strongly recommended that work halt on Skidmore, Owings & Merrill's design and that a fresh start be made with a new competition.[11] He suggested himself as one of three architects to be invited to prepare a brochure of designs that would then be distributed to high schools across the country. Students would choose the new designer of the Academy.

The committee ignored Wright's suggestion for a competition but recommended that funding for the project be withheld indefinitely, citing concern that the present design did not reflect the best traditions of American architecture. This outburst occurred a day after the new Academy was officially dedicated at its temporary headquarters in Denver. A week later Air Force Secretary Talbott presented a Senate committee with revised drawings showing a reduction in the extensive amount of glass. Talbott warned that a whole year would be lost in opening the buildings if funds were delayed. In the end a compromise was reached to restore partial funding.

Controversy continued to swirl around the project in headlines, editorials, and professional publications across the country. *Progressive Architecture*, in a letter to congressional critics, blasted the committee's qualifications to judge architectural design. Included were statements from forty-two architects, from all parts of the nation, who were overwhelmingly opposed to Congress's actions. Protesting the committee's "horse and buggy thinking in a jet age," the architects supported Skidmore, Owings & Merrill's design as an appropriate expression of function and technology.[12] To make his point, one architect sarcastically offered Congress sketches of a B-52 bomber decorated in Colonial Williamsburg style.

The Air Force Academy was catapulted into the headlines again in August 1955 when *Architectural Forum* reported on the economic motivations behind the congressional debate and shocked its readers by revealing the American Legion's 1954 plans to mount a smear campaign against Wright. Apparently, the Legion had readied another attack during Wright's testimony before Congress, when it appeared that he might have another chance to design the Academy. Upon learning for the first time of the secret opposition to him, Wright publicly attacked the Legion, declaring "I do not know why the American Legion puts me on its blackened page unless [it is] because I hate war and openly oppose it."[13] When confronted, the Legion denied everything.[14]

Although it generated more heat than light, the controversy over designs for the Academy brought the subject of modern architecture, usually relegated to academic and professional circles, to the attention of the American public, and it sparked a continuing debate on how American architecture was to reflect the country's new prosperity, technological advances, and emerging role as a world power.

—*Sheri Olson*

Notes

1. U.S. House, *Design for the New Air Force Academy,* Extension of remarks by Rep. John E. Fogarty, 84th Cong., 1st Sess., *Congressional Record,* vol. 101, pt. 7, 1955, 8781.
2. Ibid.
3. "Air Academy Design Brawl," *Architectural Forum* (August 1955): 13.
4. "Wright Favors Talbott's Aviary As Name for Air Academy," *Washington Star,* 27 May 1955.
5. Donald Leslie Johnson, *Frank Lloyd Wright Versus America: The 1930s* (Cambridge: MIT Press, 1990), 318; and Meryle Secrest, *Frank Lloyd Wright* (New York: Alfred A. Knopf, 1992), 538.
6. "Wright Assails Legion in Academy Architect Row," *Gazette Telegraph,* 12 August 1955.
7. Telegram from Frank Lloyd Wright to Richard Hawley Cutting, 3 July 1954. William Theodore Evjue Papers, State Historical Society of Wisconsin.
8. "Air Academy Design Brawl," 12.
9. U.S. House, *Military Construction Appropriations for 1956,* Hearings before the Subcommittee of the Committee on Appropriations, 84th Cong., 1st Sess., 1955, 545.
10. Ibid., 556–57.
11. U.S. Senate. *Supplemental Appropriation Bill,* 1956, Hearings before the Committee on Appropriations, H.R. 7278, 84th Cong., 1st Sess., 1955, 339.
12. Barney Seibert, "Architecture Magazine Hits Congressional Critics of Design for New Air Force Academy," *Colorado Free Press,* 22 July 1955.
13. "Wright Assails Legion for Opposing Him," *Rocky Mountain Press,* 12 August 1955.
14. "Wright Lashes Legion 'Critics' in Academy Row," *Denver Post,* 12 August 1955.

In typical fashion, Congress called upon an expert, in this case Frank Lloyd Wright, who, appearing before congressional committees, heaped scorn upon the entire project, on SOM, and on the architectural consultants.[109] The editor-in-chief of *Architectural Record* magazine suggested that Wright's dislike of the design would surprise no one: "His massive contempt for literally all save his own efforts is one of his best known and least noble traits."[110]

The design for the Chapel drew the harshest criticism. It was one of the last buildings to receive the architects' attention, and for a while they were at a loss for a design concept. Their task was exacerbated by the fact that the program for the Chapel had not yet been worked out, and it was uncertain whether the Chapel would house one, two, or three denominations, or how it would do so. During a discussion of the Chapel, one member of the design team folded a piece of white cardboard. The architects liked the effect and agreed it would provide "a good symbol" for the Chapel.[111] The folded paper recalled the technique of folded plate construction, a technique that would make the Chapel distinct from the rest of the buildings in the Cadet Area by giving it a completely different form. It had a vertical orientation appropriate to a house of worship, and a triangular shape that would distinguish it from the rectilinear buildings of the area. SOM began a study of the technique, and used it as the basis for the Chapel design as shown in the exhibition model (fig. 20). The effect this image of the chapel had on the nonarchitectural community was unimagined and brought a storm of protest. Typical were the remarks of Senator A. Willis Robertson, who protested that he did not "hear the rustle of angel's wings" when looking at the model chapel.[112]

The criticisms had their desired effect. The House Appropriations Committee, responding to the pressure, decided that to appropriate more than the initial $15 million would be "most unwise . . . until the design is more firmly established," and on 13 July 1955, proceeded to delete the Academy's funds from the Fiscal Year 1957 Supplemental Appropriations Bill.[113] This delay threatened to increase the cost of the project in added design and construction time.

23. Aerial perspective of revised site plan, late 1955. SOM drawing by Dale Byrd. In this view looking to the northwest, the Dining Hall is in the lower center of the picture. Moving counterclockwise around the Terrazzo Level are the Academic Building, broken into two parts, the Cadet Dormitory, also broken into two parts, the Cadet Social Center, the Administration Building, and the Chapel, here fashioned by the architects into a simple rectangular solid that only indicates location and avoids any indication of the style of the architecture. By the time of this drawing the ultimate location and orientation of the chapel had finally been fixed. SOM Archives, Chicago.

24. View of revised model, c. 1956. Photograph by Ezra Stoller, © Esto. In this view the Cadet Quarters are in the foreground. They now show the curvilinear landscape elements designed by Dan Kiley. Beyond this in the center of the photo are the Air Gardens, newly added to the design by Kiley and, to the right, the Chapel, still shown in schematic form.

Wright's vituperative attack and Congress's treatment of SOM triggered a supportive response that now flowed in from practicing architects. On 15 July 1955, the American Institute of Architects took a firm public stand, declaring that the architects, and the Secretary's consultants as well, were "among the most distinguished of American practitioners" and recommended that they should be allowed to get on with their work. The editors of *Progressive Architecture* magazine solicited comments from America's "ablest" architects and sent them to Talbott. The reaction of Walter Gropius, Professor Emeritus at Harvard University and international advocate of modern architecture, was unequivocal:

> **At last we have found—away from weak imitation of borrowed styles of the past—a genuine architectural expression which vigorously characterizes the present American approach in science and industry. A proud example is the design of the Air Force Academy which shows progressive American leadership in architecture. I am confident that its cultural merits will prevail against sentimentality and ignorance.**[114]

Meanwhile, SOM played its hand well, making no public reply to the criticism. The architects refused to play the naming game and declined to classify their design in terms of standard terminologies or to categorize it as Modern. When asked about it, they reportedly characterized the project "as functional, as harmonizing with the spirit of the Air Force, and as a part of the landscape in which it was set," and striving not for any evocation of a particular style or time, but for a timeless quality.[115]

The architects quietly revised their designs. Some buildings were scaled back. Glass-enclosed corridors, designed for the periphery of the Academic building, were almost entirely eliminated by moving them to the interior court, so that the amount of masonry on the exterior could be increased. Masonry also was added to other, originally all-glass buildings, such as the Cadet Social Center. The Chapel design was withdrawn, and thereafter, until a revised design was approved by the Secretary, the Chapel was represented on subsequent models only volumetrically, indicating location and mass but nothing more (figs. 23, 24).

By the time the Senate Appropriations committee met, SOM's revised drawings had been completed and the image of the Chapel suppressed. The buildings were now to be a mix of granite, limestone, and marble as well as glass, aluminum, and steel. Congress reviewed the revisions and restored funding to the project.[116]

Design and Construction With funding approved, the design and further programming of the buildings proceeded. AFACA issued and revised the "Design Directives"; SOM continued its work on the refinements of the plan and the design of the buildings; and the consultants resumed their monitoring and advising.[117]

In its designs for the Academy, the architects tried to preserve what they perceived to be the "indigenous factor" of the West. They wanted to emphasize its expansiveness, the sense they defined as "not being confined or pushed together in an artificial little community." According to Walter Netsch, the architects were constantly trying to bring the character of the land right into the built-up areas. They saw this melding of the land form into the total design as being as important as the design of the buildings. The architects also paid attention to "the interrelationship of the buildings and their spaces." They had to develop the individual buildings, but the concern for the space relationships remained dominant. The buildings would define the Cadet Area at a human and habitable scale. At the same time, the relationships of the buildings would allow the spaces between them to open out into the larger landscape. The buildings were to "contain and release and relax within an exhilarated space which is an earth-bound version of the sky." The architects above all strove to harmonize their design with the character of the landscape, particularly that of the Cadet Area with the mesa.[118]

The open side of the L configuration occurred on the southern edge of the Cadet Area, between the Chapel and the Dining Hall, permitting the extension of the sloping terrain and natural forms into the Cadet Area. This arrangement offered nature as a counterpoint to architecture. The result was a balance of hard-edge forms with the trees, scrub, and rolling slope of the site that penetrated into the center of the area and created a landscape setting for the Chapel.[119] The architects conceived the relationship between their architecture and the landscape in terms of these large concepts and broad strokes. One of the consultants, however, was critical of this approach. At a meeting in October 1955, Saarinen expressed his concern over the lack of development of landscaping concepts and elements. At his urging, landscape architect Dan Kiley was added to the project team.[120]

The Cadet Area, as the symbol of the Academy to the public, was the object of "intimate scrutiny" by the design team and the Secretary's consultants. Set against a mountain backdrop, the architectural forms had to be large enough not to be completely overwhelmed by the mountains and to provide an appropriate sense of monumentality.[121] The early decision, in line with Harmon's view, to house the diverse functions in a few large structures was the first step in addressing this design problem. However, much as the architects wanted the massive structures to be apparent from outside the complex, they did not want them to appear overpowering from the Terrazzo level. Nestling the buildings into the mesa effectively hid their bulk from the pedestrian level, allowing the architects to bring down the scale, the perceived size, of the buildings to the human range.

Nestled into the north side of the mesa, the Cadet Quarters accommodated the change of level in its design.

25. View of inside of "contrefort" retaining wall during construction. Photograph by SOM photographer, c. 1956. To create level areas for buildings and outdoor spaces, the architects regraded Lehman Mesa into a series of three large terraces with great retaining walls specially designed to hold the vast quantities of earth securely in place. Walter Netsch collection.

Viewed from below, the building loomed a bulky six stories in height; seen from the pedestrian plaza, the Terrazzo level at mesa top, it was but a sleek three stories high. Levels one and four were open loggias; levels two, three, five, and six contained cadet rooms. Level four was plaza grade. Thus, the cadets would be only two floors up or two floors down from the Terrazzo, with quick access to the rest of the academic area. Bunshaft credited Netsch with this design idea, which made the mesa a feasible location for cadet activities.[122] Interior courtyards allowed a double-loaded corridor of cadet rooms in most of the building, and provided the necessary volume to create an appropriately monumental mass for the building.

The architects decided to design the Cadet Quarters using a seven-foot module that they applied to the entire Cadet Area. This had both practical and aesthetic significance. The module times four produced the dimension of the structural bay and the standardization of the size of the beams and other structural units. Times two, it created the width of the cadet room. The module itself, or subdivisions of it, determined the sizes of windows, spandrel panels, and the detailing of the facades. The module facilitated the organization of the buildings both physically and visually, enabling the structures to differ from one another yet be "contained within one basic discipline." This module contributed to the basic, consistent discipline that the architects sought.[123]

The Cadet Quarters, the first building whose design was worked out in detail by the architects, set the scale and vocabulary for all the other buildings in the Cadet Area. A mock-up of a cadet room was prepared, to show the interior space, as well as the exterior detailing. A meeting in July exhibited the cadet room mock-up with furnishings, lighting, and cabinetry by Walter Dorwin Teague Associates, industrial designers for the project.[124]

Like the Cadet Quarters, the Academic Building extended below the level of the mesa. Here, the architects layered the building according to function, and used the change in grade to "hide" the taller laboratory level below the terrazzo. Instead of nestling the building into the mesa, however, they made the Academic Building free-standing, connected to the terrazzo level by bridges. Pulling the building away from the mesa permitted ground-level circulation all the way around the building, and allowed the architects to locate the garage and service facilities there. Level two held the science laboratories. Here, level three was plaza grade, the level that provided access to the large auditoriums. It was also entry level for the library at the northern end of the building. Levels four and five contained classrooms in clusters of five; and level six contained the faculty offices. The Air Force pedagogic program militated against windows in classrooms, and this, along with the successful campaign to increase the use of masonry, contributed to the windowlessness of much of the facade. The library, housed at the northern end of the building with the Commandant of Cadets, was articulated as a separate building from the terrazzo level upward.

The Dining Hall posed an unusual problem. The program specified that it accommodate 3,000 cadets in one sitting. In order to provide a single dining hall with no columns impeding visibility, the architects and engineers designed a huge roof structure made up of intersecting trusses, which was assembled on the ground and raised into place. The whole roof span rests on only sixteen columns that are pushed toward the periphery of the enclosed area, providing a clear span of 266 feet.[125]

The architects had wanted to locate the kitchen, staging area, and services below the main dining floor, connecting the two levels by elevators and using heated dining carts for serving food. With no service area on the dining level, all four sides could have been enclosed in glass, making the Dining Hall into a glass pavilion, a transparent screen. With this scheme, however, the architects were unable to provide the required level of food service, so that some food preparation areas had to be included on the main floor. To hide these functions, the architects had to provide an opaque facade on the north.[126]

The Social Center was initially designed as a glass box, but after congressional criticism, was redesigned with

26

substantially more stone cladding. The west facade remained glazed, however, as did part of the northern facade, the latter affording a prospect of Cathedral Rock, which the architects wanted to illuminate so that it could be viewed at night.[127] The Administration Building was designed as a long, thin bar, raised on pilotis. Entrance to the Court of Honor by the public was gained through the building at plaza level.

The architects chose structural systems on the basis of programmatic considerations. The Administration and Academic Buildings were steel frame, the Cadet Quarters composite steel and reinforced concrete flat-slab span, and the Dining Hall a long span double-truss. Similarly, the designers considered the function of the building when deciding on cladding material. For example, they chose precast concrete as appropriate for utilitarian buildings and marble facings for the classroom buildings, where there was concern for "opacity, careful scale and color."[128]

At the time that the Academy was being designed, materials that later became standard items were still under development, construction techniques were in the process of changing, and the glass curtain wall was not yet common. The architects wanted to explore new technology, and they had no trouble getting manufacturers to send samples or special fabrications to the site for review and testing, as the manufacturers were eager to find new uses for materials and processes developed during World War II. For instance, anodized aluminum was a new product. At the architects' request, manufacturers sent samples of anodized panels, some of which turned unexpected colors in the sun. Panels of stone, ceramic, and glass were also reviewed.[129] To help the Air Secretary, his consultants, the architects, and the generals in charge select cladding materials in the light of the Colorado altitude, a "billboard" of materials, 42 feet wide and 21 feet high, was erected on the site. At a site meeting in April 1956, the Secretary chose the major cladding materials, a "duller" finish aluminum for the exterior, with a "warm" white marble.[130]

Construction began in July 1955 with earth-moving and the paving of roads. The Cadet Area buildings, the first to be constructed, were far enough along to be occupied in August 1958. The Cadet Quarters and Dining Hall were virtually finished, the Academic Building met "minimum essential requirements" in July and would be complete in November, and the Social Center would be functioning in December and completed in March 1959. By November 1958, construction was 90 percent complete and ahead of schedule.[131] The scale of the project was mammoth. For the cadet area alone, the project employed 52 contractors and 6,000 workers. Two and one-half million cubic yards of earth were moved in order to reconfigure the mesa and terrace the playing fields; and two miles of retaining walls were constructed. The Cadet Quarters alone would occupy some four acres and stretch about a quarter mile in length. About 60,000 drawings and sketches were made, including 6,000 working drawings.[132] There were 32 miles of main roads and six bridges to build.[133] SOM set up an office in Colorado Springs in 1954 for shop drawings and site supervision. At one point this office employed as many as 250 people, some of them lured away from other firms.[134]

The Cadet Chapel, because of the initial controversy, was still being designed while the rest of the Academy was under construction. Unlike the other buildings of this area, the chapel was not a team project but the work of Netsch.[135] Here again the consultants played a major role. Saarinen in particular was dissatisfied with the original location of the Chapel on a hillock above the Court of Honor, which he felt was overly romantic and set too far from the rest of the Cadet Area. In October 1955, the architect was directed to restudy the location.[136] The Chapel was subsequently sited right on the Court of Honor, but still with the original east-west orientation. This too was criticized, particularly by Saarinen. Netsch then reoriented the Chapel, so that it was parallel with the mountains. The final solution integrated the Chapel in a much more satisfactory manner with the rest of the Court of Honor by placing it on the same terrace level, yet letting it remain apart by facing south (fig. 26).[137]

Early in the design process, Academy planners envisioned three separate buildings to accommodate the religious services of Protestants, Catholics, and Jews. One of the architect's schemes arranged them in linear fashion, with the Protestant chapel at one end, the Catholic at the other, and the Jewish chapel in between. Later, two chapels were

27

26. View of final model, c. 1958. Photograph by Ezra Stoller, © Esto. Looking to the east, this model shows the final Chapel configuration. Moving clockwise from the Chapel are the Administration Building, the Cadet Social Center, the Cadet Dormitory, the Academic Building, and the Cadet Dining Hall. Stoller No. 22 S 5A.

27. Central Heating plant. SOM Photograph by H. LaPlante, c. July 1958. The Academy was an entire city unto itself with elaborate provisions for water delivery, sewerage, and other utilities. SOM Archives, Chicago.

28

29

mandated, and then one building with three chapels in it.[138] By March 1957 the architects hit upon a vertical configuration, inspired by the two-level church of St. Francis at Assisi in Italy, where an upper church surmounts a lower one, sometimes called the crypt chapel. At the Academy, the architects located the Catholic chapel in the "crypt," and put the Jewish chapel there as well, with the larger Protestant chapel above. This gave a building of suitable proportions for the academic area.[139]

The final design developed from an idea Netsch had informally sketched for his colleagues on the design team.[140] After the first Chapel design, Owings had sent Netsch to Europe to study church design. In a trip described by Netsch as encompassing architectural works from "Stonehenge to Michelangelo," he was most impressed by the French Gothic cathedrals. In his final design, he sought to combine the "grandeur" of Chartres with the quality of light at Ste. Chapelle, but in new materials and with a new structural form.[141] At a March 1957 meeting, Secretary Quarles summarized the discussion of the Chapel by saying that the "inspirational quality" of the new design was well liked, and SOM should continue along these lines. The Air Force chaplains were instructed by the Secretary "not to reveal the structure or other details" of the design. The Secretary decided that the Chapel design would not be released to the public until it had progressed further, renderings had been made, and the design had been approved by Congress.[142] Having been burned once, the Secretary was going to make sure it would not happen again.

After the controversy surrounding the first Chapel plans, Congress required review of the design before it would appropriate funds for its construction. James H. Douglas, who became Secretary of the Air Force in May 1957, is reported to have told the architects that he had been before the Senate Finance Committee for over five hours: "One hour and forty-five minutes were spent on next year's entire budget for the air force, and about four and a half billion dollars, and the other three and a half hours on your damn chapel."[143] SOM received approval in January 1958 to go ahead with construction of the chapel as designed.

28. Visiting Officers' Quarters with Cadet Area in background. Photography by Stewart's, c. 1958. Although on a smaller scale than the large buildings in the Cadet Area, many of the outlying buildings shared the same modernist vocabulary. Local History Collection, Pikes Peak Library District.

29. Academy Hospital. Photograph by Stewart's, c. 1959. Viewed just after completion but before the installation of the landscaping, the hospital rises directly out of its hilltop site. Local History Collection, Pikes Peak Library District.

Achievement The cadets, faculty, and staff of the Academy occupied their new campus in the summer of 1958, although not all the buildings of the Cadet Area were completed. A visitor entering the Academy during this first year would have found much of the project in the final stages of construction.

Upon entering the site from the south, one first came upon two buildings ultimately destined for service and supply, then partially occupied and sharing space with construction field offices. On the opposite side of the road was the airfield, which would not be upgraded to Academy standards until 1972.[144] Most of the housing units in the Pine and Douglass Valleys were still under construction; only the forty-four units for senior officers were occupied.[145] Construction of the 1,200 family units, funded as a federal housing project, began in May 1958.[146] The Superintendent was installed in one of the previously existing ranch houses at the eastern end of Pine Valley, as was the Commandant of Cadets. The first phase of construction of the Community Center on Pine Ridge was completed. The stadium would be built in the early 1960s. And, up on Douglass Ridge, the Officers' Social Center was nearing completion and the Hospital, located farther west on the ridge, was under construction (figs. 28, 29). The most important area symbolically, the Cadet Area—the one that most often represents the Academy to the public—was visible on the highest ridge of the site. It was not until 1962, with the completion of the Chapel, that this ensemble of buildings was realized as intended.[147]

In its original form the Cadet Area was an extraordinarily sensitive composition of built and natural forms (fig. 30). The landform and vegetation of the site were permitted to penetrate the implied enclosure of the L shape, opening to the south and bringing into direct juxtaposition the curvilinear forms of nature with the emphatic rectilinearity of the carefully proportioned buildings. A balance was created between greenery and the walls of aluminum, glass, and marble. The Chapel, in this earlier context, was not set within a closed quadrant but was a pendant to the Court of Honor, to be viewed from the east, south, and west through a foreground of naturalistic landscape.[148]

The seven-foot grid of the module organized the buildings and the space, but never constricted or confined them as the buildings were shifted away from the corners, which were open and implied. The eye escaped through these spaces, and in the breaks in the upper levels of the Academic Building and the Cadet Quarters. The architects took care to orient the buildings in such a way that, even though a considerable visual momentum was created when one looked down their length, they never seemed to collide with one another, nor was there any sense of collision with the foothills behind. The relation of the Cadet Quarters to the vertical landmass, for instance, was mediated by the change in level and the open space of the Court of Honor, as well as by the perpendicular orientation of the Administration Building.[149] Similarly, the break in the Academic Building, in addition to providing the library with a separate identity, also forced a momentary halt in the momentum of the eye, and introduced a new staccato rhythm, which was continued in the relative verticality of the library wing and in the open space to the north. This slowing of the eye was important, as it prevented the visual collision of the Academic Building into the Cadet Quarters. Alternately, the proportion of the break in the

30. Aerial view of the Academy. Photograph by Stewart's, c. 1962. In this view looking to the southwest, the Cadet Gym is in the foreground with the rest of the Cadet Area behind, the Academic Building to the left, and the Cadet Social Center, Administration Building, and Cadet Chapel to the right. Local History Collection, Pikes Peak Library District.

Cadet Quarters, relative to the great length of the building, was not large enough to slow the eye, which leaped over it as it sped along and out into the opening at the end of the Terrazzo. This is a Modernist treatment of space, to be sure, not unique to the Academy. Yet here the great length of the buildings and the elevation of the entire terrace over the surrounding terrain created a sensation of soaring, not just of expansion.

In a word, the United States Air Force Academy at Colorado Springs could well be described as sublime. And not in any casual sense, for here the word truly refers to one of three kinds of aesthetic experience differentiated in the eighteenth century. The first is related to the beautiful, and could be exemplified by the major architectural ensembles of the U.S. Naval Academy at Annapolis, with its classical language, symmetry, smooth materials, and codified proportions (see fig. 51). The second type, the picturesque, could just as well be evoked by the buildings of the U.S. Military Academy at West Point (see fig. 49). There all the characteristics of the picturesque are evident, including a craggy, irregular outline and roughness of material. The last, the sublime, is often associated with the vastness of nature, awe-inspiring vistas, and dramatic contrast. And this is what the Air Force Academy evokes. In the siting of the Cadet Area and the contrast of the bold architectural structures against the Rocky Mountain backdrop, the academy is indeed sublime.

Sources

Unpublished

The major site for archival documents and primary records relating to the planning, design, and construction of the U.S. Air Force Academy is the Special Collections Branch of the Air Force Academy Library. Documents from this collection are cited as USAFA, with the pertinent record group (RG) and series (Ser.) numbers. Materials consulted were:

RG 101 Legislative Origins of the USAFA.

Ser. 1 Legislative Origins, 1942-64

RG 103 Early Planning for an Air Force Academy.

Ser. 1 Correspondence, 1944-56 (1960)

RG 120 Establishment of the Air Force Academy.

Ser. 17 Correspondence, "Top-Level," 1949-60.

Ser. 22 Design and Architecture, 1954-60.

Ser. 23 Construction, 1954-60

The National Archives, Rocky Mountain Region, at the Denver Federal Records Center, is the repository of documents from the Air Force Academy Construction Agency. These are cited as Denver. Documents consulted were a series from record group 461, Records of the Air Force Academy, entitled Construction Project Files. The series contains 266 boxes. The individual boxes are identified within the series, and the folder name is noted if existing. Also consulted were items in a series of 40 boxes entitled Various Records and News Releases from the same record group.

A third source is the Skidmore, Owings & Merrill archives in Chicago. These documents are warehoused and are located by transfer case or drawer number, without any other identifier included. These are referred to here as SOM, with the case or drawer number.

Materials in private hands that were used include:

Gordon Bunshaft, "Recollections," transcript, pages 92–97 concerning the Air Force Academy, SOM, New York, and reproduced in this book.

"A Conversation about the U.S. Air Force Academy," between Walter Netsch and John Burchard, 1958(?), typescript, Walter Netsch. Extensive excerpts from this are also published at the end of this volume.

Walter Netsch, "The Air Force Academy Chapel—The Very Visible, Invisible Building," 13 November 1987, typescript, Netsch.

Interviews were conducted by the author; notes on the interviews are in the author's possession. Tapes were made of most of the interviews and will be deposited with the Special Collections Branch of the Air Force Academy Library.

Interview with Jack Train, SOM Project Manager, 4 December 1992 (no taped record).

Interview with Albert Lockett, SOM Construction Manager, and Walter Netsch, SOM Project Designer, 5 December 1992.

Interview with Walter Netsch, 6 December 1992.

Interview with Dan Kiley, landscape architect, and Walter Netsch, 8 December 1992.

Interview with Walter Netsch, 20 December 1992.

Published

M. Hamlin Cannon and Henry S. Fellerman. *Quest for an Air Force Academy.* Colorado Springs: U.S. Air Force Academy, 1974.

George V. Fagan. *The Air Force Academy: An Illustrated History.* Boulder: Johnson Books, 1988.

History of the United States Air Force Academy: 27 July 1954 to 12 June 1956. Prepared by Lt. Col. Edgar A. Holt, Dr. M. Hamlin Cannon, and Dr. Carlos R. Allen, Jr. Colorado Springs: U.S. Air Force Academy, 1 August 1957.

History of the United States Air Force Academy: 13 June 1956 to 9 June 1957. Prepared by Lt. Col. Edgar A. Holt, Dr. M. Hamlin Cannon, Dr. Victor H.

Cohen, and Mr. Emory H. Dixon. Colorado Springs: U.S. Air Force Academy, 1 November 1958.

History of the United States Air Force Academy: 10 June 1957 to 11 June 1958. Prepared by Lt. Col. Edgar A. Holt, Dr. M. Hamlin Cannon, and Miss Elizabeth A. Wiley, Colorado Springs: U.S. Air Force Academy, 1 February 1960.

History of the United States Air Force Academy: 10 June 1958 to 30 June 1959. Prepared by Lt. Col. Edgar A. Holt, Dr. M. Hamlin Cannon, and Miss Elizabeth A. Wiley, Colorado Springs: U.S. Air Force Academy, 1 February 1961.

History of the United States Air Force Academy: 1 July 1964 to 30 June 1965. Prepared by Dr. M. Hamlin Cannon, and Miss Elizabeth A. Wiley, Colorado Springs: U.S. Air Force Academy, n.d.

History of the United States Air Force Academy: 1 July 1965 to 30 June 1966. Prepared by Dr. M. Hamlin Cannon, and Mr. Richard L. Martin, Colorado Springs: U.S. Air Force Academy, 30 June 1967.

See notes for periodicals and specific documents cited.

The author would like to extend her thanks to Duane J. Reed, Archivist and Chief, Special Collections Branch, Directorate of Academy Libraries and to the members of his staff, John Beardsley and Robert Troudt for their expert assistance and warm support. Thanks too, to Duane Boyle, Command Architect, Engineering Division; and to Eileen Bolger and Joan Howard of the National Archives, Rocky Mountain Region. I am grateful to Walter Netsch, Jack Train, and Albert Lockett for their time; and to Carol Krinski and Meredith Clausen for their immediate and generous responses to my queries. Thanks go to Sheri Olson and Robert Nauman, my colleagues in this endeavor. Special thanks are due Robert Bruegmann and Fannia Weingartner, for their insightful criticism and congeniality.

Notes

1. Designer Walter Netsch recalled that he visualized the site as a national park with a community in it. Interview with Netsch, 6 December 1992.

2. My thanks to Jory Johnson for clarifying the point that there are no mesas on the site, despite popular nomenclature. I refer only to the Cadet Area ridge as a mesa, as an artificial one was created there.

3. Lt. Col. A. J. Hanlon to Lt. Col. William C. Sherman, 26 November 1918. Quoted in George V. Fagan, *The Air Force Academy: An Illustrated History* (Boulder: Johnson Books, 1988), 6, without a source. (Hereafter cited as Fagan.)

4. For many years officer training was satisfactorily accomplished by the Officers Training Corps (OTC) and the Reserve Officers Training Corps (ROTC). For a discussion on the early desire for flight and officer training, see Fagan, Chap. 1, and M. Hamlin Cannon and Henry S. Fellerman, *Quest for an Air Force Academy* (Colorado Springs: U.S. Air Force Academy, 1974), Chaps. 1 and 2. (Hereafter cited as *Quest*.) For early planning efforts, see *History of the United States Air Force Academy: 27 July 1954 to 12 June 1956*, prepared by Lt. Col. Edgar A. Holt, Dr. M. Hamlin Cannon, and Dr. Carlos R. Allen, Jr. (Colorado Springs: U.S. Air Force Academy, 1 August 1957) I, 2–3, 9–11. (Hereafter the official histories will be cited as *Hist. USAFA*, with the years and volume number.)

5. Fagan, 15; *Hist. USAFA*, 1954-56, I, 11 where it is identified as the National Security Act; and *Quest*, 128, where it is called the Armed Forces Unification Act.

6. *Quest*, 94–97 and 128. In 1949, the first Secretary of the Air Force, W. Stuart Symington, worked out an agreement with the U.S. Military and Naval academies in which up to 25 percent of each of their graduating classes could volunteer to join the Air Force. Staff Study, November 1952, *Hist. USAFA*, 1954–56, IV, #90. The Secretary of the Air Force had wanted 40 percent from West Point and one third from Annapolis. Fagan, 15.

7. *Quest*, 89–90; Fagan, 13–14. There were a number of bills that designated a senator's home state, or even a representative's home district, as the proposed location for a new Academy. *Quest*, 90–91 and 128. The Bureau of the Budget wanted the Air Force Academy under the control of the Secretary of Defense. Fagan, 19. However, Gen. Hoyt S. Vandenberg, Air Force Chief of Staff, strove for the Air Force to have the primary role in the planning of the Academy. Legislation concerning the Academy was evaluated and found wanting. The Air Force then took on the task of "designing" its own bill. The evaluation was conducted under the direction of Lt. Gen. Idwal H. Edwards, Chief of Staff, Personnel. Fagan, 16.

8. This discussion also opened the way for those proponents of omnibus legislation to link the establishment of a new Air Force Academy with the

revision of the existing patchwork of legislation concerning the military and naval academies. *Quest,* 130–33.

9. Air University Study, Maxwell Air Force Base, Alabama, [1947], *Hist. USAFA*, 1954–56, I, 441–42.

10. *Quest,* 93. Air Training Command developed the *United States Air Academy Plan,* which recommended a four-year program with flight training integrated in the last two years and the installation of the air academy at Randolph in spring 1948. *Hist. USAFA,* 1954–56, I, 23–24 and 443, which cites the draft of 26 March 1948; *Quest,* 98–99, which cites Air Training Command, *United States Air Academy Plan,* 26 April 1948; and Fagan 16. In August 1948, Air Staff began planning for an air academy under the direction of General Muir S. Fairchild, Vice Chief of Staff, who "assembled a conference of senior Air Force and Army officers and eminent educators . . . to discuss plans for an academy." The Fairchild Board of fifteen civilians and military officers recommended a composite plan with no flight training. *Hist. USAFA,* 1954–56, I, 19–20. Members of the Fairchild Board were: General Fairchild; Lt. Gen. Idwal H. Edwards, Deputy Chief of Staff, Personnel; Lt. Gen. John K. Cannon; Lt. Gen. Barton K. Yount (ret); Maj. Gen. Robert W. Harper; Maj. Gen. Orvil A. Anderson; Maj. Gen. John D. McIntyre; Maj. Gen. Maxwell D. Taylor; Brig. Gen. Kenneth P. McNaughton; Col. Delmar T. Spivey; Dr. John J. Tigert, President Emeritus, University of Florida; Dr. Harry S. Roberts, President, Brooklyn Polytechnic Institute; Dr. Raymond R. Paty, Chancellor, Regents of the University System of Georgia; Rev. Hunter Guthrie, Professor of Foreign Relations, Georgetown University; and Dr. Kenneth R. Williams, Director, Educational Advisory Staff of the Air University. Fagan, 16. *Quest,* 104–5, identifies Roberts as Rodgers. Gen. Hoyt S. Vandenberg and others, however, opposed the composite plan. In August 1948, shortly after the Fairchild Board met, Vandenberg "initiated a longer range and more inclusive program to study all aspects of the Air Academy Program," and instructed that the Air Force Academy be planned as a four-year military institution like West Point and Annapolis. Maj. Gen. Robert W. Harper, Commander of the Air University and the Air University Command, was "responsible for the preparation of plans for an Air Force academy," including an interim plan. A "full-time" Air Force Academy Planning Board was established, which in turn created five task forces on various topics. Fagan, 17; *Hist. USAFA,* 1954–56, I, 20–22 and 444–445; *Quest,* 104. The Board released its report in January 1949, outlining areas of study and credit-hour distribution. It recommended a broadly based curriculum, with all cadets taking the same basic courses. Later in their education, cadets would be able to specialize on the basis of ability, just as at West Point and Annapolis. It also recommended that flying training not be a part of the curriculum. "Air Force Academy Planning Board Study: A Plan for an Air Force Academy," *Quest,* 109, 120, 122–123; Fagan, 30 and 17.

11. *Quest,* 113 and 116; *Hist. USAFA,* 1954–56, I, 15–17 and 451–53. Members included James P. Baxter, President, Williams College; Frederick A. Middlebush, President, University of Missouri; George D. Stoddard, President, University of Illinois; Edward L. Moreland, Executive Vice President, Massachusetts Institute of Technology; Maj. Gen. Bryant E. Moore, Superintendent, U.S. Military Academy; Rear Admiral James L. Holloway, Superintendent, U.S. Naval Academy; and Maj. Gen. David M. Schlatter, USAF. *The Report and Recommendations to the Secretary of Defense by the Service Academy Board; Hist. USAFA*, 1954–56, I, 453, gives the final report date of 21 December 1949; Fagan, 18, uses the publication date of January 1950.

12. The Board consisted of Gen. Carl Spaatz, USAF (ret.), Lt. Gen. Harmon, Brig. Gen. Harold L. Clark, and Dr. Bruce Hopper of Harvard University. Spaatz was appointed chair. *Quest*, 139 and 212. There had been more attempts by members of Congress to control the selection of the site. With the signing of the 1947 National Defense Act, the House Armed Services Committee was established. Representative Carl Vinson (D-Ga.), chair of the committee, wanted a particular site identified in subsequent Air Force academy bills. Fagan, 19–20. At first, the Pentagon solicited site proposals. *Quest*, 212.

13. The site proposals were reviewed between February and August 1950. Of the 354 sites proposed, approximately 150 were surveyed, 29 of which were identified as possibilities and further scrutinized. In March 1951, eight sites that met the criteria were selected. *Quest*, 213; Fagan, 27; *Hist. USAFA*, 1954–56, I, 142 and 146. *Quest* misidentifies the Chicago architectural firm as Holabird and Root and Burger, and Fagan calls it Holabird, Rout and Burger. The search was complicated by the inclusion in April 1950 of flight training in the curriculum. Thus, although there was no site requirement for an airfield in the early stages of review, this later became one of the criteria the Board had to consider. *Hist. USAFA*, 1954–56, I, 454; *Quest*, 213. The outbreak of the Korean War halted progress on the establishment of the academy, but work continued on the educational program. See Fagan, 21 and *Hist. USAFA*, 1954–56, I, 457. In the summer of 1949, the Directorate of Installations also began an investigation of "existing government installations for possible sites for a temporary location for the Academy." Fagan, 20.

14. *Quest*, 214. The other six sites were Camp Beale, Calif.; Charlotte and Salisbury, N.C.; Grapevine, Texas; Madison, Ind.; and Grayson County, Texas. The Salisbury site was later dropped. *Hist. USAFA*, 1954–56, I, 147.

15. *Quest*, 215; Fagan, 28; *Hist. USAFA*, 1954–56, I, 146–47. The Board was disbanded in December 1952. *Quest*, 214.

16. Vandenberg created the Office of Special Assistant for Air Force Matters, and appointed Harmon to head it. *Quest*, 136; Fagan, 21. Harmon's duties included securing proper legislation from Congress. Both the Service Academy Board and the Air Force Academy Planning Board had been formed not only to assess the situation and recommend solutions, but also to establish a body of information that could be used to convince Congress and the public of the need to create a third academy. *Hist. USAFA*, 1954–56, I, 452 and 454.

17. Air Training Command, *Air Academy Plan* (Draft), 13, cover letter dated 27 March 1948; Air Training Command, *United States Air Academy Plan,* 26 April 1948, Tab F; Memo from Col. Leo J. Erler, Acting Director of Installations, to Logistics Plans Group, 11 May, 1948, USAFA, RG 103, Ser. 1. It was also observed that the layout of Randolph's existing buildings was not suitable for an academy, and that the structures, built for an air base and not a campus, were not up to "collegiate standards." Erler to Logistics, 11 May 1948.

18. Ornamental pools were specifically mentioned as contributing to this effect. The statement proposed "pools . . . in connection with some of the approaches to the administration and memorial buildings," or grass and plantings "to develop the same formal appearances." It also suggested the option of postponing a decision until "full cognizance is given to the geographical location, the existing terrain of the selected site and further study of the facilities which are to be incorporated in the various buildings." This is a one-page typescript sheet that refers to a series of sketches which are no longer in evidence. No author is indicated. "Suggested Architectural Treatment for the Air Force Academy," 5 January 1949, USAFA, RG 103, Ser. 1.

19. Harmon was referring to the Hotel El Panama in Panama City; see "Hotel Made for the Tropics," *Architectural Forum* 94 (April 1951) 138–45. The associated architects were Mendez and Sander. Harmon realized that the building had been designed for its tropical site but thought that "the general style might very well be adapted to any climate in this country." Harmon to Brig. Gen. Colby M. Myers, 28 August 1951, USAFA, RG 103, Ser. 1. Myers agreed: "The modern architecture of this hotel is very good; and if well studied and modified slightly, it would be suited to the Air Academy requirements." Myers to Harmon, 13 September 1951, USAFA, RG 103, Ser. 1. Note again the confusion in architectural terminology. Is Harmon referring to the collegiate Gothic of West Point as the "classic tradition"?

20. There would be restrictions and externally dictated construction standards. Understanding the symbolic importance of the project, Air Force planners expressed their concern: "Because the Academy will be a national monument, as are West Point and Annapolis, the assumed construction standards are higher than those authorized by law. However, because of the nature of this project, it is earnestly hoped that Congress will waive the present restrictions in this instance." *Summary of Plans for Permanent Air Force Academy*. Reproduced in *Hist. USAFA,* 1954–56, III, #33. The document is not dated but probably was produced between 1952 and 1954, that is, after the Site Selection Board and before the Site Selection Commission.

21. Husted had been a member of the Air Force "long range planning commission" and had top-secret clearance. Memo for Record by Lt. Col. Thomas L. Sheldrake, Office, Special Assistant for Air Force Academy Matters, 27 March 1953, USAFA RG 103, Ser. 1. I have not seen the sketches.

22. Memo for Record by Col. Robert O. Good, 11 January 1952, USAFA, RG 103, Ser. 1. Good admitted being unsure of Saarinen's name, thought it was "Aero," and noted that "the doc [*sic]* from which this info [*sic*] was taken spelled the name Soerinen and gave no first name."

23. Memo for Special Assistant for Air Force Academy Matters, from Brig. Gen. H. W. Ehrgott, 8 January 1954, USAFA, RG 103, Ser. 1; Memo for Record by Col. William G. Hipps, 28 April 1953, in *Hist. USAFA*, 1954–56, IV, #76. Although he was to prepare "studies for an Air Academy situated on a hypothetical site," Husted studied the final site reports. This time the site reports are said to have been those done by "Holabird, Roote and Burgee." Memo for Record by Sheldrake, 27 March 1953.

24. The former firm was composed of Eric Gugler, Richard A. Kimball and Husted; John F. Harbeson, William J. H. Hough, William H. Livingston, and Roy F. Larson constituted the latter, which was the successor firm to Paul Cret's. The associated architects were awarded the contract on 26 May 1953. Memo for Special Assistant for Air Force Academy Matters, from Ehrgott, 8 January 1954.

25. As for the buildings, consideration was given to the "flexibility offered by clear spans and moveable partitions." "Notes on the Air Academy Study Project," attached to a letter from Husted to Harmon, 15 December 1953, USAFA, RG 103, Ser. 1.

26. The size of the cadet chapel (2,000 capacity) and the auditorium for the entire cadet wing (2,500) was determined at this time. The placement of

toilet facilities in the cadet quarters was also discussed, as it would be again in the future. Harmon thought that the location of showers and lockers in the basement, as at West Point, was acceptable, but agreed with the architect's idea of providing a toilet room between every two cadet rooms. Memo for Directorate of Installations from Harmon, 24 November 1953; Memo for Maj. Gen. Washbourne and Col. H. C. Person from Harmon, 24 November 1953, USAFA, RG 103, Ser. 1. Harmon also expressed his preference for a library with "six large reading rooms nicely furnished, each with a fireplace and wall space for paintings." Memorandum of Conference in General Harmon's Office, 27 November 1953, USAFA, RG 103, Ser. 1.

27. "Study of Proposed U.S. Air Force Academy, Hypothetical Site," 15 February 1954, USAFA, Special Collections; and "United States Air Force Academy Cost Analysis Sheets and Diagrammatic Drawings for Preliminary Estimate," both prepared by Gugler, Kimball and Husted, and Harbeson, Hough, Livingston and Larson, Associated Architects, 15 February 1954, USAFA, RG 103, Ser. 1.

28. When the Husted group was preparing its plans and models, Air Force personnel at Air University were anxious that they "all be in a position to pass judgement on the project." Thinking of their own previous experience with the school-facility consultant for the provision of suitable facilities at Maxwell Air Force Base, they realized they needed to educate themselves. While they acknowledged that one trip there would not make them "experts . . . at least it might keep us from making grave and irreparable blunders." Col. Dale O. Smith, Director of Education, USAF HQ, Air University, to Col. A. E. Boudreau, 25 May 1953, USAFA, RG 103, Ser. 1. Carlos Lazo was the chief planner and coordinator for the new University of Mexico campus. See *Architectural Record* 111 (June 1952) 12–13, 364.

29. Functional planning was not the only concern: "We believe the plans should also take into account the advantage of providing buildings and grounds of beauty which will inspire young men to strive for an Air Force career." Request for Clearance for Flight to Mexico, 25 May 1953, USAFA, RG 103, Ser. 1.

30. "Report of Trip to University City in Mexico City, Mexico," by Col. George B. Dany, 6 July 1953; and "Report of Group Visit to University City, Mexico City, Mexico," by Dale O. Smith, 9 July 1953, USAFA, RG 103, Ser. 1.

31. "Report of Trip to University City," Dany, 6 July 1953.

32. "Report of Trip to University City," Dany, 6 July 1953; and "Report of Group Visit to University City," Smith, 9 July 1953. Walter Netsch recalled that a second trip to Mexico City was made, this time with Lt. Gen. Harmon and with architects Nathaniel Owings, Gordon Bunschaft, and Netsch. Of interest to Air Force Staff and architects on this trip was the use of mosaics on many of the buildings. This second trip probably took place in late 1954. Telephone conversation with Walter Netsch, 28 February 1994.

33. Harmon to Kuter, 1 March 1954, USAFA, RG 103, Ser. 1. Harmon's comments are in response to "Ideas on the Forming of an Air Academy." Memo from Brig. Gen. Dale O. Smith to Lt. Gen. Laurence S. Kuter, 19 February 1954, USAFA, RG 103, Ser. 1.

34. Smith to Kuter, 19 February 1954. It is interesting here to quote the recommendation of Admiral Hall, Superintendent of the Coast Guard Academy, and Harmon's response. Hall "stressed the advantage of having a nearby first-rate girls college because it (a) keeps cadets at home, (b) keeps them from traffic accidents on weekends and (c) encourages high-class brides leading to future marital success and adjustment in the service. All graduates of USCGA I questioned . . . have married graduates of the Connecticut College for Women and all seem eminently satisfied." Smith to Kuter, 19 February 1954. Harmon replied that the Air Force was "all for girls too," but that they did not see this issue as "a controlling factor in site selection." Harmon to Kuter, 1 March 1954.

35. Harmon to Kuter, 1 March 1954.

36. *Quest*, 217. The press conference took place on 19 March 1953. The elections of 1952 changed the country's leadership, as Republican candidates won the White House and the House of Representatives, and progress on the Academy accelerated when Eisenhower took office. *Quest*, 153. Charles E. Wilson became Secretary of Defense, Harold E. Talbott Secretary of the Air Force, and Dewey Short Chair of the House Armed Services Committee. On 29 January 1953, Short introduced a bill to establish an Academy "almost identical" to one Vinson had earlier introduced. A revised version of the bill, H.R. 5337—that is, the one that was ultimately passed—was introduced on 21 May 1953. It was supported by Eisenhower, passed by both houses, and signed into law on 1 April 1954. Fagan, 22–23 and *Quest*, 217.

37. *Quest*, 154 and 176.

38. Randolph "has a fine type of architecture, and its conversion to Academy use and gradual expansion will be far less costly than would be a

complete new installation." Memo from Harmon, 4 March 1953, USAFA, RG 103, Ser 1. Senator Lyndon B. Johnson questioned Talbott about the location of the Academy, and "wanted assurance that all Texas sites would receive full consideration." Fagan, 25. Perhaps not sure of his influence with the Secretary of the Air Force, or any decision-making body the Secretary would appoint, Johnson tried to see to it that the decision was made in a committee over which the Senate had control. He asked Talbott whether he would object to having "a provision inserted in the bill requiring approval of the site choice by the House and Senate Armed Services Committee." Talbott made it clear that he would indeed object. *Quest*, 218.

39. *Quest*, 154, 176, 217. The House had passed an amended version of the bill on 21 January, and the Senate passed its amended version on 8 March 1954. The conference committee worked out an agreement, and on 29 March 1954, Public Law 325 of the 83rd Congress, Second Session, was passed. *Hist. USAFA*, 1954–56, I, 1–2.

40. Talbott said at this time that "preliminary designs [were] already underway." Memo for Record by Lt. Col. William B. Taylor, 9 January 1954, 2, USAFA, RG 101, Ser. 1. Privately, Talbott admitted that "he did not think the present architect, Mr. Hustead [sic], was large enough to handle the architectural designs." Talbott wanted a cost estimate for a permanent site at a minimum cost, and he thought a $175 million figure was too high and would "kill the project." Yet he was also concerned that Husted's estimates of some $125 million were about $50 million too low. For congressional testimony, Talbott said they should "state not less than $150,000,000." Major General L. B. Washbourne agreed that "Hustead's figures were weak." The architect had estimated $9,000,000 for the airfield, but Washbourne knew one "couldn't get much of an air field for that." Harmon estimated that 1,200 family quarters would be needed, but thought that Congress would balk at that figure, so suggested asking for only 100 units. Memo for Record by Taylor, 9 January 1954, 2–3; *Quest*, 156; Memo for Record, by Washbourne, 28 January 1954, USAFA, RG 103, Ser. 1.

41. The 1949 figure was for capital costs. Director, Personnel Planning, "Air Staff Summary Sheet," 1 April 1949 and 1 December 1949, *Hist. USAFA*, 1954–56, IV, #152, #128; and Memo from Lt. Col. Easton, 12 May 1949, USAFA, RG 103, Ser. 1, suggesting $6 million for planning and $165 million for construction. Another estimate for the cost of land preparation, total facilities, and 10 percent contingencies was $150,120,300. This figure seems not to include $69,000 for site selection and the 4 percent design fee of $6,000,000, but this is not clear. Memo from Brig. Gen. James B. Newman, Jr., to Gen. Nugent, 28 February 1949, USAFA, RG 103, Ser. 1. A third estimate put the cost, including airfield construction, at $164,678,970. This document lists site selection at $69,000; design, $6,000,000; land acquisition, $1,800,000; land preparation, $1,600,000; total facilities, $134,273,000; contingencies, $13,827,300; engineering, architecture, and supervision, $9,210,030; and airfield construction at $3,368,640. Again, it is unclear whether the $6,069,000 for site selection and design is included in the $164,678,970 figure, or whether it should be added to it to equal $170,747,970. Memo from Col. Edward B. Gallant to Col. Dau, 10 May 1949, USAFA, RG 103, Ser. 1. In 1950, the estimate for construction was $153,272,390. This includes architectural and engineering fees. Director of Installations to Special Assistant for Air Force Academy Matters, 17 February 1950, *Hist. USAFA*, 1954–56, IV, #120. The Assistant Secretary of Defense told the Speaker of the House in 1951 and again in 1953, that the estimate for the academy was $148,000,000. Daniel K. Edwards to Sam Rayburn, 20 June 1951; and Roger Kent to Joseph W. Martin, Jr., 5 January 1953, *Hist. USAFA*, 1954–56, IV, #101, #83.

42. *Summary of Plans for Permanent Air Force Academy.*

43. It also excluded air-conditioning, which would add another $5,159,280. The figures were based on a Chicago cost index. "Summary of Preliminary Estimate for Proposed USAFA," 15 December 1953, USAFA, RG 103, Ser. 1. The estimate was prepared by Gugler, Kimball and Husted, and Harbeson, Hough, Livingston and Larson, in consultation with Turner Construction Co., Ammann and Whitney, Consulting Engineers, and Guy B. Panero, Engineers, Inc.

44. *Quest*, 173, 176; Fagan, 24.

45. Public Law 325, 83rd Congress, 2d Session, Sections 3 & 9. A copy of the act can be found in *Hist. USAFA*, 1954–56, IV, #54.

46. *Quest*, 157, 177.

47. The others were Dr. Virgil M. Hancher, President, State University of Iowa; Lt. Gen. Harmon, Special Assistant for Air Force Academy Matters; Merrill C. Meigs, Vice President, Hearst Corporation; and Gen. Carl A. Spaatz, USAF (ret). Staff to the Commission were Col. Arthur E. Boudreau, Secretary and Recorder; Col. Max Boyd, Public Information Officer; and Col. James Moore, Agent Finance Officer. The Commission decided not to elect a chair. *Quest*, 219–22; Fagan, 29; *Hist. USAFA*, 1954–56, I, 148.

48. *Quest*, 219; Fagan, 30.

49. *Hist. USAFA*, 1954–56, I, 152–53; *Quest*, 223. The Commission also visited Annapolis and West Point. "Report to the Secretary of the Air Force by the Air Force Academy Site Selection Commission," 3 June 1954, in *Hist. USAFA*, 1954–56, III, #52.

50. *Quest*, 220–221. These points are contained in the "Report to the Secretary of the Air Force by the Air Force Academy Site Selection Commission," 3 June 1954.

51. *Hist. USAFA*, 1954–56, I, 154; *Quest*, 228.

52. "Record of Interview of Brigadier General Charles A. Lindbergh," by Maj. Holt, USAFA Historian, 3 January 1957, 1, in *Hist. USAFA*, 1954–56, III, #3.

53. *Quest*, 227; Fagan, 33; "Report to the Secretary of the Air Force by the Air Force Academy Site Selection Commission," 3 June 1954. As might be expected, Senator Everett H. Dirksen (R-Ill.) and former Secretary of the Air Force, Senator W. Stuart Symington (D-Mo.), favored the Illinois site. Fagan, 34.

54. *Quest*, 231; Fagan, 35, 47. The state of Colorado had already established the State Land Acquisition Commission in April, so that it would be "ready to acquire land for the Air Force Academy if and when a Colorado site" was selected. "United States Air Force Academy," *SOM News* (15 June 1956).

55. *Quest*, 234.

56. Fagan, 48.

57. Quoted in Fagan, 48, from *Hist. USAFA*, 1958-59, III, 678.

58. The Office of the Secretary had determined how an architect would be selected for the project, "a plan for controlling the construction of the proposed air academy" was created, and there had been discussions of "[t]ypes of architecture and some of the leading architects of this and other countries." Memo for Record by Ferry, 11 March 1954, with enclosure "Suggested Procedure for Initiating the Construction for the New Air Academy," USAFA, RG 103, Ser. 1; Memo for Record, by Taylor, 9 January 1954.

59. Press Release, 17 May 1950, USAFA, RG 103, Ser. 1.

60. The Project Office would prepare and issue information for prospective architectural and engineering firms. Requirements specified that firms competing for the project should have "a combination of joint venture, master planning, architectural engineering and supervisory personnel." Memo for Record, by Ferry, 11 March 1954, with enclosure; Memo for Record from Washbourne, 12 March 1954, USAFA, RG 103, Ser. 1. At this point, Washbourne was Assistant Deputy Chief of Staff, Operations. *Hist. USAFA*, 1954–56, I, 239–40; Memo for Special Assistant for Air Force Academy Matters, Deputy Chief of Staff, Personnel, from Washbourne, now Assistant Chief of Staff, Installations, 26 March 1954, USAFA, RG 103, Ser. 1. Staff consisted of Lt. Col. C. A. Eckert, Officer-in-Charge; Lt. Col. J. R. White; Mr. J. P. Huebsch; Mr. R. S. Rio; and a clerk-stenographer.

61. Memo for Record from Washbourne, 12 March 1954.

62. Memo for Secretary from Harmon, 31 March 1954, in *Hist. USAFA*, 1954–56, IV, #58.

63. Walter Netsch, "The Air Force Academy Chapel—The Very Visible, Invisible Building," 13 November 1987, manuscript, unpaged. The Board would consist of the Secretary of the Air Force, the Special Assistant for Installations, the Deputy Chief of Staff, Installations, the Deputy Chief of Staff, Personnel, Harmon and two or three prominent architects hired as consultants. Memo for Record, by Ferry, 11 March 1954, with enclosure. After initially agreeing with the idea of a civilian board of architects, Harmon reversed himself and urged an advisory board consisting only of the Secretary, Washbourne, the head of the Air Force Academy Project Office, and himself. That is, the Board would contain no one with architectural training. Harmon seems not to have understood that the practice of an architect centers on design critiques, and that the dialogue between designer and critic is what contributes to an improved outcome. Especially in this situation it would be beneficial to have critics independent of the selected firm. Memo from Harmon to Washbourne, 31 March 1954, USAFA, RG 103, Ser. 1.

64. Memo for Record by Ferry, 11 March 1954, with enclosure.

65. Delano addresses Whitney as "Sonny." William Adams Delano to Cornelius V. Whitney, 28 March 1949, USAFA, RG 103, Ser. 1.

66. The memo mistakenly identifies it as Raymond Lowry Associates. Memo for Record, by Lt. Col. William B. Taylor, 9 January 1954, 4, USAFA, RG 101, Ser. 1.

67. Welton Becket Associates was in joint venture with Airway Engineering Corporation of Washington, D.C.; Quinton Engineers, Consulting Engineers; and Murray Erich Associates, Structural Engineers. Jack B. Beardwood, of Welton Becket Associates, aggressively pursued the contract through political

connections. Beardwood had served on Eisenhower's staff in Europe and was close enough to the President to have attended his "stag dinner" in June 1954. After all his efforts, Beardwood was angry when his firm was "not called for interview by the Academy Architectural Selection Board," and therefore "did not have an opportunity to personally present our qualifications." He was outraged when the smaller and less experienced Pereira and Luckman was called for an interview, especially as the latter had "served the previous administration and...[one of its principals] is a close friend of Harry Truman." Beardwood felt better when the "Democrat-headed firm" did not get the contract, and SOM, "a fine firm with an excellent record and background," did. Senator Thomas H. Kuchel to Talbott, 16 June 1954, Denver, RG 461, 6/266, Folder REL 1-2; Talbott to Beardwood, 6 April 1954; Charles Willis, Jr., to Talbott, 31 March 1954; Beardwood to Willis, 29 March 1954 and 24 June 1954; Sherman Adams to Beardwood, 25 June 1954; Memo for Col. Burroughs from Lt. Col. William G. Draper, 28 June 1954; and Brig. Gen. Joe W. Kelly to Beardwood, 1 July 1954; Beardwood to Adams, 13 July 1954; Beardwood to Willis, 14 July 1954 and 27 July 1954, USAFA, RG 120, Ser. 17. I have yet to locate a similar body of correspondence for SOM or any other competitor, but it is likely that other firms pursued similar political avenues and social connections.

68. These letters, and many more like them, are located in the National Archives, Rocky Mountain Region, Denver Federal Records Center, RG 461, 6/266, folder REL 1-2, Congressional Inquiries, 1 May–15 September 1954. Kennedy wrote on behalf of the H. E. Fletcher Granite Co. of West Chelmsford, Massachusetts. The joint venture letter that Dirksen forwarded was from a principal of the Roberts and Schaefer Company (Chicago) which was associated with Hellmuth, Yamasaki and Leinweber (St. Louis and Detroit), Karsunky, Weller and Gooch (Washington), Justement, Elam and Darby (Washington), Kuehne, Brooks and Barr (Austin), Page, Sutherland and Page (Austin), Phelps, Dawess and Simmons (San Antonio), Stone and Pitts (Austin), Carber Burgess (Fort Worth), Linder, Hodgson and Wright (Denver), and Horner and Shifrin (St. Louis).

69. *Hist. USAFA*, 1954–56, I, 243; Frederick Gutheim, "Washington Perspective," Progressive Architecture 35 (September 1954) 4.

70. Talbott to Rep. John McCormick, 11 September 1954, Denver, RG 461, 6/266, Folder REL 1-2. Talbott was explaining after the fact how the architect was selected.

71. *Hist. USAFA*, 1954–56, I, 242; "A Proposal to Furnish Architect-Engineer Services for The United States Air Force Academy," 40ff, Denver, RG 461, 50/266, Folder 17. And there was of course the firm's corporate work, as exemplified by the Lever House office building on Park Avenue in New York City. "The Architects from 'Skid's Row'," *Fortune* (January 1958) 4–6.

72. "Proposal to Furnish A-E Services," 2 and 21. In the context of the joint venture, Moran, Proctor, Mueser and Rutledge were to provide the "civil engineering, soils and foundation engineering including airfield pavements and roads," and Syska and Hennessy would provide the "mechanical, electrical and power engineering for structures and site utilities, including airfield lighting, petroleum, oil and lubrication engineering." The cover letter is addressed to Secretary of the Air Force, attention Col. E. V. N. Schuyler, and is dated 17 May 1954.

73. "News," *Architectural Forum* 101 (August 1954) 52. Ferry is listed as head of the Board. Saarinen is said to have sketched his design during the interview. Interview with Albert Lockett and Walter Netsch, 5 December 1992.

74. "Netsch, "Chapel." After his presentation at the interview, Owings was asked whether he would "design the academy in sandstone," as Frank Lloyd Wright had indicated he would. Owings remembered replying "General . . . would you build an airplane of sandstone?" Nathaniel Alexander Owings, *The Spaces In Between: An Architect's Journey* (Boston: Houghton Mifflin, 1973) 152. The idea for the screen came from work Netsch had done for the U. S. Armed Services in Japan and at the U. S. Naval Post Graduate Academy. Telephone conversation with Netsch, 28 February 1994.

75. "Air Academy Design Brawl," *Architectural Forum,* 103 (August 1955) 9.

76. It included Graham, Anderson, Probst and White (Chicago); Mitchell and Ritchie (Pittsburgh); Bush-Brown, Gailey and Hefferman (Atlanta); Kump and Associates (San Francisco); Burns and Roe (New York); Robert and Co. (Atlanta); and George B. Cunningham (Fort Lauderdale). "Air Academy Design Brawl," 9; and James H. Duff to Talbott, 21 July 1954, Denver, RG 461, 6/266, Folder REL 1-2.

77. Telegram from Wright to Cutting, 3 July 1954, William Evjue Papers, State Historical Society of Wisconsin. My thanks to Sheri Olson for bringing this to my attention. Wright later claimed he knew nothing of the American Legion threat and had withdrawn for his own reasons. "Academy gets Building Funds; Wright hits American Legion," *Architectural Forum,* 103 (September 1955) 28; "Air Academy Design Brawl," 9

78. *Hist. USAFA*, 1954–56, I, 243; "Record Reports," *Architectural Record*, 116 (August 1954) 15.

79. "Air Academy Design Brawl," 9. The Secretary wanted an Advisory Board that would include "three or more distinguished civilian architects" to

advise him "in all matters pertaining to the initial construction of the Academy." Memo for Record from Washbourne, 12 March 1954. Beardwood was happy to accept the consultant's position on Becket's behalf. Beardwood to Willis, 27 July 1954. Gordon Bunshaft thought Becket's presence on the consultants committee was a political appointment. Gordon Bunshaft, "Recollections," 94. "United States Air Force Academy," *SOM News* (15 June 1956).

80. Interview with Lockett and Netsch; Owings, *Spaces,* 152. Bunshaft, in his recollections, also thought Mrs. Talbott influenced the selection of the architect. Bunshaft, "Recollections," 93.

81. *Hist. USAFA*, 1954–56, I, 243.

82. Netsch was responsible for the Court of Honor buildings—the Administration Building, the Cadet Social Center and the Chapel—and was assisted by Ralph Youngren. Youngren also headed the Academic Building design team. William Rouzie led the Cadet Quarters team, and Gertrude Peterhaus the one for the Dining Hall. Stan Gladych directed the master planning team, which included Quig Lewis and Otto Starck. Other teams leaders were: John Hoops, service and supply, and airfield; Carl Kohler, housing; John Weese, Senior Officer housing; and Don Ryder, Officers Club and Quarters. Contacts with the engineers were lateral, and formed as the project demanded. Telephone conversations with Netsch, 28 February 1994 and 18 August 1993. The composition of the leadership was unusual for its time in that besides having Peterhaus, a woman, head a design team, it also had Ryder, an African-American, in a prominent position. Although head of the Dining Hall team, Peterhaus was "prevented from participating in design presentations to the client," and was "excluded from the site visit to witness" the raising into place of the roof truss she had designed. Gertrude Lempp Kerbis (formerly Peterhaus), Statement, 25 June 1993, provided courtesy of Sheri Olson.

83. AFACA was located within the Office of the Assistant Chief of Staff, Installations. *Hist. USAFA*, 1954–56, I, 233, 229. The Project Office for the Air Force Academy had been established in Installations in March 1954. Installations would also monitor AFACA's work, review the preliminary plans and engineering studies, and the site and final inspections. In March 1955, an ad hoc committee was set up "as an adjunct to the Installations Board" to review Air Force Academy planning and "to make certain the requirements are not exaggerated, that standards are adequate, and that the sum total of the initial installations does not exceed the $126,000,000 presently available." The Committee would report to the Installations Board, which in turn would advise the Chief of Staff. However, in October 1955, with the establishment of the Air Force Academy Panel, "to consider all the construction program at the highest level below the Secretary and the Chief of Staff," the Installations Board was relieved of all master planning and design responsibility. *Hist. USAFA*, 1954–56, , 230, 239, 234, 260–61; Memo from Gen. Thomas D. White, Vice Chief of Staff, for Deputy Chief of Staff, Personnel, Special Assistant for Installations, and Assistant Chief of Staff, Installations, 3 March 1955, Denver, RG 461, 33/266; Robert H. Warren to Air Academy Panel on Design and Construction Matters, and Assistant Chief of Staff, Installations, 14 October 1955, USAFA, RG 120, Ser. 23.

84. On 31 August, Installations submitted "a detailed list of facility requirements" to Harmon. Once Academy personnel were appointed, they would be asked for comments, requirements and recommendations. Input was requested by 21 October. However, it was noted that the "initial submission of comments from the entire Academy did not preclude constant analysis of requirements and the submission of recommended changes at later dates." *Hist. USAFA*, 1954–56, I, 244–45, 260, 250.

85. The description here is based on the organization chart published in SOM News. The procedure was not fixed, and changed over the life of the project, often at the preference of the Secretary. Ferry to SOM, 7 September 1955, USAFA, RG 120, Ser. 23. An earlier procedure had SOM reporting to AFACA, which in turn was responsible to Installations, as noted. In this diagram too, Harmon has a dotted-line relation to the Chief of Staff. Netsch to Merrill, 31 August 1954, SOM, #125, AFA Design Reference File.

86. John Hoops went to Washington with Netsch. "A Conversation about the U. S. Air Force Academy" between Netsch and John Burchard, 1958 (?), II-4, 5; Gertrude Lempp Kerbis, Statement, 25 June 1993.

87. "Conversation," II-4, 6; *Hist. USAFA*, 1954–56, I, 270; Interview with Lockett and Netsch. About four years ago, the Academy investigated the renovation possibility of locating a toilet room between every two cadet rooms.

88. The members of both site selection commissions had been aware of the importance of their charge, particularly with regard to the appearance of the site. A major concern was that the "natural surroundings" of the site be suitable for "its status-to-be as a national monument." *Hist. USAFA*, 1954–56, I, 141.

89. “Conversation,” I-4.

90. “Conversation,” I-5, 8. In the words of Netsch: “Every architectural study involves a search for all the limits of the program that may help to define it or at least give direction to it. To solve an architectural problem which has no such limits is the hardest thing for an architect, not a freedom which he would covet. So we searched for these definers.” “Conversation,” I-5. The Secretary, his staff, his consultants, representatives of AFACA and members of SOM met in Colorado Springs in August 1954, to inspect the site at the same time early planning conferences were conducted. SOM Record of Consultants Meetings, 17–20 August 1954, Denver, RG 461, 69/266, REL 5, Conferences; “Conversation,” I-6.

91. That is, this one runway was appropriately oriented with regard to the direction of the wind for 93 percent of the conditions experienced. The reorientation was necessary to accommodate a diurnal wind shift. Interview with Lockett and Netsch; “Conversation” I-4, I-5.

92. “Conversation,” I-6, I-9. The identification of three major components and the use of a perimeter road sounds very like the arrangement proposed by the Husted team and the Air Force planners over a year earlier.

93. “Conversation,” I-8, I-7. While the architects “were trying to get the programs together and to make logical decisions,” they “were also putting [their] eyes and senses to work.” “Conversation,” I-7. With the support of Saarinen, who as a competitor indicated he would locate the Cadet Area on Lehman Mesa, Harmon was made to see “that once you had a mountain site, it was foolish to cower down in the valley and that the development of the mountain area did not have *ipso facto* to be flamboyant.” This is Netsch’s recollection; “Conversation,” I-7 to I-9. Saarinen may almost be said to have indeed chosen the site, as he literally showed it to Bunshaft and Netsch. Bunshaft “Recollections.”

94. “Conversation,” II-9.

95. Netsch interview, 20 December 1992; “Conversation,” I-7, I-10.

96. “Master Plan, United States Air Force Academy,” 1 June 1955. Submitted by Skidmore, Owings and Merrill, Syska and Hennessy, Robert and Co., and Moran, Proctor, Mueser and Rutledge, Tab S2; *Hist. USAFA*, 1954–56, I, 261, 275.

97. Owings, *Spaces,* 153. In a very explicit statement of the belief in form following function, Owings continued: “Among the Secretary’s advisers in the military some were surprised, others amused and still others chagrined when our benign deceit was discovered—totally unaware that in approving the functional integrity of this design they had also approved a contemporary design for the academy buildings themselves.”

98. *Hist. USAFA*, 1954–56, I, 248.

99. The housing component would cause SOM considerable trouble. Ultimately, it would be funded and administered as a Title VIII (Capehart) Housing Project. SOM was required to affiliate with a firm experienced in the process, and chose Clark and Enerson of Lincoln, Nebraska. Memo for Record, Samuel Hanenberg, Assistant General Counsel, 25 April 1957, USAFA, RG 120, Ser. 22; Carroll L. Tyler to AFACA, 21 May 1957, Denver, RG 461, 68/266, Installations 4, Family Housing; and Stoltz to SOM, 22 May 1957, Denver, RG 461, 69/266, Reading File 1957, #23.

100. “Master Plan,” Tab A3.

101. This advice came from Col. Max Boyd, Chief of the Public Information Division, Office of Information Services. Quoted in *Hist. USAFA*, 1954–56, I, 276–77, from a memo from Boyd to Ferry, 1 April 1955.

102. *Hist. USAFA*, 1954–56, I, 279; and “Credit Panel for Lobby Display—Fine Arts Center,” USAFA, RG 120, Ser. 22, which identifies Adams’s work as “planned photography.”

103. Husted, as the AFACA’s consultant, and the Secretary’s consultants, who at this time were Saarinen, Becket, and Belluschi, were also invited. *Hist. USAFA*, 1954–56, I, 279–81.

104. Talbott was somewhat unhappy with the location of the airfield, and wanted it reoriented so that the highway would not have to be moved. Talbott to SOM, 16 May 1955, SOM, #140, AFA Design Reference File.

105. Dewey Short to Talbott, 26 May 1955, SOM, #140, AFA design Reference File.

106. John Stennis to Talbott, 27 May 1955; SOM, #140, AFA Design Reference File.

107. *Hist. USAFA*, 1954–56, I, 283, 298, 299.

108. “Air Academy Design Brawl,” 13; *Hist. USAFA*, 1954–56, I, 302–303, where there is an expanded quotation by Fogarty, which goes on to say that the materials were “alien to and will not meet the demands of American monumental design.” The editorial from the *San Francisco Chronicle* is

reproduced in "Air Academy Design Brawl," 13.

109. *Hist. USAFA*, 1954–56, I, 298. Wright's remarks on the qualifications of SOM were nasty, those on Saarinen and Belluschi were demeaning, and those on Becket pathological. Of Becket, Wright said that he did not know the man, but "I wish that something would happen to him soon. I would hate to see his things going as they are now." "Air Force Academy Design Brawl," 9.

110. Wright's "continuing eagerness to do the job himself" was also observed, casting doubt on the objectivity of his criticism. John Knox Shear, Editorial, *Architectural Record* 118 (August 1955) 132a. Wright spoke before the House Appropriations Committee on 7 July 1955.

111. Netsch, "Chapel." Netsch remembered it as being Karl Kohler who offered the folded cardboard. Owings, Spaces, 159, said they were serious about the first Chapel design; and Lockett recalled that he was sent to Denver to learn folded plate construction, Interview with Netsch and Lockett.

112. *Hist. USAFA*, 1954–56, I, 297.

113. Owings, *Spaces,* 157.

114. Gropius was Chair of the Department of Architecture, Graduate School of Design, Harvard University, from 1938 to 1952. "Top American Architects Express Opinions Of House Appropriations Committee Denial of Funds for Construction of U.S. Air Force Academy," attached to letter from Bradford Wilkin, publisher, to Talbott, 19 July 1955, USAFA, RG 120, Ser. 23.

115. "Air Academy Design Brawl," 9. Some characterized the Academy architecture as "definitely modernistic in a conservative way." *Hist. USAFA*, 1954–56, I, 282–83.

116. The revised design was described as being modern but not "ultra-modernistic." The Senate Committee voted to restore $79 million to the Bill. A Conference Committee had to be called and a compromise with the House was reached at $20 million. Yet "considerable delay resulted from the fact that Congress had temporarily withheld funds." *Hist. USAFA*, 1954–56, I, 306, 307, 300–302.

117. Although work proceeded, the master plan and "basic design" of the buildings were not approved by the new Secretary of the Air Force, Donald A. Quarles, until February 1956. The exception to this was the Chapel which, because of the controversy over its design, was thereafter treated as a separate issue. Its design would not be resolved until 1958. Quarles replaced Talbott in August 1955. John Ferry to Welton Becket, 1 March 1956, USAFA, RG 120, Ser. 22.

118. "Conversation," I-8-10, II-11; *Hist. USAFA*, 1954–56, I, 292.

119. Interview with Netsch, 6 December 1992. This balance was upset, and the setting for the Chapel destroyed, when the second cadet quarters was built in the mid-1960s.

120. Consultants Meeting Minutes, 1 October 1955, 2, USAFA, RG 120, Ser. 23. Consulted in 1955, Kiley began actively working on the project in 1956. He concurred that nature was a major part of the design of the Cadet Area, and worked on the integration of nature into the plaza, and the transition of the hillock west of the Chapel and the upper terrace. Interview with Dan Kiley and Netsch, 8 December 1992.

121. Netsch, "Chapel;" "Conversation," II-8; Interview with Lockett and Netsch.

122. Bunshaft, "Recollections," 95. Lore at the Academy says that this is a "West Pointer" idea. Bunshaft moved to Chicago from New York for a few months and worked on locating the major buildings.

123. "Conversation," II-3. The decision to use the module was based on Netsch's experience in Japan.

124. At that meeting, the Secretary also considered the color and material of retaining walls as well as the selection of paving stone. Consultants Meeting Minutes, 28 July 1956, Denver, RG 461, 69/266, REL 5; Interview with Lockett and Netsch.

125. *Hist. USAFA*, 1954–56, I, 268. A cantilevered overhang of 21 feet surrounds the exterior of the building. The roof span is made up of 23 warren trusses in each direction, intersecting at right angles 14 feet on center. Computers were used to solve the 86 simultaneous equations necessary to design the structure. Interview with Lockett and Netsch; and Peterhaus statement.

126. "Conversation," II-7. Cornell University Hotel School consultants were used by SOM. "One objective was to serve two eggs sunny side up at the same temperature to all cadets." Peterhaus statement. With the closure of the cadet area by the later addition of a second cadet quarters, this transparency is missed.

127. Interview with Netsch, 6 December 1992.

128. "Conversation," II-3.

129. For instance, when a gray panel turned red. Interview with Lockett and Netsch. Robertson Ward's contribution to the project, as head of the architectural technology research team, cannot be overestimated. Netsch interview, 20 December 1992.

130. Netsch interview, 20 December 1992; Consultants Meeting Minutes, 16 April 1956, Denver, RG 461, 69/266, REL 5. See also SOM's record of the meeting, prepared by Ralph Youngren, 19 April 1956, SOM, #140, Design Reference File. Making the decision was Secretary Quarles.

131. "Comparison of Completion Dates Schedules," 17 October 1958, USAFA, RG 120, Ser. 23; News Release, 7 November 1958, Denver, RG 461, 20/40, #148.

132. Interview with Lockett and Netsch. These figures were compiled by Lockett for an address he delivered at the Academy on the occasion of the twenty-fifth anniversary of its opening. And *Hist. USAFA*, 1954–56, I, 312.

133. The bridges, two for the railroads and four for the highway, had superstructures of precast, prestressed concrete girders and cast-in-place decks. "Approach Bridges: United States Air Force Academy," *Architectural Record* 123 (April 1958) 239–40, which says that the girders were both pre-stressed and post-tensioned.

134. This office was headed by Edward Merrill and supervised by Albert Lockett. The site office opened in 1954 and closed in 1959. Interview with Lockett and Netsch. Jack Train recalled hiring talent away from the Chicago firm of Holabird & Root, who, in Train's opinion, had the best technical staff at that time. Interview with Train, 4 December 1992. Design and working drawings were executed in Chicago.

135. Netsch, "Chapel." In retrospect, Netsch was not displeased with the controversy, because it gave him both the impetus and the time to rethink the Chapel's setting, form, and relation to the rest of the Cadet Area; at the time, however, the criticism and the controversy were devastating. Netsch was in his early thirties when he began working on the project. "Conversation," II-12.

136. Netsch interview, 20 December 1992; Netsch, "Chapel." Belluschi was critical of the treatment of the area around the Chapel and others agreed the Chapel should be restudied. Consultants Meeting Minutes, 1 October 1955, 3, 5, USAFA, RG 120, Ser. 23.

137. Netsch, "Chapel"; "Conversation," II-12.

138. Interview with Lockett and Netsch. The "Design Directive" issued in June 1955 on the Chapel instructed that two chapels be designed: an Academy Chapel that would house a 1,600-seat Protestant chapel and a 100-seat Jewish synagogue; and a Cadet chapel for Catholics with a 600-person capacity nave. An amendment in October 1955 reduced the Protestant seating capacity to 1,200. "Design Directive," FY 1955, #42, 1 June 1955, and #42A, 18 October 1955, SOM, #53, Central Files/Design Directives. By the end of 1956, the respective capacities for the Protestant, Jewish, and Catholic facilities were 900, 100, and 500. "Design Directive," FY 1957, #6, 27 December 1956, 3, SOM, #53, Central Files/Design Directives.

139. Consultants Meeting Minutes, 12 March 1957, USAFA, RG 120, Ser. 22. Bunshaft credits himself with the idea of a two-level church, and cites Assisi as his inspiration; he credits Netsch with the form of the Chapel and the use of tetrahedrons. Bunshaft, "Recollections," 96. Netsch remembers being influenced by the two-level Church of Ste. Chapelle in Paris. Interview with Lockett and Netsch.

140. From this time, the Chapel began to take shape, with the support of Owings, Bunshaft, and Saarinen. Netsch credits colleagues Ralph Youngren, his chief assistant, Robertson Ward, architectural technician, and Ken Naslund, in engineering, with help on the design. Netsch, "Chapel."

141. Interview Lockett and Netsch.

142. Consultants Meeting Minutes, 12 March 1957, 4 and 3. The Chapel design was widely published in September 1957, some months before its approval.

143. Owings, *Spaces*, 158. Secretaries of the Air Force during the initial planning, design, and construction of the Academy were: W. Stuart Symington (September 1947–April 1950); Thomas K. Finletter (April 1950–January 1953); Harold E. Talbott (February 1952–August 1955); Donald A. Quarles (August 1955–April 1957); James H. Douglas, Jr. (May 1957–December 1959); Dudley C. Sharp (December 1959–January 1961); and Eugene M. Zuckert (January 1961–September 1965). Douglas was among those who had long-term involvement with the project, from the time he was Under Secretary to Talbott to his own term as Secretary. Superintendents included Harmon, who became Superintendent on 27 July 1954, resigned on 27 July 1956 because of illness, and died in February of the next year; James E. Briggs, who remained in that post until August 1959; and William S. Stone, who served until 1962. Of the consultants, Saarinen is remembered by Netsch and Train as the one who would really roll up his sleeves and work on the project. Interview

with Train, 4 December 1992, and Netsch, 6 December 1992.

144. *United States Air Force Academy Base Comprehensive Plan: Service, Supply and Airfield Master Plans,* prepared by Skidmore, Owings & Merrill, September 1990, 9, 10.

145. These units, which contained 1,750 square feet each, were for the Academy's professors, and made up the only part of the housing component that SOM held on to after being directed to affiliate with a firm experienced in Capehart housing. "Design Directive," FY 1955, 8 November 1956, SOM, #53, Central Files/Design Directives; Comparison of Completion Dates Schedules, 17 October 1958. And see notes 99 above and 146 below.

146. *Hist. USAFA*, 1957–58, II, 715–16, and 1958–59, I, 170, where the date of the start of construction is mistakenly given as May 1959 instead of 1958. SOM had first proposed a Dymaxion-type house which, either suspended or cantilevered from a single vertical support, would require the least disruption to the natural terrain of the valleys. This scheme was quickly rejected. SOM then designed a series of cluster-planned modern houses. AFACA turned these down, and funding for the housing was changed to a Title VIII (Capehart) federal housing project. SOM was required to affiliate with Clark and Enerson, and the housing produced was a watered-down version of the modern design. Telephone conversation with Netsch, 28 February 1994.

147. Unfortunately, the Cadet Area existed in this state for just a few short years, as its character was dramatically altered in the 1965 expansion program. This expansion program enclosed the Terrazzo level with the construction of the second Cadet Quarters, turning the open L into an enclosed courtyard. It also extended the Academic Building, added the field house, and included a number of smaller additions.

148. That is, a reconstituted landscape, for very little of the site of a major construction project can be considered natural.

149. One need only look at the unfortunate Sijan Hall to see the contrast, and the care with which the earlier quarters was located. Sijan seems to ram its adjacent landmass, at the same time that it creates the only closed corner of the cadet area.

31

32

31. Elevations of one of the colonels' houses. What the architects thought of as simplicity and elegance in this scheme apparently did not appeal to Air Force officers, and the houses were heavily remodeled. SOM Archives, Chicago.

32. Presentation drawing of early unbuilt scheme for the Academic Building. Rendering by George Rudolph. This perspective drawing rendered in gouache (an opaque water color) was probably prepared for the Colorado Springs Art Center exhibition but never used because the design for the Academic Building changed. SOM Archives, Chicago.

Architects at Work
DESIGN DRAWINGS

In the course of designing any project as large as the Academy the architects make thousands of drawings. These range from the small sketches, often jotted on the backs of envelopes or napkins at restaurants, in which a design idea is first recorded, to elaborate perspective views rendered in color, in which designs are presented to the client. There are also drawings in which the architects work out their ideas, and working drawings, the detailed drawings that are used for actual construction. Included on these pages are some examples of drawings prepared in the course of designing the Air Force Academy.

–Robert Bruegmann

33

33. Perspective study of library. In this drawing, which matches the finished building fairly closely, the architects explored spatial relationships and the effect created by various colors and finishes. SOM Archives, Chicago.

34. Study for interior of room in Cadet Quarters. This perspective sketch was probably prepared for a meeting of the architectural consultants. The scheme, which would have concealed untidy beds, was promptly discarded. SOM Archives, Chicago.

34

37

36

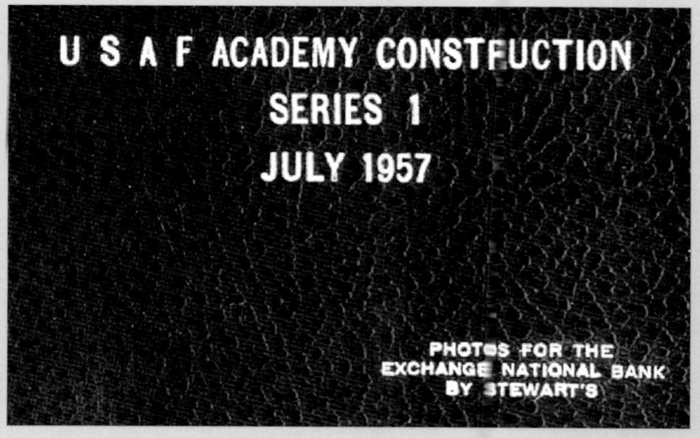

35

Documenting Construction:
PHOTOS BY STEWART'S

The Colorado Springs photography firm of Stewart's photographed the Academy construction from July 1957 through May 1965, providing documentation for the architects, the contractors, and the subcontractors. Although the firm was not directly employed by Skidmore, Owings & Merrill, many of its photographs were purchased by the architects and used in marketing and disseminating the Academy image. With funding from the Exchange National Bank in Colorado Springs, copies of Stewart's prints were compiled on a monthly basis, beginning in late 1957, and were then used as a catalogue for future reference. Clarence Coil of Stewart's was responsible for the ground photographs, while Cloyd Brunson provided the aerial photographs.[1] The photographs range in style from elegant, formally composed images to informal views that have a snapshot quality. They are important documents in recording how this facility was actually constructed, used, presented, and perceived.

–Robert Nauman

Notes

1. This information was provided by Cloyd Clarence Brunson in a telephone conversation on June 3, 1993.

39

38

35–37. The July 1957 Exchange National Bank book, volume 1 in the series of 70, records construction of some of the essential structures and buildings housing basic services at the Academy. Many of the photographs record steel erection, for example, at the heating plant where the framing has been erected around a great boiler, or at the Academic Building. Stewart's Nos. 1-8, 1-5.
38–39. By Series 60 in June 1962 most of the major buildings had been finished, but the Stewart's photographers continued to chronicle events at the Academy, including the construction of the Stadium and a visit by Vice President Lyndon B. Johnson. Stewart's Nos. 60-79, 60-32.

40

40. In this photograph three cadets accompany Cadet Col. Robert D. Beckel (left) up the stairs in the Dining Hall. The curving staircases were designed to contrast with the right angles that prevail elsewhere. Photograph c. 1959 by William Belknap, © National Geographic Society.

41. By positioning the camera parallel to the facade, photographer William Belknap created a view which echoed the elevation drawings made by the architects. The primary colors of the glass mosaics derive from Bauhaus designs. Photograph c. 1959 by William Belknap, © National Geographic Society.

42. In the *National Geographic*'s Academy there are also light moments. Here two carefully posed cadets share a joke in their quarters. Photograph c. 1959 by William Belknap, © National Geographic Society.

The *National Geographic* Visits the Academy

Of all the articles on the newly opened Academy, by far the most lavish was that in the June 1959 issue of *National Geographic*. Splashed across thirty pages of the magazine, spectacular full-page Kodachrome photographs and a highly enthusiastic text treated the Academy in much the same way the *National Geographic* dealt with Hawaiian volcanoes or the visit of Queen Elizabeth to Ottawa. In each case stirring events were captured as they unfolded in a colorful and exotic locale. At the Academy the glistening facades of the buildings formed the backdrop for the pomp and ceremony of the public life of the Academy. In William Belknap's dramatic photographs, perfectly groomed cadets, whether marching across the Court of Honor or at ease in their quarters, provided the ideal counterpoint to the sleek modern buildings.

–Robert Bruegmann

41

42

43, 44

Raising the Roof:
THE DRAMATIC CONSTRUCTION OF MITCHELL HALL

One of the most spectacular of the many structural and technical innovations that Skidmore, Owings & Merrill incorporated in its design of the Air Force Academy was the construction of the two-acre roof over Mitchell Hall, the cadet dining facility. A large, uninterrupted space was desired for the dining hall to promote an esprit de corps among the 3,000 cadets assembled for meals. According to Gertrude Lempp Kerbis, an architect on the project, the Academy wanted the ability to "serve 2 eggs sunny side up at the same temperature to all cadets".[1] Due to the roof's enormous clear span, 266 feet, a two-way system of prefabricated Warren trusses was assembled on the ground and then jacked into place utilizing equipment and techniques normally reserved for precast concrete lift slab construction. Structural engineers at the American Bridge Division of the U.S. Steel Corporation came up with the idea of using this specialized concrete building method in which roof and floor slabs are cast, usually at ground level, and then raised into position by jacking. With the application of this construction technique to Mitchell Hall's roof, it became the first long-span steel structure to be lifted into place.[2]

Despite the fact that most of the trusses that make up the dining hall roof were prefabricated, twenty-seven welders were required, along with 11,500 pounds of welding rod, for the final assembly at the building site. The American Bridge Division of the U.S. Steel Corporation was the contractor for fabrication and erection and Vagtborg Lift Slab Corporation was subcontracted for the actual lift. The 308-foot-long trusses around the perimeter of the building are 8' 6" deep and have parallel top and bottom chords that present a uniform fascia on the elevation. The bottom chords of the spanning trusses are flat, but the top chords slope up from the fascia at a rate of a quarter inch per foot toward the center of the roof to form a maximum truss depth of 11' 8 1/2". All joints, splices, and intersections were welded to provide structural continuity. Structural calculations were required for each of these connections. The senior structural designers at Skidmore, Owings & Merrill saved hundreds of man hours by using a computer system that was then being developed at the University of Illinois for massive number crunching. This was one of the earliest applications of the new computer technology for structural analysis.[3]

In six hours on January 6, 1958, the 308' X 308' roof was raised 24' 2" into the

43. Mitchell Hall roof resting on the ground before being lifted into place. Photograph by Stewart's, c. 1958. The steel truss roof over the Cadet Dining Hall was the first structure of its type to be fabricated on the ground and lifted into place. Local History Collection, Pikes Peak Library District. Stewart's No. 5-3.

44. Jacks on Mitchell Hall columns. Photograph by SOM, Jan. 1958. Hydraulic jacks on each column were synchronized through four manned consoles on top of the trusses and rose with the roof as it was lifted. SOM Archives, Chicago.

45. Mitchell Hall roof in place. Photograph by SOM, Jan. 1958. SOM Archives, Chicago.

45

air by hydraulic jacks on top of the sixteen freestanding columns. (fig. 44) Four manned control panels connected by telephones were placed on top of the truss and went along for the ride as the structure was lifted. To coordinate the movement, and keep the structure level as it rose, valved high-pressure hydraulic lines passed through the interconnected control panels to the jacks. Each jack had two lifting rods which passed through the cap and base plates of the jack and were held in position by locking nuts. The roof framing was picked up by engaging the rods in a lifting frame connected below the bottom flange of the roof truss. The lifting process was simple in principle: by pushing up the cap plate of the jack and the attached lifting rods, the hydraulic jack pulled the truss up into place. The pressure was then released from the hydraulic piston, and heavy springs between the cap and the base plate slowly pulled the cap back down into its low position, ready for the next lift. In this way the roof was lifted three inches at a time.

The roof came to a rest two inches above its final position and its load was then transferred to hydraulic jacks mounted on temporary heavy timber posts. Cables fastened the four corners of the roof structure to interior columns to provide temporary bracing. The jacks were removed from the steel columns and replaced with two-ton caps. Next, the structure was lowered to its final position and steel braces were welded to the roof grid and the caps to support the truss system after the temporary timber supports were removed. The cap consists of a ball-and-socket joint which allows the structure to move under the stresses of wind thrusts and thermal expansion. The ball is a 6"-diameter stainless steel hemisphere, and when it is coupled with the upper socket plate, the 1,150-ton-roof literally floats above the ground. The construction of Mitchell Hall's roof marked a new and faster way to fabricate and erect an extremely long-span steel roof.[4]

—Sheri Olson

Notes

1. Gertrude Lempp Kerbis, Chicago, to Franz Schulze, Lake Forest, Ill., 26 June 1993. Statement transmitted with letter. Transcript in U.S. Air Force Academy Archives, Colorado Springs.
2. "New Way to Raise the Roof," *Architectural Forum* (March 1958): 126.
3. Letter from Kerbis to Schulze.
4. Andrew J. Brown and Wayne Teng, "Jacks on Columns Erect Two-Acre Roof at AF Academy," *Engineering News-Record,* 23 January 1958, 26.

PART 2

INTERPRETING THE ACADEMY

46. View of Cadet Area from the east. Photograph by Stewart's, 1961. This shows the Academic Building (left) and the Cadet Dormitory (right) from a slightly oblique angle, but the brilliant sunlight on the east-facing facades and crystalline clarity of the day makes the photograph read almost like an architect's elevation drawing. Local History Collection, Pikes Peak Library District.

Robert Bruegmann

Military Culture, Architectural Culture, Popular Culture

If ever an architectural project seemed to demand monumental treatment, it was the United States Air Force Academy. As a relatively new branch of the American military, the Air Force wanted an architectural ensemble as impressive as West Point or Annapolis. It also needed a complex that would be able to stand up to the grandiose natural setting that had been selected for it at the base of the Rocky Mountains.

The Academy, moreover, had to function as a national monument. It was one of the largest commissions of the American government at the moment when the United States was starting to exert its influence more directly than ever before on the world's political and economic scene. It would inevitably serve as one of the most important representations of American military power during the Cold War. Finally, the need for a monument was critical in another "cold war," the battle in the world of architecture over the "Modern Movement." The Academy was widely seen as an opportunity to demonstrate once and for all that Modern architecture could rise to the grandest occasions, sweeping away the historical styles of the nineteenth century.

Thus, three different constituencies; the military, the general public, and the architecture and design community, all demanded a monument. They got one. Today, perched securely in its vast natural setting and familiar from endless photographic reproductions, the Academy has the kind of apparent inevitability common to many architectural monuments (fig. 46). But, as is also true of many of these monuments, this apparent inevitability masks a history of false starts, fundamental clashes in beliefs, compromises, and bittersweet conclusions. This essay will consider three key moments in the making of a monument at Colorado Springs.

Selecting an Architect After thousands of words describing the site selection, program formulation, and organization of the Construction Agency for the Academy, a voluminous manuscript history in the Academy Archives abruptly disposes of the selection of an architect in two terse, but typically bureaucratic, sentences: "As a result of the Air Force announcement that it desired applications from architect-engineer firms, more than 260 individual organizations applied for selection. The successful applicant was Skidmore, Owings and Merrill of Chicago."[1] We are told the final result, but hardly anything more. Who were the 260 architects? What were the criteria for choosing? What was said in the discussion? Why was SOM chosen?[2]

We may never know the answers to these questions.[3] So far, no records of the proceedings have been found, and few of the participants from the military seem to have left accounts. It is likely that this absence of information was quite intentional on the part of the Air Force, merely standard operating procedure in dealing

with important, politically sensitive decisions. For historians, however, this silence is particularly frustrating because the juxtaposition of two very different worlds, the Air Force hierarchy and the architectural community, raises some particularly intriguing questions.

It is not that the American military had had no previous experience with architecture. From the earliest days of the Republic the American Army had created ensembles ranging from the flimsy frame buildings surrounding dusty parade grounds at Western forts to the vast masonry piles at the great arsenals in Springfield, Massachusetts; Rockford, Illinois; and elsewhere.[4] In virtually every case, the buildings had rational plans and sober facades. Important buildings might be dressed up with some ornament, but it was usually restrained in quantity and conservative in style. In other words, considerations of function and engineering efficiency usually took precedence over aesthetics. In fact, in many military buildings, engineering technique became its own, often highly satisfying, aesthetic.[5]

The most direct and obvious precedent for the Academy was the complex then known as the "West Point of the Air," Randolph Air Force Base in San Antonio (fig. 48). From the time of its completion in 1930 by the Army through the early 1950s when it served the newly created Air Force, this impressive 2,300-acre installation provided the most important training for Air officers . The buildings, laid out along radiating streets in the center of a large airfield, were nominally Spanish colonial in style. As was the case at many bases, the majority of buildings were fairly utilitarian, but the two most prominent structures, Chapel One and the so-called Taj Mahal, an extravagant domed structure that housed the base's administrative offices and disguised a water tower, were considerably more elaborate.[6]

During World War II the scale and complexity of military construction increased enormously. To keep up with the demands, the Army and the Navy increasingly turned to civilian architects and engineers, and, by necessity, allowed them somewhat greater freedom in design decisions. Although some of these architects believed that they were still unnecessarily hampered by bureaucratic demands and constricting guidelines, the results often compared favorably with the most advanced designs for American corporations.[7] Many of America's most prominent Modernist firms, Skidmore, Owings & Merrill among them, received their first major commissions from the military during this period.[8]

The most conspicuous military building erected in the decade before the Academy was, of course, the Pentagon, the new home of the War Department in Arlington, Virginia (fig. 47). Rushed to completion during the early years of World War II, it was one of the largest buildings ever erected, and it incorporated all of the latest transportation and communications technology.[9] Exterior expression posed something of a problem. The main purpose of the building was to house an enormous number of offices, a program which appeared to dictate a very large but simple box wrapped around a rabbit warren of cubicles inside, all lit by endless rows of regular windows. To house the top officials of the American Army in a building that looked like a warehouse or factory, however, was clearly unacceptable, so the architects clad the building in stone (limestone after President Roosevelt vetoed marble) and added a modest cornice at the top, slight projections at the center, and a series of porticoes that gave the entire ensemble a thin veneer of monumental grandeur. It was a kind of working-class relative of the much more expensive and ambitious classicism seen in the monumental core of Washington, for example, in the buildings of

47

48

47. Aerial view of the Pentagon. Photograph by MSgt. Bill Thompson. The architects of the Pentagon applied a thin classical veneer onto what was otherwise a factory-like structure. U.S. Department of Defense.

48. Aerial view of Randolph AFB, San Antonio. Air Force photograph taken 1931. The base was located in the center of the airfield. The Taj Mahal is on the circumference of the circle to the right. Hangars line the exterior of the base. Randolph AFB Archives.

49

50

49. Aerial view of United States Military Academy from above Hudson River. Photograph by Kepler, 1953. Visible are several of the most prominent Cram, Goodhue and Ferguson buildings, including: in the far left foreground, the Power and Steam Generating Building, 1909; next to it on the right the long, low wall of Thayer (formerly Riding) Hall, 1911; behind Thayer Hall the towered Headquarters and Administration Building, 1910; and, above all of the other buildings, the Cadet Chapel, 1910. In the left foreground the building with the hipped roof in the center of a group of three is Cullom Hall, 1897–99, by McKim, Mead, and White. USMA Archives.

50. Headquarters and Administration Building, United States Military Academy, West Point. Photograph by White Studios, early 1930s. Constructed in 1910, this building, one of the first from the designs of Cram, Goodhue and Ferguson, set the tone for much of what would follow. USMA Archives.

51. Aerial view of United States Naval Academy, Annapolis. Photograph by Forsberg, probably early 1950s. This view looks toward Bancroft Hall at the center of the courtyard facing Annapolis Harbor. Behind Bancroft Hall is the domed Chapel, which faces a courtyard opening onto the Severn River. USNA Archives.

the Federal Triangle or in John Russell Pope's National Gallery and Jefferson Memorial.[10] This kind of stripped classicism proved to be immensely popular in the 1930s and 1940s, becoming a governmental vernacular not just in Washington but in Berlin, Moscow, and around the world.[11]

The military buildings that loomed largest in the process of planning the new Air Force Academy, however, were not buildings in Washington but the two largest existing service academies, the United States Military Academy at West Point and the United States Naval Academy at Annapolis.[12] Both had started as modest installations, but by the late nineteenth century the Army and Navy had raised their architectural standards and had started to turn to prominent civilian architects for ambitious new building schemes. At West Point, the earliest buildings, which surrounded a parade grounds at the base of dramatic high bluffs along the Hudson River, were joined in the late nineteenth century by polished classical structures by the well-known New York architects Richard Morris Hunt and McKim, Mead, and White.[13] But while these architects created compositions that were indeed more elegant than the earlier buildings at West Point, the classical style clashed with the existing Tudor and Gothic modes. In an effort to gain more coherence, the Academy sponsored a competition in 1903 which was won by Cram, Goodhue and Ferguson of New York, known for their scholarly Gothic churches. These architects produced a plan that called for new buildings to be clothed in local stone in a stripped-down Gothic style so that they would appear to rise directly out of the steep site, culminating in a great Gothic chapel on the hillside well above the parade grounds. The architects themselves designed only seven buildings, but almost all later architects paid homage to this precedent, creating, by the outbreak of World War II, a dramatic, unified complex rising up above the Hudson (figs. 49, 50).

At Annapolis, located on the low land at the point where the Severn River empties into Chesapeake Bay, the Naval Academy's site allowed a more regular configuration of buildings.[14] The presence of Maryland's gracious eighteenth-century capital city behind the campus virtually guaranteed that its buildings would be classical in style. The earliest structures, again fairly modest, almost completely disappeared during a massive rebuilding scheme started in 1898 to designs by Ernest Flagg, one of New York's most accomplished practitioners of the lavish classical style American architects had learned at the Ecole des Beaux-Arts in Paris (fig. 51).[15] This rebuilding, partly a response to the nationalistic fervor stirred up by the Spanish-American War of that year and the vital role naval warfare played during the hostilities, included a vast courtyard facing Annapolis Harbor with an imposing classical structure, Bancroft Hall, at its center. Another courtyard, at right angles to it and facing the Severn, culminated in a huge domed chapel designed in a severe French Baroque style. At Annapolis, as at West Point, there were alterations and additions in the interwar years, but the essential character of both places was well set by mid-twentieth century.

A high percentage of early Air Force officers had attended one or the other of the two schools, particularly West Point, and this architectural setting, the scene of their initiation into military life, remained indelibly stamped in their memory. Over and over during the planning for the new academy, memories of life at West Point

51

would surface as Air Force generals tried to imagine what it would be like to be a cadet in the buildings they were envisioning. But if tradition could act as a positive force, it could also mean an unthinking reliance on old ways. The Air Force, newly created as a separate branch of the American military, wanted to distinguish itself, to demonstrate its interest in new technologies, and to prove that it was not held back by restrictive traditional thinking. "West Point has 160 years of tradition unhampered by progress," was a commonly heard piece of Air Force wisdom.[16] The critical

52. Project for Air Force Academy by Ellery Husted, 1954. This scheme featured a moderate Modernist design. U.S. Air Force Academy Collection.

importance of air power during World War II, displayed again in the air lift to Berlin in 1948-49 and in the Korean conflict, led many Air Force officers to see their branch of the Armed Services as the ascendant military force of the postwar era.[17] Their Academy should somehow reflect this position.

How to translate these ideas into architectural design? The top military officers often had a considerable amount of engineering training but usually had little firsthand familiarity with the world of architecture or the fine arts. If the record of their buildings is any indication, they were not at all averse to trying new technologies or even new styles, but they had a deeply rooted conservatism when it came to the design of public structures, as the serviceable but pallid postwar buildings at West Point and Annapolis suggest.

The size of the Academy project and the requirement that the selected team must have competence both in architecture and engineering narrowed considerably the field of plausible contenders for the Academy commission. The most obvious candidates were large architect-engineer firms like Graham, Anderson, Probst & White of Chicago, Pereira and Luckman of Los Angeles, or Skidmore, Owings & Merrill of Chicago, all of whom made the final round in the Air Force Academy competition, the latter two on their own and Graham, Anderson, Probst & White as part of the Kittyhawk team. A partner in one of these firms shared a number of attributes with a top military officer. Usually highly trained, he too was aware of belonging to an elite profession, one that, like the military, had a long and impressive history, and one that, again like the military, if not always appreciated or understood, at least commanded considerable prestige among the population at large.

In other ways, however, the world of architecture was a very different world. Unlike the military, with its heavily hierarchical, top-to-bottom authority that tended to impose a certain unity and stability, the architectural profession in the postwar years found itself in the throes of a major debate over the "Modern Movement." According to the accounts of its advocates, the Modern Movement, although prefigured by a number of developments in the nineteenth century, had really come into its own in Europe in the early years of the twentieth century as a fusion of various avant-garde positions.[18] The avant-garde, originally a military term referring to the small advance party sent to scout out new positions, became a metaphor for the cultural shock troops of artistic Modernism. To be culturally avant-garde meant to resist prevailing attitudes. In architecture the particular enemy for avant-garde groups like the Italian Futurists or members of the Bauhaus was the classical tradition that had been the dominant mode for public buildings from the time of the Renaissance. A great many of the avant-garde architectural figures were far to the left politically. Disenchanted with conditions in the modern capitalist world, they advocated the end of the bourgeois-dominated liberal democratic governments and the creation of a new, rational, classless, egalitarian society. Although radical politics did not necessarily go hand in hand with radical aesthetic ideas, many radical Modernists considered all traditional ideas of beauty suspect, part of the bourgeois effort to keep control of the economy and society. The most radical avant-garde figures proposed doing away with the idea of aesthetics altogether. If a building were fit for its purpose and structurally sound, that was enough. Certainly the palace, the church, the opera house, the museum—all of the monumental buildings that represented the control of bourgeois authority—needed to be replaced by new egalitarian monuments: the efficient factory, the communal housing block, the workers club.

European avant-garde Modernism first came to the attention of most American architects in the 1930s. In the United States it

was championed by a small cadre of zealous followers. Although they often had a considerable disdain for the great mass of the American middle class, these advocates rejected out of hand the leftist political stance of the Europeans. For American architectural critics like Henry-Russell Hitchcock and Philip Johnson and the curators at the Museum of Modern Art—the most visible American institution promoting the new architecture—modern architecture was not about social reform. It was about the creation of a new style, one they dubbed the "International Style."[19] This term created considerable confusion. Ironically, it was anathema precisely to most of the European avant-garde architects whose work the Americans most fervently championed. The European avant-gardistes believed that they had abandoned style altogether in favor of a universal, timeless architecture. They believed that their architecture was simply modern and that it would never go out of style. In America, however, the term struck a resonant chord. It suggested something up-to-date and technologically advanced, and the very presence of the word "style" repudiated the more alarming political and social implications.

By the early 1950s the debate over Modernism had produced a situation of considerable complexity. At one end of the ideological spectrum were the conservatives who were unwilling to jettison traditional styles in favor of the new International Style. Although hardline classicists no longer dominated the American architectural world, in the 1950s most public buildings in the country were still built in a style that could be called classical. That many Air Force officers favored this kind of design is apparent from the many favorable comments about the architecture of Randolph Air Force Base found in Air Force documents.

In the middle of the architectural spectrum, many of the largest American firms committed themselves to no single architectural position. They felt free to use elements from any source. Many were happy to apply Modernist details on buildings that were still fundamentally classical in their overall plan and configuration. Early indications might have suggested that this kind of cautious, eclectic approach was exactly what the Air Force wanted. In 1947, for example, Air Force officials engaged a New York architect, Ellery Husted, to help with site planning and preliminary designs. Husted

53

53. Illinois Institute of Technology. Photograph by Hedrich-Blessing. Designed by Mies van der Rohe starting in 1938, IIT was, in the early 1950s, one of the few complete campuses in the United States in the Modern style. Chicago Historical Society. HB 13666 E.

54. Aerial view of the University of Mexico. One of the largest ensembles of Modernist buildings in North America, this university featured brilliantly colored murals and mosaics that warmed up the austere surfaces seen in European Modernist design. Organization of American States.

had worked in the office of James Gamble Rogers, the brilliant designer of Yale's Gothic and classical quadrangles erected in the 1920s. It appears that Husted was quite catholic in his design ideas, an attitude that allowed him to act as consultant for numerous government bodies for decades, even though architectural tastes shifted dramatically during that time.[20]

A site plan produced by him for the Academy in 1954 followed traditional notions of axial symmetry and classical order (fig. 52). The major group of buildings formed a U-shaped composition with a large domed structure at the end of the U and a series of pavilions on either side. This arrangement recalls strongly one of America's most famous campuses, Thomas Jefferson's University of Virginia. The buildings seen in Husted's rendering seem to have been vaguely classical but highly stripped down. They were obviously intended to be Modern—that is they were certainly not literal copies of any past style—but they were definitely not in the new International Style. Instead they were closer to the moderate Scandinavian Modernism of the interwar years.[21] This kind of moderate, flexible stance on architectural style was seconded by the chairman of the Air Force's architect selection committee, John M. Ferry. Although he stated that the Pentagon wanted a design "suitable to the forward looking view of the Air Force," he immediately qualified this with the reservation "We're not looking for. . . something very startling."[22]

If it appeared from hints that had been dropped publicly that the Air Force favored an architect with a fairly flexible attitude toward what was "Modern," in the end the choice came down to several firms clearly identified with a more aggressive Modernist style.[23]

The Depression, political upheaval and World War II had brought European avant-garde Modernists themselves to the United States. By the late 1930s many of the most influential figures had arrived on these shores, notably the German architect Ludwig Mies van der Rohe. In the United States Mies soon abandoned whatever radical social and political ideas he might have had and reduced his buildings to sleek steel and glass prismatic solids, creating what was dubbed by one critic the "stainless steel" standard for American commercial architecture. His designs would be adopted and copied endlessly over the next few decades for corporate structures and elegant apartment buildings.

But Mies himself was never a popular architect. His was a small office that operated like an artist's atelier; he had a

54

perfectionist bent so strong that it drove off many potential clients; and he had inflexible ideas about style. This proved to be a particular problem with public buildings. Mies's design for the Illinois Institute of Technology in Chicago, for example, his only large-scale public commission executed before 1960 and perhaps the only example in the United States of an entire university campus designed in the European Modernist mode, was apparently never even mentioned in connection with discussions about the architecture of the Air Force Academy, probably because it was considered insufficiently monumental and too factory-like (fig. 53). Instead, Air Force planners flew to Mexico City where the strikingly modern university under construction there employed European stylistic elements but adopted them to local conditions, warming up the flat machine-like surfaces with spectacular murals and other ornamental features (fig. 54).[24]

Many of the most successful large American offices did the same thing. One of these was the office of Edward Durell Stone, whose El Panama Hotel in Panama City was praised by Superintendent Harmon. In this building the intricate grilles, serpentine curves and elaborate palate of materials and surface treatments emphasized the decorative aspects of Modernism over its strictly functional and structural elements (fig. 55). In the early 1950s Stone was still included, if with growing reservations, in the Modernist camp. The same was true of architects like Wallace Harrison who had been involved with some of America's most important structures, from Rockefeller Center in the 1920s to the United Nations in New York in the early 1950s.[25] Although he certainly considered them "Modern," Harrison's buildings were routinely dismissed as half-modern by advocates of the European avant garde and by much of the American architectural press.

To be considered thoroughly Modern but still attract commissions from relatively conservative American businessmen was a feat achieved by only a handful of architects. One of the most successful was Eero Saarinen. At the General Motors Technical Center in Warren, Michigan, for example, Saarinen, with his famous father Eliel, forged a stylistic vocabulary that grafted elements drawn from Mies, Le Corbusier, and other European avant-garde designers, with standard American industrial practice, seen for example, in the work of their Detroit-area neighbor, the firm of Albert Kahn, America's largest and best-known industrial architect. The Warren complex, with its dramatic site plan, sleek steel and glass curtain walls, brilliantly colored tile end walls, and ingenious

55

use of new technologies, was greatly admired in the architectural world of the 1950s and made Saarinen a prime candidate for the Air Force Academy commission (fig. 56).[26]

For all his design skill, however, Saarinen could not, in the end, compete with the scope or experience of the SOM organization. Like Saarinen, the SOM designers offered a rich amalgam of elements drawn from both Mies and the Europeans and also from standard American practice. In the case of the SOM office, the great Chicago skyscrapers of the late nineteenth century by architects like Burnham & Root, Holabird & Roche, and Adler & Sullivan loomed particularly large. These buildings, which were being rediscovered in the 1950s, seemed to provide a particularly American prototype for Modernist architecture.[27] The SOM designers were backed up by a work force much larger than Saarinen's and organized in much the same way as the large American business corporations which the firm served. With several offices and hundreds of architects and engineers, they commanded the technical expertise to design and supervise even the largest projects.

Businessmen as well as artists, the SOM partners shared many of the political and social ideals of the American corporate leaders. By the time of their selection as architects of the Academy, they had brought European avant-garde design ideas into the mainstream of American architectural practice and made them acceptable to American business.[28] In SOM's open, transparent facades American industrialists found a perfect expression of their attempts to present a cool, technologically advanced image to the world. Lever House, designed by Gordon Bunshaft in the early 1950s for a prominent site on Park Avenue in New York City, for example, was an early and conspicuous merging of American skyscraper design and ideas borrowed from Le Corbusier and Mies[29] (fig. 9). The new headquarters of Connecticut General Life Insurance Company in the suburbs of Hartford, Connecticut, used a similar vocabulary, perhaps influenced as well by Saarinen's General Motors Technical Center (figs. 57, 58). Designed by Bunshaft in the early 1950s and under construction during the same years as the Air Force Academy, the Connecticut General project was apparently quite influential in helping Skidmore, Owings & Merrill get the Air Force commission. From the scant evidence that remains, it appears that the selection of an architect for the Academy was not made by Air Force officers but by Harold Talbott, the civilian Secretary of the Air Force.[30] It appears that Talbott, a businessman, had been heavily influenced by a fellow business leader, Frazar Wilde, president of the insurance company.[31] Certainly in its site plan, its treatment of the surrounding

56

55. El Panama Hotel, Panama City, 1950. Photograph by Ezra Stoller © Esto, c. 1950. This building, designed by Edward Durell Stone, exemplified a softer, more decorative Modernism than the astringent designs of Mies. Stoller No. 115 L:3.

56. Air view of General Motors Technical Center, Warren, Michigan. Photograph by Balthazar Korab. This complex by Eero Saarinen had a major influence on the design of the Air Force Academy.

57

57. Aerial view of Connecticut General Life Insurance Co. Headquarters, Bloomfield, Connecticut. Photograph by Ezra Stoller © Esto, c. 1957. Built between 1954 and 1957 to designs of Gordon Bunshaft of Skidmore, Owings & Merrill, this work was apparently highly influential in getting SOM the commission for the Air Force Academy and shares many design features with it. Stoller No. 51 S:1.

58. View of courtyard of Connecticut General Life Insurance Company. Photograph by Ezra Stoller © Esto, c. 1957. One of four courtyards in this building designed by the eminent artist Isamu Noguchi. Stoller No. 51 S:54.

58

landscape, and its use of interior courtyards, the Connecticut complex prefigured many of the design features seen slightly later at the Academy.[32]

For American Modernist architects, the Academy was more than just another commercial commission. While such architects had done well in several competitions for major public buildings, there were hardly any examples of major built work for government bodies or public institutions in America at the time the Academy competition was announced.[33] Here was a golden opportunity. The International Style seemed particularly appropriate for a military academy. Unlike the users of most government buildings, who could clutter up the clean lines of the buildings with inappropriate personal effects, the military could impose a discipline on the way the buildings were used. At a more basic level, moreover, one of the most important tenets of Modernism was a belief that architecture could not just influence its inhabitants but could play a major role in molding individuals and society. This coincided perfectly with the idea of the military academy, in which every aspect, from the most important educational program down to the smallest detail of the daily routine, was formalized and regulated as part of a conscious effort to mold behavior and character.[34]

Reviewing the Designs After the selection of the architects in 1954, the real work of designing the Academy began, as the architects, their associated engineers and consultants, the Construction Agency, and officials of the Academy refined the program and drew up plans. In the process it became clear that the desire of designers at Skidmore, Owings & Merrill to create an entire ensemble using the new style would have to be modified. Early in the design stage, for example, the architects proposed a highly futuristic housing scheme intended to minimize the impact on the landscape. In this scheme each house was cantilevered from a narrow concrete stem which was the only part of the house to touch the ground.[35] But while Air Force officers could accept a Modernist dormitory or gymnasium, they drew the line on the houses in which they would live. The architects were forced to acquiesce.

Although there were many other disputes during the design process, it is likely that by the time the masterplan was complete, both the architects and the Air Force officers felt that they were in basic agreement.[36] They had used a rational planning process and had created what they believed was an efficient and appropriate design for the Academy. Whatever their differences, the top military brass and the architects had a heavy investment in the design, and they took great pains to present it in the most convincing manner at the Colorado Springs Art Center in May 1955 (figs. 74-79).

Different groups reacted quite differently to the designs. Not surprisingly, military figures were largely silent. Whatever their personal opinion, most military officials were constrained in what they could say in public about a design that had the tacit support of the Secretary of the Air Force.[37] At least in remarks made for public consumption, the architectural community's reaction also appeared to be highly favorable. Although many architects obviously did not like the design, they, too, were constrained in their reaction, in their case by the architects' professional code of ethics. Many thought that criticism of the work of fellow architects was both unprofessional and harmful to the profession as a whole. Others believed that they had the right to criticize, but the American Institute of Architects strongly disapproved of any architect doing anything that might look like he was trying to take away a commission once it had been fairly awarded to a fellow practitioner. The one architect who breached this ethical code, Frank Lloyd Wright, came in for especially bitter criticism from his colleagues.[38]

The most public voice of the profession was the architectural press. Because, by the 1950s, these journals had taken an editorial stance favorable to International Style Modernism, their reaction to the selection of a confirmed Modernist for such a large project can be described as almost ecstatic. "In my opinion, Skidmore, Owings & Merrill as architects-engineers for the Academy have developed one of the most remarkable and natural accommodations of an architectural complex to terrain that has ever been achieved in any major project," wrote George A. Sanderson, editor of *Progressive Architecture*. He went on to describe the design as efficient, flexible, and simple, concluding that the architects had reached their goal of making it, "above all, beautiful, lastingly beautiful."[39]

The unidentified author of a piece in *Architectural Forum* went further. After stating that the assembled critics and Congressmen had pronounced the design a "solid hit," he continued, "Thus passed, quietly, the eclectic era in government architecture. With the new embassies abroad and the Air Academy at home, the US has come to grips with architectural reality."[40] Among many architects, even those jealous of Skidmore, Owings & Merrill's success, the Colorado Springs exhibition was a millennial event.

Although neither the architects nor the military expected that Congressional and public approval would be automatic, it is unlikely that any of them expected the controversy that ensued when their design was presented via the media to the ultimate client, the American public. Popular opinion was probably just as divided as that of the military or the architectural profession, but because the general public was not inhibited by the same professional constraints, critics could be considerably more vocal. Public opinion was channeled most directly through the country's newspapers and magazines, where the reviews ran the gamut from highly positive to vociferously negative and from sketchy to quite sophisticated (fig. 59).[41] To the considerable consternation of both architects and Air Force officials, the negative criticism also found an even more effective outlet, the Congressional hearing room. The buildings are "not American," stated Representative John E. Fogarty of Rhode Island, who quickly became the architects' nemesis. The designs relied on untested new materials, and were cold, impersonal, and mechanical in appearance, others chimed in.

In the end, although Congress held up funds for construction, temporarily endangering the project, the Air Force and its architects prevailed, and the designs were built with only minor modifications. The issue that was forcefully raised, however, was the question of who the real client was and the relation of elite, self-regulating professions like architecture to the public at large. Writers in the architectural press reacted angrily to the Congressional hearings. They condemned Congress for presuming to judge matters architectural. The American Institute of Architects took the extraordinary step of making public a letter backing the architects and praising their abilities, although it was careful not to make judgments about the design itself. The implication was that matters of judgment on aesthetic issues should be left to the profession itself. Although this had been a perennial debate, the controversies surrounding the design of the Academy marked a distinct escalation in the ability of the public at large to challenge the architects' assumptions and translate their views into political action.[42]

The alliances made during the debate on the Academy were complex and shifting. Aesthetic conservatives who would have preferred a classical design, for example, found common cause with groups representing the masonry industry which felt that public buildings should have palpable weight and solidity. Both found an ally in Frank Lloyd Wright, who used the congressional hearings for his own purposes.[43] The fact that the style of the buildings had been dubbed the "International Style" by the Museum of Modern Art also caused considerable suspicion at a time of strongly resurgent nationalism in America when even the arts were considered a Cold War battlefield.[44]

In retrospect it seems likely that the vast majority of Americans did not object to the use of Modernist architecture for most of the buildings. They may well have thought it appropriate for the dormitories or the classroom buildings, even for the dining hall. The cadet chapel was another matter. For architects and for Air Force officials, the major issue at the time they were designing the chapel was a planning problem: where to put it and how best to accommodate the various denominations. No one seems to have spent a great deal of time worrying about the exact appearance of the building.[45]

Thus did the architects and the Air Force back into one of the knottiest problems of Modernist architecture, the problem of the monument. This issue had not been a major concern for the Modernist pioneers because their commissions usually involved factories, apartment blocks, and small houses.[46] As soon as the Modernists ceased being a group of rebels and actually received the commissions for important public buildings that they had for so long coveted, the problem of monumentality became quite apparent. Delayed by depression and war, this moment arrived immediately after World War II. The problem of the Modernist monument obsessed many of the most prominent architects and critics during the 1940s and the 1950s.[47]

The dilemma consisted of two parts. The first concerned the desirability of monumental expression in the first place. Many Modernists argued that all of the great monuments of the past from the Great Pyramids to the Capitol in Washington, were symbolic expressions of power and coercion. A true modern democratic society should need no such monuments since there should be no need to express power and no desire to create invidious hierarchical distinctions between civic structures and housing blocks, factories, and other buildings types.[48]

If one agreed with what was probably the majority of Modernists who still felt the need for monuments, how could one give to these buildings the kind of weight, dignity, and associations with long-standing traditions that had been possible in classical architecture, without using classical styles of architecture? In fact, one of the major reasons that many Modernists preferred asymmetrical buildings made of materials so light that they seemed to defy gravity, was that these traits deliberately contradicted the most basic principles of classical architecture, which was based on a palpably heavy system of masonry walls, columns, arches, and beams arranged in regular, symmetrical configurations.

The idea that one could create a genuine monument, which by definition meant a structure that reflected the values of all the people, in a style that was avant garde, that is, by definition in opposition to prevailing tastes, must have seemed even to many Modernists to be contradictory on the face of it.[49] Traditional monuments had worked, in great part, because their forms had long been associated with specific meanings drawn from the rich history of architecture. The Modernists, in their desire to sweep away all merely conventional design elements, could not draw on this source of meaning. Although the issue surfaced in discussions about public buildings, for example over designs for the permanent home of the United Nations in New York, the problems came most clearly into focus with the design of churches.[50] If the new architecture was a rational architecture, based directly on program and structural necessity, how could one deal with a building type whose very program attempted to transcend the rational?

One way architects dealt with the problem can be seen at the chapel designed by Mies van der Rohe for IIT (fig. 60). It consisted of a simple box-like structure with virtually no overt reference to religion at all. Although enthusiasts of Mies's work claimed that this solution reduced the idea of chapel to its universal essentials, space and light, critics were quick to point out that it could not be distinguished on the exterior from the classroom or dormitory buildings around it. Rather than reducing religion to its universal essentials, these critics believed, Mies's plan reduced it to nearly total poverty.[51]

The more promising method devised by Modernists to get around the apparently inevitable conflict between monumentality and their own ideas about functional and structural rationalism, was to depart quite frankly from mere physical program requirements, justifying these departures by invoking the need to experiment with new materials. In many of the most memorable churches of the postwar years, reinforced concrete allowed the creation of dramatic, sculptural form. In this way the entire structure could be treated like a large piece of modern sculpture, thus getting around

59. Cartoon from the *Denver Post,* 13 July, 1955. Drawn by Paul Conrad. This is one of dozens of cartoons published around the country during the debates following the Colorado Springs presentation. Reprinted by permission Paul Conrad, Los Angeles Times Syndicate.

59

the vexing problem of justifying elements that could not be justified by strict programmatic and structural requirements. This was the route taken by Le Corbusier in the most famous religious structure of the postwar era, the pilgrimage church of Notre Dame de Ronchamps in eastern France. It also informed the design of the chapel at the Benedictine abbey of St. John's in Minnesota.[52] Here architect Marcel Breuer animated a simple rectangular plan with walls of elaborately folded concrete plates. The creased cardboard representing the chapel on the model at the Colorado Springs presentation bore a considerable resemblance to the Breuer building.

The problem of the church was particularly acute in America in the 1950s. Far from dying away as many leftist European Modernists had expected, religion enjoyed something of a resurgence in the United States in the postwar years as the church, along with the family and other community institutions, was seen as part of a national bulwark against social disintegration and Communism.[53] As the number of new churches rose sharply, there were constant debates over whether they should be traditional or modern.[54] These debates took their most public form in the controversy over the most public American religious building constructed in the 1950s, the Cadet Chapel at the Academy. When the Academy chapel was condemned because of its resemblance to a factory, this commentary was less about style per se than about major social, political and religious conflicts in America.

Although most Americans might not have agreed on the exact appearance of the chapel, most would have agreed that it should look very different from a classroom, a dormitory, or a power plant and that, because the Academy was an American institution, it should evoke American traditions in religious architecture. The final design apparently mollified some critics, but for others it exacerbated the problem. What relationship did a building inspired by Gothic cathedrals, built by kings and princes of the church, have with contemporary society in democratic America? Debate over the chapel never really ended. It would resurface as soon as the building was finished.[55]

Judging the Finished Buildings At the time the Academy opened to the first classes of cadets in 1958 and again when the chapel was finished in 1962, the old debates were rejoined as thousands came to see the buildings themselves and millions experienced them through the articles that appeared in publications throughout the world. Accompanying the text in these publications were photographs supplied by the architects and the Academy that showed perfectly groomed and uniformed cadets marching in precise formations in front of equally precise architectural backgrounds and perfect summer skies. So controlled were these images, particularly the immaculate prints of Hedrich-Blessing, that it was often difficult to determine whether they were, in fact, the finished buildings or the architects' models. The Academy photographs suggested a Modernist utopia with everything from the largest building down to the buttons on the cadets' uniforms perfectly in place, tightly controlled, and free from the distracting clutter of the outside world (fig. 61).

The response of the military, at least in statements issued to the press, was, predictably, enthusiastic. The Air Force used the image of its new buildings over and over. Privately, however, many individuals at the Academy and in the federal government were less than completely happy. Although almost everyone agreed that the basic layout, arrangement of buildings, and architectural character were satisfactory, there had been cost overruns during construction, controversy over the architects' fees, and, at completion, numerous functional problems, notably a notoriously leaky roof on the Chapel, leaks from the Air Garden pools and the Cadet Quarters courts, and window panes that broke or were blown out of their frames during high winds. Although most of these problems were eventually fixed and perhaps constituted no more than the usual "shake-down" problems inherent in any construction project of this size, some problems were never really resolved and left a residue of bad feelings at the Academy.[56]

Among the general public, reaction appears to have been largely positive. An aesthetic that had still seemed somewhat startling in the mid-1950s apparently had less ability to shock by the early 1960s. As pictures of the Academy appeared on the pages of newspapers and magazines around the country and the world, almost all of the writers stressed the newness of the buildings. Wrote David Boroff in *Harper's:*

> **At the older academies, there are always reminders of the glorious past—at West Point, a statue of General Patton, pearl handled pistols on his hips, his martial gaze fixed on the distant plain; at Annapolis, anchors and memorabilia everywhere. But at the Air Force Academy . . . there are only the bright mountain air, the exhilarating sense of space and**

60. Chapel at Illinois Institute of Technology. Photo by Hedrich-Blessing. Although many admirers of Mies believed that in this structure he had reduced the idea of church to its universals—space and light—others thought that there was nothing left to distinguish it from a factory building. Chicago Historical Society: HB 15691 D.

the clean, hard lines of intransigently modern buildings. The Air Force souvenirs—a supersonic fighter and a ballistics missile perched in the middle of the campus—are more advertising for the present than mementos of the past.[57]

In the national press, authors most often described the buildings as awe-inspiring and beautiful. Even the Chapel, which had been so controversial nearly a decade earlier, came in mostly for praise. An article in *Time* entitled "Spires that Soar" was typical. Concluded the author: "Most important of all, the building's metallic majesty, visible across the countryside like the church spires of rural Europe, is in perfect harmony with the spirit of the academy. Its materials and basic forms are largely those of an airplane, and its spires do not merely point, they soar."[58]

At first, reactions in the world of architecture appeared to be similar. Most of the rev ews were, at least on the surface, positive. Almost all stressed the scale and historic importance of the design. Under the banner "The Air Age Acropolis" a writer in *Architectural Forum* proclaimed, "On a base scaled to rival the grandest pedestals of antiquity stands the nation's first monument in the modern style—the new Air Force Academy."[59] Writing in *Architectural Record* in December 1962, one critic called the chapel a "unifying symbol for its several creeds that is particularly appropriate for our democracy in a world of conflict."[60]

Although there were still many conservative architects who resisted Modernist design, the Academy was tangible evidence of the way Modernist style had become orthodoxy. It had, in the words of John Burchard and Albert Bush-Brown, "uttered a stentorian shout," proclaiming that "modern design had won the battle of the campuses as it had earlier won the battle of the residence, of the factory, of the office building, of the church, of the school."[61]

Paradoxically it was this acceptance into the mainstream that contributed to suspicion and outright hostility elsewhere in the architectural world. The avant garde, because it had championed the overturning of all widely accepted norms in favor of new, innovative designs, had inexorably prepared the way for the disavowal of the very forms it had championed. By the time the International Style was acceptable for a large-scale commission from the United States military, it had long since ceased being avant garde. From an early date, reviews of the Academy in the architectural press contained evidence of this growing realization. The negative voices of the early 1960s were not those of the conservatives who had blasted Modernist architecture at the time the design was first presented. By the early 1960s most of these individuals had either given up the battle against Modernism or had moved on to other targets of criticism. Instead, the most telling criticism came from the left, from individuals who believed that the new Academy, while representing a triumph of Modernist style, at a deeper level represented a betrayal of the Modernist spirit, the abandonment of the dream of a new society and a capitulation to middle-class, capitalist America.[62]

In a June 1959 review in *Architectural Record*, for example, the writer of what started out as a largely positive review concluded with questions that undermined much of what had gone before. Are the buildings, he asked, "suitable to the great national monument they will in fact be? Or . . . do they signify merely the latest expression of what some observers have chosen to call an SOM style; perhaps crisper and handsomer than usual but nonetheless expression of a corporate esthetic rather than of intrinsic purpose?"[63] In 1958, just as the Academy was opening, the writer of a *Fortune* article quoted an anonymous architect who echoed an increasingly common judgment about Skidmore, Owings & Merrill: "Rigor mortis

is setting in. They're becoming a conservative force in U. S. architecture—they stopped inventing."[64]

The objections of San Francisco critic Allan Temko went deeper. While praising the academic complex generally, he blasted the Chapel, not just for its design but for the way it was placed in the center of the composition. For him this represented "not merely an architectural failure but a social and spiritual fiasco."[65] Underlying his architectural objections was a belief that the focus on a chapel rather than a library or an educational building represented a repudiation of the rational humanist thought of the Modernist pioneers, a retreat from the problems of a thermonuclear age and an escape into mystical metaphysics.

For Temko the style of the building merely compounded the problem of siting. He believed the chapel to be a sentimental pastiche of Gothic forms. Worse still were the decorations, mostly not designed by SOM but commissioned from other designers by the chaplains. For Temko, the chapel with its decorations constituted a monument to "mass-cult," a phrase that clearly evoked the expression "mass culture," used by many intellectuals of the 1950s to designate what they felt was one of postwar democratic America's

61. Cadet formation in front of Chapel. Photograph by Stewart's, c. 1963. The machine-like precision of the Chapel facades provide an appropriate backdrop to the daily formation of the cadet corps witnessed by more than a million visitors every year. Local History Collection, Pikes Peak Library District. Stewart's No. 69-37.

greatest problems, a leveling of culture to the lowest common denominator.[66] Although no other criticism was this stinging, many individuals in the world of architecture probably shared with Temko a bitter disappointment that Modern architecture, far from bringing in the millennium, had succeeded only in buttressing what observers on both the political right and left felt was an emerging anti-democratic oligarchy, an isidious coalition that C. Wright Mills called the "power elite" and Dwight Eisenhower the "military-industrial complex."[67]

Certainly the paradoxes were readily apparent. Most Modernist architects and designers believed that a piece of architecture should reflect the time in which it was built, and many architects believed that the International Style could do just this. Yet many of the same architects also believed that what they did should transcend style and the era in which in was built. Nathaniel Owings, for example, stated that the Air Force Academy would be "as styleless as the most modern guided missile—timeless."[68] Furthermore, if, as many Modernists believed, men's needs were universal and so justified an "international style," how then could these buildings relate successfully to a very specific location and function as a monument to a specific institution in a specific country? Above all, if the architects were successful in finding a style that could win acceptance in the general public, how could they still satisfy the need of Modernists to resist reigning conventions and constantly "make it new"?

By the time of the completion of the chapel it was clear that the Modernists' desire to reconcile all of these apparent contradictions had run into unexpected difficulties. Certainly the hope of creating a timeless architecture as "styleless as a missile" had faded. Even a missile, it turned out, was marked by the style of the era in which it was created. In the architectural world the first volleys of a mounting attack on Modernist certainties had already been fired.[69] Many of the designers involved in the Academy designs, including Walter Netsch, Gordon Bunshaft, and Eero Saarinen, had already started to turn to heavier, more complex expressions, often with increasingly overt references to history.[70] At the Academy, many of the hopes of the founders were likewise compromised. Air Force Secretary Talbott, who as much as any individual had set his stamp on the design of the Academy by his role in choosing the architects, had long since resigned over questionable business practices.[71] Nor was the Academy immune to the cheating scandals and other problems that had plagued West Point and Annapolis.[72] The suburban sprawl that the architects had hoped to avoid was starting to spread toward the hills opposite the Academy gates.

The anguished debates that greeted the Air Force Academy are not unusual. They have occasioned the birth of virtually every really important piece of architecture, and the more conspicuous the buildings the longer it takes for the design to settle, either by agreement or sheer exhaustion, into a comfortable niche in the history books. This process is obviously still underway in the case of the Air Force Academy. One thing that does seem clear from the perspective of the 1990s, however, is that what distinguishes the Air Force Academy is not, as Nathaniel Owings had hoped, its timelessness (fig. 46). It is clearly a product of the 1950s. In fact, it is one of the grandest and, thanks to a relentless maintenance program by the Air Force, most intact ensembles of that era to be seen anywhere in the world. What may be most compelling today is exactly the opposite of what Owings had desired. The Academy has not escaped time and history. It is precisely because the Academy has changed so little while the world around it has changed so much that it functions as one of the great monuments of an era that seems so near to us in time but in other ways appears to belong to a past almost beyond recall.

Notes

1. Holt et al., *History of the United States Air Force Academy: 27 July 1954 to 12 June 1956,* 243.

2. For an interesting editorial criticizing the competition see Frederick Gutheim, "Washington Perspective," *Progressive Architecture* (September 1954): 4.

3. Perhaps the most informed conjecture came from *Architectural Forum* in "Air Academy Design Brawl" (August 1955): 15–16.

4. About American military architecture remarkably little has been written. There have long been books on specific topics such as American forts, particularly those of the earliest period and those constructed in the West and used in the Indian wars. See, for example, Willard Robinson's *American Forts, Architectural Form and Function,* 1979. But until recently many of the largest military installations, for example, the arsenals and shipyards, remained largely unstudied. Within the last decade there has been a growing interest, spurred in part by the fact that a great number of these installations have been or will be closed by the military. Documentation has often accompanied their transfer to other uses.

5. For example, the Brooklyn Army Terminal building, along the waterfront south of downtown Brooklyn, designed by Cass Gilbert in 1918, was one of the country's largest and most severe structures of reinforced concrete. On this building, see Elliot Willensky and Norval White, *AIA Guide to New York* (1988), 617.

6. In a way not atypical of these installations, the overall plan and many of the buildings were designed and constructed by the Army itself. On the more pretentious buildings local architects were hired, but their work was strictly monitored. On Randolph Air Force Base, see "Randolph Air Force Base: Preserving the Past; Building for the Future," an undated recent publication. I would like to thank Kirk Cordell of the National Park Service Air Force project for his help in obtaining information about Air Force bases.

7. A good example can be seen at the Naval Ordnance Depot at Hunter's Point in San Francisco by Ernest Kump. Finished in 1947, this building had an extremely elegant curtain wall that gave it a crystalline character. On this building see the *San Francisco Chronicle,* 2 January 1945, 4, col. 6, and Talbot Hamlin, *Forms and Functions of Twentieth Century Architecture,* 1950–52, vol. 4, 202. According to Louis Wall, Coordinator of Cultural Resources for the Navy in the Western Division, the building was abandoned ten years ago and is in ruin. Kump was included in the Kittyhawk team submission in the Air Force Academy competition.

8. On SOM's war work, see Nathaniel Owings, *The Spaces in Between,* (1973), 134–35.

9. It was one of the first buildings designed in conjunction with an expressway system and contained an entire network of tunnels, ramps, and bridges to ease circulation. Considering its size and prominence, remarkably little is known about the Pentagon. A good recent study can be found in Alfred Goldberg, *The Pentagon: The First Fifty Years,* 1992. The cheif designers of the Pentagon were George Bergstrom and David Whitmer.

10. On the buildings of the Federal Triangle, see Sally Kress Tompkins; *Quest for Grandeur: Charles Moore and the Federal Triangle,* (1993).

11. For the monumental architecture of the 1930s see, for example, Franco Borsi, *The Monumental Era: Europe: 1929–1939,* (1987), or C. W. Short and R. Stanley-Brown, *Public Buildings: Architecture under the Public Works Administration 1933–39* (1939).

12. For a good introduction to the design of the service academies, see "Brass Factories," in Lois Craig, *The Federal Presence: Architecture, Politics and National Design* (nd), 228–33.

13. On West Point, see Theodore J. Crackel, *The Illustrated History of West Point* (1991). For the buildings, the best source is a document entitled *Historic Structures Inventory, United States Military Academy,* produced by the Historic American Buildings Survey and Historic American Engineering Record in four volumes in 1984.

14. On Annapolis, the most accessible source is Jack Sweetman, *The U.S. Naval Academy: An Illustrated History* (1979).

15. On Ernest Flagg, see Mardges Bacon, *Ernest Flagg,* (1986).

16. Quoted in David Boroff, "Air Force Academy: A Slight Gain in Altitude," *Harper's Magazine* (February 1963): 86–98.

17. On the position of air power within the American military, see Monro MacCloskey, *The United States Air Force* (1967), 61–73, and the last pages of the excellent work by Michael Sherry, *The Rise of American Air Power* (1987). For a brief review of the role of the Air Force in the reluctant involvement of the United States military in world affairs, see Edward A. Kolodziej, *The Uncommon Defense and Congress, 1945–63* (1966), 75–81.

18. For the standard, Modernist version of the story of modern architecture, see Nikolaus Pevsner, *Outline of European Architecture* (1943); Sigfried Giedion, *Space, Time and Architecture* (1944); and Henry-Russell Hitchcock, *Architecture: Nineteenth and Twentieth Centuries* (1958).

19. This term was coined for the catalog of an exhibition at the Museum of Modern Art in 1932. Edited by Philip Johnson and Henry-Russell Hitchcock, this catalog was entitled *The International Style: Architecture Since 1922.*

20. About Ellery Husted surprisingly little is known. An obituary appeared in *Progressive Architecture* (November 1967), another in the *New York Times,* 19 July 1967, and the records of the Air Force contain several notices, but none of these sources gives more than a bare outline of his career. Born in 1901, he received his architecture degree from Yale University in 1927. He worked for one year with Douglas Orr in New York, then for six years as junior partner with James Gamble Rogers, also in New York, during which time he helped on the designs of the Columbia Presbyterian Medical Center in the same city. During World War II he

served with Naval Intelligence and retired as a Commander. After the war he joined with the firm of Gugler Kimball to create the new firm of Gugler, Kimball and Husted in New York. From this time onwards he seems to have been increasingly involved in consulting for government agencies, including the CIA, the Army Corps of Engineers and others, as well as the Air Force. After he retired he moved to Portugal, where he died in 1967.

21. The Husted design recalls, for example, the buildings of Cranbrook Academy at Bloomfield Hills, outside Detroit, designed by Eliel Saarinen in the 1920s and 1930s.

22. *Architectural Forum* (August 1954): 52.

23. Frank Lloyd Wright had designed Florida Southern College in Lakeland, Florida, but this work was too eccentric and personal, as well as too far off the beaten path, to garner much interest from campus planners.

24. Whereas before World War II, the architectural meccas for Americans were primarily European countries such as the Netherlands and Germany, during the 1950s Latin America enjoyed a considerable vogue as projects like the University of Mexico or Brazil's new capital city of Brasilia seemed to give the best foretaste of the new Modernist world. See the catalog of the Museum of Modern Art, *Latin American Architecture Since 1945,* by Henry-Russell Hitchcock (1955), and I. E. Myers, *Mexico's Modern Architecture* (1952).

25. One of the architects involved in both of these sets of buildings was Wallace K. Harrison. For a very good portrait, see Victoria Newhouse, *Wallace K. Harrison, Architect* (1989).

26. Walter Netsch, for example, remembers hearing that Saarinen, during his interview, made a sketch for the Academy that "created a sensation." Saarinen's assistant and later partner, Kevin Roche, has stated that Saarinen made no drawings, however. Letter from Kevin Roche to the author, June, 1994.

27. The major figure in the rediscovery of late nineteenth century Chicago buildings was Northwestern University professor Carl Condit. His books, *The Rise of the Skyscraper* (1952), and *The Chicago School of Architecture* (1964), were very influential in the architectural design community.

28. The best-known early article on SOM in general-circulation magazines was entitled "The Architects from Skid's Row," in *Fortune,* January 1958, 215. According to the author, "SOM took Mies's stainless-steel standard, warmed it up and sold it as a prestige package to the U. S. businessman." The situation was actually much more complex since, on the one hand, Mies had already adapted himself to American practice, and, on the other, SOM designers were adept at using elements from a wide variety of sources, American and European, but this formulation represented what soon came to be accepted wisdom within and outside the architectural community.

29. The influence of Mies on buildings like Lever House has been greatly exaggerated. Already in the interwar years many American firms had been experimenting with the curtain wall. The initial design idea for Lever House probably came from Charles Wiley, a designer in the SOM Chicago office, working with Nathaniel Owings, and the influence of American industrial designers, Le Corbusier, and the United Nations complex was probably more important than Mies.

30. Talbott had long been active in aviation-related businesses and in the Republican Party.

31. Both Gordon Bunshaft and Nathaniel Owings have left accounts of the architect selection process. They imply that the decision was effectively made by Talbott himself and had already been made by him before his selection board had met. See Nathaniel Owings, *The Spaces in Between,* 150–53, and Gordon Bunshaft, taped recollections in the archives of SOM, New York, 96 (reprinted in the last part of this book). By 1956, it is clear from testimony during the congressional budget hearings, Talbott had taken a deep personal interest in the appearance of the Academy.

32. On Bunshaft, see Carol Krinsky, *Gordon Bunshaft of Skidmore, Owings & Merrill* (1988). Both the Hartford corporate headquarters and the Academy featured prismatic rectangular buildings in the middle of carefully tended, pristine landscapes. In both cases these large buildings were clad in clean metal and glass curtain walls with large windows looking back out onto the exterior landscape and to inner courts. The courtyards at Connecticut General were designed by the famous Japanese-American sculptor Isamu Noguchi. The original designs for the courtyards in the cadet quarters, by Dan Kiley, were similar in many ways.

33. Among the most prominent of competitions of the interwar and immediate postwar years were those for a new building for the Smithsonian Institution, the Jefferson Memorial, and the National Gallery of Art, all in Washington. In none of these cases was a thoroughgoing Modernist design built, although Eliel and Eero Saarinen won second prize in the Smithsonian competition. On these competitions, see James Kornwolf, Ed., *Modernism in America* 1937–41 (1985).

34. On military education, see John W. Maseland, *Soldiers and Scholars* (1957). It must also be remembered that the Air Force Academy was launched during the apogee of behaviorism in American universities.

35. According to Walter Netsch this "Buck Rogerish" scheme was indebted to Buckminster Fuller. The drawings for these houses have not been located.

36. On some of the tensions between the architects and the Academy officers, see the conversation between Walter Netsch and John Burchard in the last section of this book.

37. That there were significant internal splits among the top officers in the Air Force itself can be seen in the interchanges between Talbott and Harmon cited in George Fagan, *The Air Force Academy, An Illustrated History* (1988), 84.

38. See, for example the scathing criticism of Wright in *Architectural Record* (August 1955): 16–18.

39. George A. Sanderson, "Air Academy, U.S. Air Force Exhibits Plans at Colorado

Springs," *Progressive Architecture* (June 1955): 90.

40. "The United States Air Force Academy," *Architectural Forum* (June 1958): 102.

41. Newspaper columns and editorials appeared all over the country. Among the huge number of newspaper editorials on the subject were "Tradition and All That" in the *Boston Herald,* 15 July 1955, "Let's Break with Tradition," in the *Baton Rouge Morning Advocate,* 28 June 1955, "Too Many Amateurs," in the *Denver Post,* 13 July 1955, and "Architecture and the Air Academy," in the *New York Herald Tribune,* 14 July 1955.

42. *Architectural Record,* in its August 1955 issue, for example, printed the remarks of Rhode Island Congressman John E. Fogarty, whom they pointedly identified as a "former bricklayer," and then a set of "Professional Views Sought by the *Record,*" all of which rebutted Fogarty. The Academy debate was, of course, just one in a long line of similar debates, perhaps the most conspicuous of which in recent years have been the struggles over the Maya Lin design for the Vietnam Veteran's Memorial. These cases suggest that the power of the public has, if anything increased since the 1950s.

43. On the various tactics used in the congressional investigations there is a fascinating analysis in "Off They Went into the Wild Blue," by George Orick, *The Reporter,* 22 September 1955, 28–29.

44. In historical scholarship, for example, one of the strongest currents in immediate postwar America was a search for characteristics that could be called distinctly American modes of expression. A good example can be found in John McCoubrey, *American Tradition in Painting*, 1963. In the field of criticism, a number of prominent leftists of the interwar years, mostly notably Clement Greenberg, shifted focus from international developments to the national scene and championed American arts and artists. See Serge Guilbaut, *How New York Stole the Idea of Modern Art* (1983), and Jackson Lears, "A Matter of Taste: Corporate Cultural Hegemony in a Mass-Consumption Society," in Lary May, *Recasting America* (1989), 38–57. For some interesting comments on this process in connection with the Air Force Academy, see Richard Gid Powers, "The Cold War in the Rockies: American Ideology and the Air Force Academy Design," in *Art Journal* (Summer 1974): 304–13.

45. Although later testimony is contradictory about how much care went into the building represented in the model, the testimony of Gordon Bunshaft, "Recollections," (excerpted at the end of this volume), is convincing in its suggestion that for him, and by extension, for many of the other design participants, the siting of the Chapel was of considerably more importance than the exact appearance of the building. At least for him the Cadet Chapel shown in the model at the Colorado Springs presentation was there primarily to give an idea of location. It also appears that very few of the most important participants in the design process were much interested in any form of organized religion.

46. Among the early Modernists, if monumentality was considered desirable, it was a monumentality that completely inverted the usual logic of the monument. Walter Gropius and Le Corbusier, for example, suggested that the real monuments of the twentieth century were anonymous grain elevators or hydroelectric installations. Where Modernist architects spoke about building monuments, it was usually in connection with factories and housing projects.

47. For an excellent discussion of this topic, see Christiane C. and George R. Collins, "Monumentality: A Critical Matter in Modern Architecture," *Harvard Architecture Review* 4 (Spring 1984): 14–35. The authors chronicle the shift of the term from its earlier meanings where it referred to a written document, a legal marker, or a commemorative design at a burial place, to its current architectural meaning. See also Sarah Ksiazek, "Architectural Culture in the Fifties: Louis Kahn and the National Assembly Complex in Dhaka," in *Journal of the Society of Architectural Historians* (December 1993): 417.

48. An early and powerful argument of this kind was made by John Summerson in a paper read at the Architectural Association in London in 1941 called "The Mischievous Analogy," published in Summerson's *Heavenly Mansions* (1949). See especially pages 203–9 in the 1963 Norton reissue. Other arguments against the need for monuments can be found in the pages of the British journal *Architectural Review* (September 1948): 117–27, which contained transcriptions from a symposium sponsored by the journal titled "In Search of a New Monumentality," with contributions by some of the best-known architects and critics of the day, including Walter Gropius, Henry-Russell Hitchcock, Sigfried Giedion, and Albert Roth. See, especially, the comments by Gregor Paulsson, who maintained that "monumentality can arise only from dictatorship," and those by Albert Roth.

49. See for example, the interesting essay, "Nine Points on Monumentality," written by the prominent Swiss critic and historian Sigfried Giedion with Fernand Léger and José Luis Sert for a symposium in 1948 and published in Sigfried Giedion, *Architecture, You and Me; The Diary of a Development* (1958), 48–51.

50. Collins, "Monumentality," 25.

51. Perhaps the most amusing version of this criticism is found in the anti-modernist polemic of Charles Jencks, *The Language of Post-Modern Architecture* (1976), 16–17 where Jencks suggested that the chapel looked much less like a religious structure than did the boiler house, which at least required an impressive smokestack.

52. On the Breuer chapel, see *Architectural Forum* (July 1954): 148–55.

53. On the connection between religion and patriotism, see Chapter 5, "Under God, by Act of Congress," in Paul A. Carter, *Another Part of the Fifties* (1983), 114–40. According to research by Sarah Ksiazek, the number of churches constructed rose dramatically in the 1950s as new congregations were formed and established congregations outgrew older buildings.

54. I am indebted to Sarah Ksiazek for a number of the ideas developed here.

55. For an excellent collection of commentaries on the Chapel after the design

modifications, see *Architectural Record* (December 1957): 9ff.

56. There was a great deal of acrimony all around. While the Air Force charged faulty architectural design in the case of the windows, for example, the architects faulted the Academy itself for putting gravel on the roofs that, during high winds, blew into the glass and broke it. Leaky roofs, on the other hand, were caused, according to some government officials, by poor design; but, according to the architects, they were the result of the substitution of flashing materials by the Construction Agency. The architects attempted to raise their fee, citing a great many design revisions requested by the Academy during the course of design and construction. They were not successful in proving their case, and, according to the testimony of Nathaniel Owings, lost over a million dollars on the job. Nathaniel Owings, *The Spaces in Between,* 150. When the architects for the 1965 expansion ignored previous SOM site plans and placed the new cadet quarters to the south of the Court of Honor, blocking off what the original architects had thought of as an important link with the natural landscape, it is likely that there was a certain sense of satisfaction among everyone concerned that the influence of SOM had been broken. Although this scheme was attacked by many of the original designers, it can be seen as a rational response to the emerging critique of the open, asymmetrical character of Modernist planning and the rising sentiment in the profession in favor of well-defined, closed public spaces.

57. Boroff, "Air Force Academy," 86.

58. *Time,* 27 July 1962, 39.

59. *Architectural Forum* (June 1959):158.

60. The Chapel won a prestigious Reynolds Award in 1963.

61. John Burchard and Albert Bush-Brown, *The Architecture of America: A Social and Cultural History* (1961), 486.

62. For an interesting parallel to this situation, see "Did Success Spoil the United States? Dual Representations in Postwar America," by Warren Susman, in Lary May, ed. *Recasting America,* 19, where Susman writes that by the end of World War II America had succeeded beyond any expectations in achieving what it had been striving for since the nineteenth century but that the triumph contained within it the seeds of a new sense of anxiety.

63. *Architectural Record* (June 1959): 153.

64. "The Architects from Skid's Row," 215.

65. Allan Temko, "The Air Academy Chapel—A Critical Appraisal," in *Architectural Forum* (December 1962): 75–78. See also the letters in response in the February 1963 issue of the *Forum*, 19.

66. On the use of the term "Mass Culture" in the 1950s, see the essays in Bernard Rosenberg and David White, Editors, *Mass Culture, The Popular Arts in America,* 1956. See also Susman, "Did Success Spoil the United States," 24, and an excellent discussion in Sarah Ksiazek, "Architectural Culture in the Fifties: Louis Kahn and the National Assembly Complex in Dhaka," in *Journal of the Society of Architectural Historians* (December 1993): 417. Temko, in a telephone interview with the author in February 1994, stated that he felt that his criticism of the Chapel had stood up well. For him, it marked the first "wrong turn" by SOM leading to post-Modernism and what he considers the irrational eccentricities in the later work of Netsch. For Temko, the best of the Academy buildings was the Dining Hall, the most Miesian of the buildings at the Academy.

67. Eisenhower used the phrase in his Farewell Address of January 1961. The *Power Elite* was the title of Mill's most famous book, published in 1956. In it Mills argued that an industrial and military oligarchy in America effectively controlled most major decisions. For interesting observations on the increasing convergence of military and industrial bureaucracies, see Morris Janowitz, *Sociology and the American Military Establishment* (1959), 15–18.

68. "The Architects from Skid's Row," 215.

69. From the anti-Modernist writings of Lewis Mumford in the early 1950s, the tide of criticism reached flood stage in the 1960s. The two most conspicuous books in this literature were a small volume by Robert Venturi, published in 1964, entitled *Complexity and Contradiction in Architecture,* and a volume by the Italian architect Aldo Rossi, *l'Architettura della Citta,* published in the same year. In very different ways each met head-on many of the most cherished notions of Modernism.

70. One recurrent theme of critics was the thinness of the Academy buildings and the way they seemed to stand out in contrast to the landscape. See, for example, Vincent Scully, *Modern Architecture,* revised edition (1974), 36, where he described the academic buildings' "thin, icily gleaming screen wall, endlessly repetitive and expressive of that utter separation from the place. . . characteristic of America's earliest works," or in Scully's *American Architecture and Urbanism* (1969), 190, where he described the Academy as "hard to beat in the Americanized (sharpened, smoothed) Mies of the dormitories and so on, but abortive in the wigwammy chapel, which seeks to invoke, a little like late Wright at Elkins Park or at Taliesin itself, the Rocky Mountain's serrated forms." Scully would contrast the Academy with the increasingly weighty work of Louis Kahn, just then emerging as a figure of national importance in architecture.

71. Talbott resigned in 1955. On his business dealings, see *New Republic,* 1 August. 1955, 5.

72. The old problem of cheating on exams, which had plagued West Point in 1951, resurfaced in an even more disturbing form at the Air Force Academy in 1965 and would recur. On the cheating episodes at the Academy, see J. Arthur Heise, *The Brass Factories,* 15–16, and 38–41, and Fagan, *The Air Force Academy,* 151ff.

Jory Johnson

Man as Nature

Bring me men to match my mountains,
Bring me men to match my plains
Men with empires in their purpose,
And new eras in their brains.

Sam Walter Foss, "The Coming American" (1895)[1]

Nowhere in the continental United States are the plains and the mountains more decisively and dramatically conjoined than at the Front Range of the Rocky Mountains. To the east, the softly undulating plains—once great inland seas—rest firmly on a buried geologic platform that extends well into Canada. At the Front Range this calm has been shattered by violent uplifts and intrusions of igneous rock which heaved marine fossils to the peaks of the mountains (fig. 62).[2] Here, geology is destiny. The Rocky Mountains have been celebrated in verse, prose, paintings, and the movies as an idealized landscape of purity, challenge, and greed. "Pikes Peak or Bust" was the cry of adventurers in the nineteenth century, and, more recently, a monument to Olympic-medal winners was dedicated at the summit of Pikes Peak. In the late 1800s, adventurers, prospectors, and those who preyed on them rushed past the High Plains and into the mountains. They seldom paused, as do today's tourists, to contemplate the broad plains and gentle valleys of the Platt and Arkansas Rivers. "Can you see Kansas from here?" is frequently heard at the top of Pikes Peak. The High Plains are slow and settled, the short grasses ideal for the leisurely ruminations first of buffalo and now of cattle.

62. Air view of the site. Photograph by William Garnett, 1955. The Front Range and the plains extend into infinity.

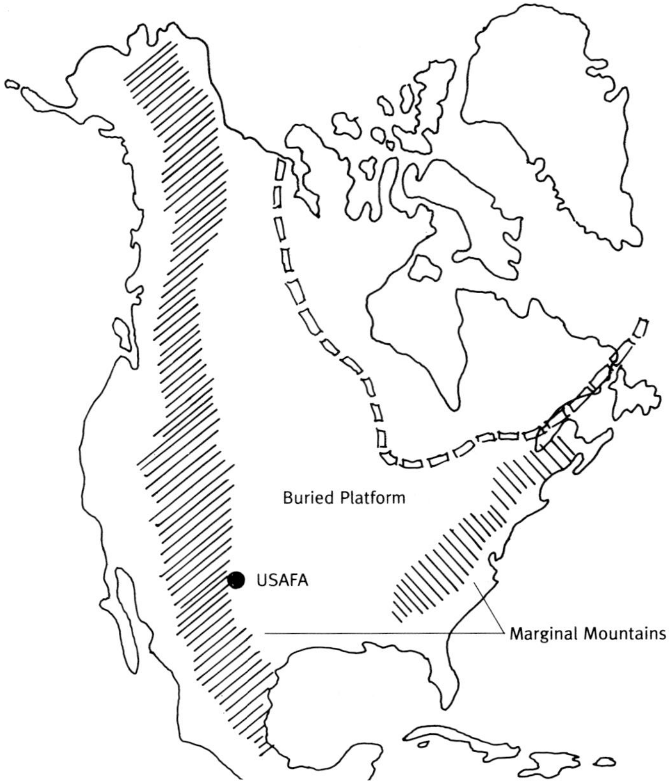

Most tourist cameras at the Front Range are trained on the snow-capped majesty of Pikes Peak—the view from which inspired Katherine Bates to write "America the Beautiful"—or the culturalized geologic curiosities such as the Garden of the Gods or Cathedral Rock, improbably huge sandstone formations which resisted the weathering and erosion that leveled the High Plains. But the panoramic grandeur outflanks even the widest camera lens. It is above all a landscape whose infinite measure cannot be captured in books or film.

When Skidmore Owings & Merrill's teams of architects, engineers, and geologists flew above or walked on the site of the future Air Force Academy, the firm's lead designer, Walter Netsch, remembers that they wondered: "How can we compete with infinity?"[3] Since Academy facilities and infrastructure requirements seemed equally infinite, how could the designers in a few short years meet the challenge wrought by millions of years of intense geological collisions? Conventional expectations were either the appropriation of the landscape as a scenic backdrop to an independently derived architecture (such as the Gothic Revival architecture at West Point) or a romantic or "organic" design which used local materials to mimic or make reference to the natural forms of the landscape.

Dan Kiley, the landscape architect for the Academy, argued that neither model was appropriate to the twentieth century. "It's not man and nature," Kiley insisted, "Man is nature."[4] There should be no attempt to blend into the sheer face of the mountains or to build a pretentious, self-conscious monument; both man and nature should to their own natures be true. Men should build as men, taking the raw materials of the land and fashioning them into practical and meaningful geometries.[5] Beauty and meaning come from looking for the simple truths of proportion, scale, and the integration of land and buildings over the whole site. The complexities, irregularities, and vastness of the landscape would be brought into the life of the Academy, but never as trite miniaturizations or self-conscious symbols. The master plan and landscape design conceived by Skidmore Owings & Merrill and completed by Dan Kiley is equal in boldness and confidence to the landscape, marrying the typical demands of a large institution and the pageantry, discipline, and idealism of a military academy with the magnificent site.

Unfortunately, this vision was never fully realized. Many critical landscape components were vitiated by bureaucratic intransigence

63. The structural geology of North America. Diagram by Jory Johnson, based on data from Mel and Lynerell Rubright, *Colorado, A Biography.* The Academy rests on the margins of the Buried Platform and the Marginal Mountains.

64. Cross-section of Colorado geology from Colorado Springs to Grand Junction. Drawing by Jory Johnson, based on data from Erickson and Smith, *Atlas of Colorado,* and Varnes and Scott, *General and Engineering Geology of the U.S. Air Force Academy Site.* The Continental Divide reaches its highest elevations in Colorado, but it is the difference in elevations that make the Front Range especially dramatic and photogenic.

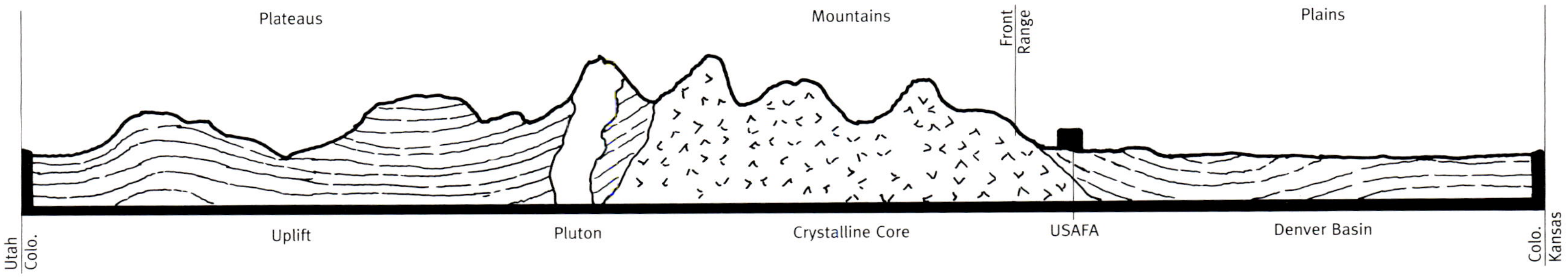

64

or stillborn because of budget setbacks. In other cases, in part because of the tight construction schedule and the sheer scale, the architects and landscape architects did not always give the implementation of the landscape plans their full attention, or they hoped that the landscape would be completed later. In the mid-1970s, the essence of the landscape design was irrevocably neutralized by the construction of Sijan Hall, which fully enclosed the Cadet Area, blocking both the view of and access to the immediate natural landscape.[6] However, enough remains of the original plan to recognize its greatness as a monument to the confidence and mastery of a particular time and place in American landscape architecture. Therefore, this essay will concentrate almost exclusively on the Academy as it existed in conception and construction from 1955 to 1961.

The Land As the Front Range of the Rocky Mountains began its final uplift seventy million years ago, the gray, gravely sedimentary rocks were swept down the eastern side of the range, leaving the huge granite batholiths (irregularly shaped masses of intrusive igneous rock) like Pikes Peak and the lower peaks of the Front Range. The sediments that washed out of the rising peaks filled in the irregularities of the former seabed, creating the long inclined slope from the Front Range to the Kansas border (figs. 63, 64).

The jagged peaks of the Front Range are inscribed on Colorado's license plates—the facade and image of the state. The mountains immediately adjacent to the site are called the Rampart Range. Like military ramparts, they are forbidding, almost vertical earthworks—the bulwarks of the Rocky Mountains. The rising sun lights up the Rampart's gray-green visage, and the evening sun casts the Cadet Area into shadow twenty minutes earlier than the Academy airfield on the eastern edge of the site.

Everything that passes over the Rampart Range—the weather, transportation, flora and fauna, and, of course, human beings—is dramatically transformed. The Rocky Mountains are a right-angle barrier to the prevailing westerly winds, inscribing a "rain shadow" on the eastern slope and the High Plains. As the prevailing westerly winds rise over the mountains, the air cools and loses its ability to retain moisture. The Rocky Mountains get 35 to 40 inches of precipitation per year, while only 13 to 15 inches make it across the Front Range. However, as the Academy learned in 1957 when 40

65. Natural vegetation between Colorado Springs and Grand Junction. Drawing by Jory Johnson based on data from *Atlas of Colorado.* The composition and appearance of the forests in Colorado change dramatically at the different elevations.
66. View of Academy site. Photograph by Ansel Adams, all rights reserved, 1955. The flowering plants and occasional trees create a very open, inviting landscape.

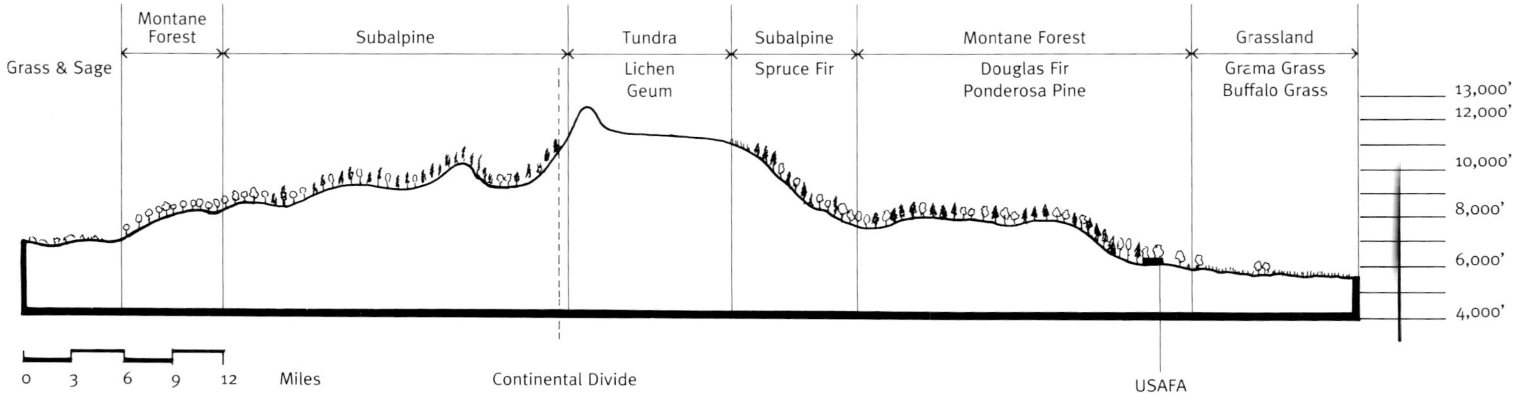

65

inches of snow fell in two days, this enormous atmospheric tension sometimes explodes in impressive climatological aberrations. The high Rampart Range also produces a venturi effect on the Academy site with recorded gusts of 135 mph.[7] Though seldom that severe, the wind velocity was strong enough to create a major problem in aligning the air strip. In the end, the architects were forced to reroute a stream.[8] But despite the occasional extremes, the area enjoys a relatively benign temperate climate with clear skies, cleansing winds, and January temperatures averaging 32 degrees and July temperatures of around 74 degrees. Even on warmer days, the low humidity allows most Academy buildings to be comfortable without air-conditioning.

Biomes in Colorado are constrained by elevation and moisture (fig. 65).[9] The Academy site is part of a montane forest, which exists between 6,000 and 9,000 feet. Within the site, microclimates create smaller biomes, the most important being the south—facing slopes with deep-rooted ponderosa pine with its irregular cylindrical crown and short stout branches, and thick, gnarly three- to six-foot stands of mountain mahogany, scrub oak, and juniper. Opposite, the north-facing slopes are dominated by the bluish-green pyramids of the cold-resistant Douglas fir.[10] The cattle ranches kept much of the landscape in native grasses, which bunch in short clumps one to two feet high. While not as colorful as the high valleys of the Rocky Mountains, in the warmer seasons the Academy site features small, flowering plants seldom more than eighteen inches high, whose flower colors include the yellow of the tickseed and coreopsis, the reddish shades of Indian paintbrush, and the blue of anemones. The spiky yuccas, whose three-foot-high stalks of yellow flowers wither to brown and the prickly pears lend a desert flavor (fig. 66).

It is an open, inviting landscape. Except for the occasional thickets of scrub oak, one can walk anywhere. Colorado Springs was a health Mecca, the thin, cool, dry air making the city a natural sanitarium. Only one day in six is overcast, but the sky is seldom bland. Dark, billowing clouds loom over the Rampart Range, Pikes Peak is often shrouded in white, and to the east clear rainless skies gently fold over the distant horizon.

Since the cadet's daily schedule leaves little time for hiking or strolling, the visitor to the Academy is more apt to encounter mule deer or flocks of intimidating wild turkey than cadets. In the trees,

66

the raucous crows and Steller's jays squabble; while falcons—which are captured and trained by cadets—stealthily circle above (fig. 66).

The People The only radical difference between the landscape studied by Skidmore Owings & Merrill and the one explored by Zebulon Pike in 1806 is the absence of vast herds of bison. Native Americans never settled near the Academy site. The Front Range was a border between the agrarian tribes in the mountain parks and the nomadic Apache on the High Plains. By the eighteenth century, horses had realigned tribal boundaries, and raiding parties of Comanches, Navajo, and Sioux galloped through the site. When silver was discovered in the mountains, white settlers ignored or abrogated previous treaties and drove or forcibly relocated all Native Americans to other states. During the massacres and retaliatory attacks in the 1860s, a sawmill near the Academy site sustained heavy casualties.

By the 1870s white settlers had a free hand in Colorado and the base of the Rampart Range soon became a major north-south transportation route. The Denver–Colorado City stage ran alongside Monument Creek , followed by the Denver and Rio Grande Railroad (1871), the Atchison Topeka & Santa Fe (1887), U.S. Highway 85/87 (1933), and Interstate 25 (1960). But today's densely populated urban corridor from Denver to Colorado Springs did not develop until after World War II, when high technology, military bases, and defense contractors began moving into the state. As always, the patterns of development were controlled by the Front Range, as houses and manufacturing spread out north and south along the base of the mountains with small fingers of suburban and recreational development creeping up the base of the mountains.

In 1954 the Academy site was occupied by four or five large ranches and a small community in Pine Valley consisting of about fifty residences, several motels, a tavern, and a small airport with a gravel runway. The Superintendent of the Academy and the Commandant of the Cadet Wing moved into the largest homes, but with the exception of a log cabin (circa 1860) and a few incidental structures, both the landscape features and artifacts were ignored or obliterated.

The urge to build anew is an essential heritage of Colorado. Boom-bust cycles of gold, silver, coal, molybdenum, uranium, and

67. Long section through Cadet Area. Drawing by Jory Johnson, based on SOM working drawings. The "two up and four down" building section complements the existing topography of the site.

other extracted materials, the tourist trade, and the post–World War II high technology/military expansion all demanded instantaneous construction. As Kenneth Helphand observes, the landscape has always been modern.[11] Mining towns, railroads, center-pivot irrigation, water diversion projects, and ski resorts were all products of technology, function, and the landscape. It was within this tradition that teams of architects, engineers, geologists, and Air Force officers flew over the site, probed beneath it, and soon began to fit the Academy to the land.

The Master Plan "The Academy is a bridge to the future, gleaming with the promise of peace in a stable, sane world," intoned Secretary of the United States Air Force Harold Talbott in 1955.[12] It was to be a "national monument" like West Point and the Naval Academy, but also a bridge to the future built not according to preconceived styles or symbols but on the basis of scientific, rational planning and design. Because there were no "man-made restrictions such as existing communities or industry," the planning team could develop "An ideal plan. . . . the best solution for each problem took into account the topography and geology. [The Master Plan] reflected the physical nature of the site itself more obviously than . . . [plans for] existing urban centers."[13]

The Academy was designed from flow diagrams which charted both the flow of human beings through the site (cadet, visitors, pilots, cars, etc.) and the flow of the natural processes and land forms.[14] In retrospect, the engineering and geological studies appear to have been quickly done but were essentially accurate. For example, the U.S. Geologic Survey team noted that the site "is not one of unique geologic interest [and that] the time allowed for geologic investigations preceding design and construction is very short ."[15] If the project had begun in the 1990s instead of the 1950s, the various environmental impact statements, permits, and reviews would dramatically swell the environmental studies and probably lengthen the planning process by several years, depending on local or national opposition.[16] The limitations of hand-drawn maps and the contemporaneous state of the art environmental technology meant that the "best solutions" were based primarily on general assumptions and professional expertise.[17] However, the gravely soils and good depth to bedrock meant that the necessary grading would be relatively inexpensive and that the steeper slopes would be the only major building constraint, except in the case of the airfield where the necessity of extensive areas of relatively flat land meant that there was only one possible site.

The Cadet Area, due to its size and the desire to keep facilities centrally organized, was almost equally geographically predetermined. The most dramatic and romantic site—Cathedral Rock—was too close to the northern property line. Douglass Valley lacked drama and visitors would "look down" on the cadets from the roads on the neighboring ridges. While some felt this modesty to be a virtue, most concurred that the Academy should not, in Walter Netsch's phrase, be "tucked away." Schematic plans for damning up Douglass Valley to reflect both the mountains and the Academy were scraped as frivolous in a dry landscape. And so the base of the Rampart Range overlooking Lehman Valley became the "ideal plan" in terms of geology and topography, both visually and pragmatically.

The topography and flow diagrams determined the rest of the land-use plan. The appropriately named Eisenhower Golf Course was inserted into the South Lehman Valley, whose deep alluvial deposits allowed the course to be planted to look less like Colorado and more like a heavily wooded course in the eastern United States.[18] The heavy tree canopy allows the golf course to

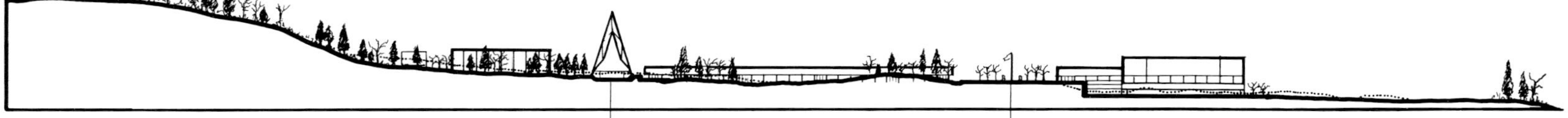

recede back into the woods thus preventing the Academy from looking like a resort from adjoining ridges.

"Pity the poor Cadet. If we don't, no one else will."[19] The Cadet Area is immense, covering about a fifth of a square mile. In a sense, the construction continued the geological erosion by pushing the sedimentary material downhill to construct a series of terraces or mesas.[20] Ten thousand lineal feet of retaining walls leveled the Court of Honor and the chapel to 7,176 feet, with the Terrazzo Level and Air Garden 13 feet below, the lower cadet quarters 44 feet below, and the parade grounds 72 feet below. The constructed mesa is exposed, rugged, and Spartan, in marked contrast to the domestic domiciles in the more benign valleys.

There are some aspects of the complex that recall the architecture of the southwestern United States, for example, the Acoma Pueblo in New Mexico, built high on a mesa for defensive purposes. One is also struck by the visual similarity of the chapel's serrated profile and the angular peaks of the Rampart Range, especially since such homage to distant mountains was common in Native American architecture (though Netsch maintains that such associations were unintentional (fig. 67).[21]

Skidmore Owings & Merrill resisted the Air Force generals' desires for a traditional typological hierarchy—the idea that buildings such as a library should be more impressive than more "ordinary" buildings such as dormitories.[22] But since both West Point and Annapolis have magnificent chapels, the decision to make the Air Force Chapel architecturally prominent was almost inevitable.[23] Architecture critic Allan Temko questioned the propriety of the prominent chapel, arguing that a library or observatory should have been the symbol of the Academy. Visiting the Academy soon after completion, Temko wrote that "against the formidable background of the front range of the Rockies, the chapel [registers] a thinly, strident, silvery note amidst dark, massive harmonics."[24] But had the chapel been less of an architectural departure from the rest of the Academy buildings and had the landscape matured to make the chapel less visually exposed, the landscape orientation and the centrality of the cadet and his relationship to the natural environment would have been apparent. But unfortunately, the vitiation of the original landscape plan (much of which was never planted) and the chapel's soaring tetrahedral "wings"—however striking—upstage the more profound humanist relationship to nature. If one focuses on the daily life of the cadet—not the visitor experience—a very different relationship emerges.

Consider the compass orientation of the cadets' lives. Meals, classes, and athletics are all on the north-south axis which links the dining hall to the dormitories and the athletic fields, while the east-west axis leads to special events: chapel, parades, and social affairs. In the plan, the chapel is framed on the western side by the grove of Douglas firs extending from the Court of Honor and on the eastern side by the constructed hill. Since the chapel is also 13 feet above the Terrazzo Level, it is somewhat removed from the dormitories, dining hall, and academic buildings. Today, without the trees on either side, the chapel visually intrudes into the Terrazzo Level.

Renaissance humanists referred to gardens as a third nature, the first being the primal, unmediated world and the second being what we today call the built environment. Human beings transform the first nature into the second—raw materials, agriculture, and even recreation like hiking and camping. It is in the third nature, or landscape design ("gardens" is used in a much narrower sense by the general public today than in the Renaissance, when it referred more to the design of an entire property and not just the part set aside for flowers), that art and nature come together. As historian

68. Diagram of original quadrangle, University of Virginia (right), and of Air Force Academy Cadet Area (left). Drawing by Jory Johnson. The clear demarcations among the three natures at the University of Virginia. Nature is welcomed into the Academy.

John Dixon Hunt explains, "landscape design is the expression or representation of a culture's position vis-à-vis nature."[25] At the Cadet Area, nature is experienced as measures of control on a continuum from the ordered geometry of the Air Garden, the controlled "art forms" of the courtyards, to the minimal management of the larger site.

If we take a comparative look at the disposition of the three natures in Thomas Jefferson's design for the University of Virginia—where the natural landscape never intrudes into the formal lawn or the dormitory wings—we can read the difference between the relative position and perception of nature and culture in the eighteenth century and the modern amalgamation and synthesis represented in the Academy plan (fig. 68).

The jets and rockets of the Air Force itself bear witness to the idea that it is no longer possible to demarcate a separation between ourselves and nature. The "natural" air, plants, and animals have all been and are being transformed by technology and our burgeoning population. While this is heretical to many, including those who cherish romantic ideals of the purity of nature and environmentalists who urge restraint in the exploitation of natural resources, for Dan Kiley—who served as landscape architect for the Academy—it offers man an exhilarating freedom: "Man is Nature. Isn't that exciting to realize? It's not man and nature. Man is nature, just like the trees. Both live and grow."[26]

Like Kiley, geologist Stephen Jay Gould sees the question of culture and nature as one of appropriate geometries: "Our geometries tend to operate at the integral values of 1, 2, and 3 or in the regular geometries of lines, planes, and simple solids. Nature builds in the fractional domain between 2 and 3 . . . . Every flower is far too irregular to reconstruct or copy or to use as a model for anything of much use to human beings. So we melt, pound, and shape materials into right angles and regular shapes."[27]

The regular shapes of the cadet wing—their living quarters—open and lift to form a series of apertures that capture reassuring retinal images of pines and wildflowers. Looking north-south (never directly into the rising or setting sun) the architecture frames and focuses the eye without competing for attention. The apertures don't culturalize or comment on the landscape. They resist naive ornamentation or symbols of flight.

The forms come from the dynamics of the cadet's life—geometrical and disciplined—but are visually directed to the limitless freedom of the landscape. The Doolies—as the freshman cadets are nicknamed—literally walk only on the marble strips that define the 28-foot modules of the Terrazzo Level terrace. This "marching module" geometrically interlocks with the 7-foot module on which the buildings are based. This carefully proportioned architecture and the landscape architecture frame and clarify the cadet's relationship to the physical, transcendental truths of the Rampart Range.

Refining the Plan Dan Kiley was not hired until the master plan had been presented to the Air Force,[28] but he was so sympathetic to its concepts that there was little he would have challenged. "The steel and architecture were so strong in their relationship to the site. I could really build on it."[29] Saarinen urged Skidmore Owings & Merrill to get Kiley on board as soon as possible, knowing that not only would he make the design stronger by extending the architecture, but that a different landscape architect might want, in the fashion of the times, to subvert the architectural concept by "softening" the buildings with vegetation.[30]

Dan Kiley attended the Harvard Graduate School of Design in the mid-1930s, but his real graduate education came at the end of

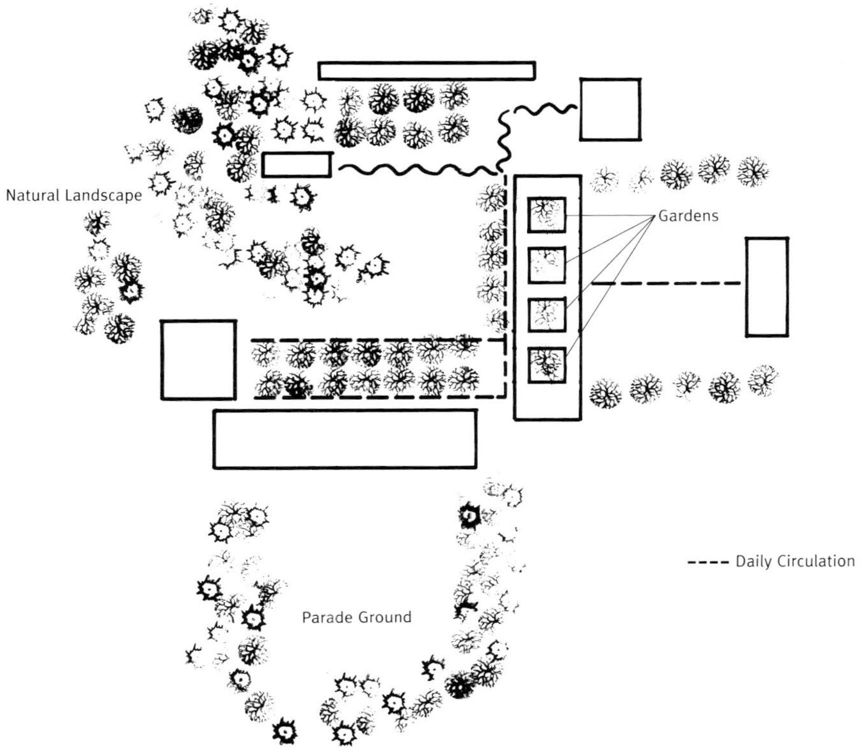

USAFA

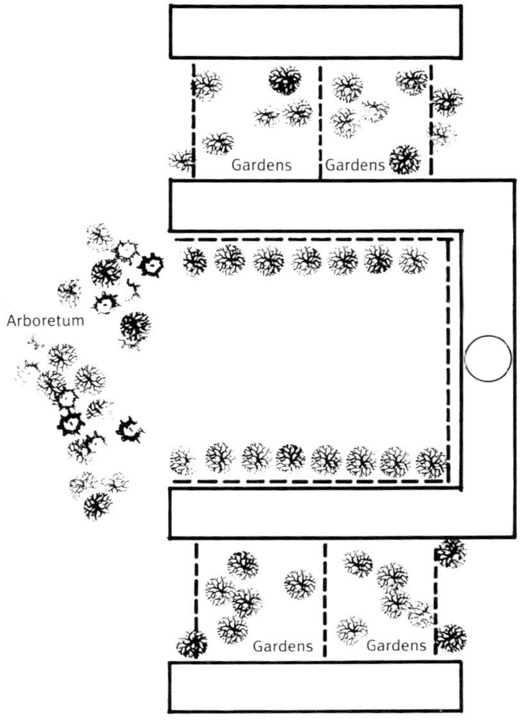

UVA

World War II, when he stayed in Europe as a designer in the Office of Strategic Services located in Paris. While designing the courtrooms for the Nuremberg trials and other postwar projects, Kiley found time to visit Vaux-Le-Vicomte, Sceaux, Versailles, and other classical French gardens designed in the seventeenth century by André Le Nôtre. A skeptical empiricist who trusts only firsthand experience, Kiley had been bored by the stately glass lantern slides at Harvard. But walking on soft gravel paths, he was astonished and transformed by the spatial power and beauty of the gardens. Nothing in America compared with the clarity and sensual elegance of the bosquets, the tapis verts,[31] the allées, the gravel walks, the tightly spaced trees, and the terraces. Kiley was also struck by the fact that Le Nôtre's gardens were not self-indulgent extravaganzas; they were built for people to use. "Boulevards were built to shoot cannonballs down them," Kiley explains. "That's what 'boulevard' means. Now it's an avenue which means 'welcome' and it works beautifully, but it was originally for defense. They weren't just planting a bunch of trees to make some kind of art."[32]

Returning to the United States, Kiley was increasingly dissatisfied with the biomorphic forms, zigzags, amoebas, kidneys, and asymmetrical lines typical of the designs by his former classmates Garrett Eckbo and James Rose. The courtyards designed, but never executed, for the Cadet Quarters at the Air Force Academy are a vestigial example of the lingering influence of such twentieth-century artists as Joan Miró, Jean Arp, and architects Le Corbusier and Alvar Aalto. Increasingly, Kiley thought that such designs tried too hard to be "new" and "up-to-date" so that the modern architecture of the house would not appear to be attached to an "old-fashioned" landscape or garden. Such designs were also supposed to reflect the informalities and outdoor games and barbecues of the 1950s.

In Kiley, Skidmore Owings & Merrill had a landscape architect who would vigorously defend their ideas. Instead of trying to be "one with nature" by hiding the buildings, Kiley is more sympathetic to Woody Allen's quip, "I am two with nature." Kiley is "two with nature" by knowing what he is and what nature is. He complains that Frank Lloyd Wright's shifting axes and angular geometries at Taliesin West, built in 1937 near Phoenix, Arizona, confuse the way Native Americans hunted with the way they lived. "Camouflaging, rotating, bending, that's how Indians hunt, but not

69. Original landscape design for Cadet Quarters Courtyard. Detail from architects' drawings. Dan Kiley's schematic designs for the cadet courtyards are an unusual departure from the ordered geometries for which he is best known.

how they live. Look at the Pueblos or the Teepees. They were always geometric with strong axes. They didn't try to hide or blend into the desert. They had a distinct relationship with the Universe."[33]

Kiley's designs were more readily appreciated by architects than by landscape architects. The spatial structure and experience of his designs are dependent on geometric bosquets and allées that need more time to mature than landscape designs dependent on built structures, sculpture, or picturesque effects. Kiley wrote very little, and in the typical architectural photographs taken soon after the landscape was installed, his work sometimes appeared thin and insubstantial. The Miller residence in Columbus, Indiana—now almost universally acknowledged as one of the masterpieces of modern landscape architecture—won only a merit award from the American Society of Landscape Architecture in 1962. Many landscape architects were convinced that straight lines and modern architecture were incompatible with natural landscapes. At the ASLA Convention held in Denver in 1962, Vice-President Eldridge Lovelace echoed the prevailing view when he described some of the area sights: "You can go to the Rocky Mountain Park and see Man with Nature or you can go to the Air Force Academy and see Man against Nature."[34] When Kiley and architect Hugh Jacobsen were trying to win a commission together, the latter advised Kiley "to go easy on the geometry" when talking with their potential client "because you're thought of as a neo-classicist." "Forget the neo," Kiley snapped, but duly showed slides of Frederick Law Olmsted's Central Park, instead of Le Nôtre, and they got the job.[35]

Simplicity Although he hadn't worked with Kiley before, Netsch recalls that he knew they would get along:

> **Because we worked the same way. He solved things visually and practically. One of the first things we looked at were the two entrances to the site and when Dan began talking about wind breaks and large panels of Ponderosa pine that would blend with the pines in the existing landscape and not be static points, I knew he was perfect for us.**[36]

Kiley's Yankee pragmatism extended to his drawing board. Because the job and the drawings were so enormous, Kiley "invented" tree stamps by carving symbols of evergreens, large deciduous trees, and smaller trees and shrubs on rubber stamps (this was before such stamps were sold commercially). His eyes light up as he remembers them:

> **I laid out the huge drawings on this beautiful hardwood floor on the second story of my office. My sons helped stamp the drawings. . . . I would let them play around in the areas we weren't really planting just to indicate the existing or revegetation. There are only two kind of trees out there so they could just stamp away.**[37]

Much of Kiley's energy was expended in trying to stop costly proposals by the Air Force Construction Agency like the seven miles of lighting on the loop road, security lighting being a common feature of all military bases. Kiley pleaded: "All you need to light is the road and that's what headlights are for. All the parkway lights do is blot out night views of the mountains, the sky, and the Academy buildings. And it also costs half a million dollars!"[38] Over the added objections of Skidmore Owings & Merrill, the lighting was installed, but a decade later it was removed.

Kiley fought another battle over plans to irrigate the median

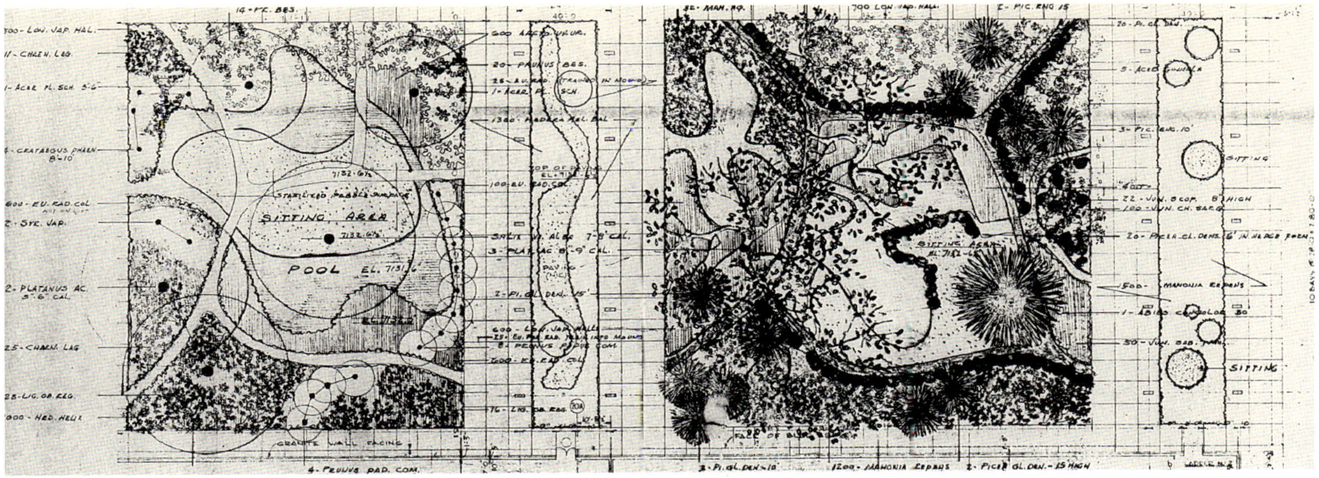

strip on the same road . He wrote that "[the] only apparent excuse for spending 2.1 million dollars on an irrigation system is to maintain roadside plantings of inappropriate, non-indigenous material which otherwise would have no chance of survival. I cannot see the slightest excuse—ecological, functional or esthetic—for this arbitrary, labored and utterly unnatural treatment . . . ."[39] He suggested planting native grasses to "give us the character, dignity and great scale essential to the area." Landscape architects who know only the geometric character of most of Kiley's urban work, might be surprised to read his vigorous arguments in favor of native plants and what we now call ecological design, but for Kiley it was not a matter of dogma, but appropriateness. To overcome suspicion of a landscape architect from the East working in Colorado, Kiley relied on George Kelly, who ran a small nursery near Colorado Springs. "He was a very nice man who really knew plants. We used Russian Olive. It's not native, but it takes the harsh conditions and its gray color is a very nice shade for the native grasses. I don't care if it is native or not, but whether or not it is appropriate—both ecologically and visually."[40]

Another struggle Kiley lost was the hill next to the entrance road. While its 1.5:1 slope was steeper than the engineering standard of 2:1, Kiley argued that since it had been holding for hundreds of years, the bulldozers should leave well enough alone. Instead, the Air Force Construction Agency heeded its construction standards instead of Kiley's common sense, especially since a landslide would have blocked access to the Academy entrance. The hill was carefully regraded and replanted at considerable cost and loss of native vegetation.

The limits of construction were carefully observed to minimize environmental impact. Kiley was particularly jealous of the natural intrusion below the chapel. Once he found bulldozer operators casually moving some of the earth and angrily confronted them with "Goddammit, put that hill back."[41]

The Court of Honor Kiley's design for the Court of Honor uses a motif of a geometricized landscape metamorphosing into the natural landscape (fig. 70). At the Court of Honor, a ceremonial grid of trees gradually becomes looser until it blends with the trees of the hillside. Deciduous trees from the hillside "infiltrate" the geometrical plantings so there is a transition of both geometry and the type of trees. The motif of geometry merging and leading into the natural landscape became a magical interplay between gridded bosquets of small deciduous trees and Douglas firs. Unfortunately, the trees were never planted so we could never have the experience Kiley described:

> **I always am excited with the idea of man as clearly recognizable in nature—projecting his designs in clear strength and letting the natural landscape lap its shores, modifying and breaking it up until total assimilation has taken place. I am delighted and amazed when I set a little bit of geometry in space and see it develop and grow and seek its infinite relationships outward with the universe.**[42]

The Cadet Dormitory Courtyards These cadet dormitory courtyards were to be a break from both the Terrazzo Level and the natural

70. Original landscape design for the Court of Honor. Redrawn by Jory Johnson from working drawings. Kiley's original design for the Court of Honor continued to bring nature into the geometry of the Academy.

71. The Air Garden at night. Photograph by Stewart's, c. 1958. At night a serene elegance and beauty settled on the Air Garden. Local History Collection, Pikes Peak Library District. Stewart's No. 38-27.

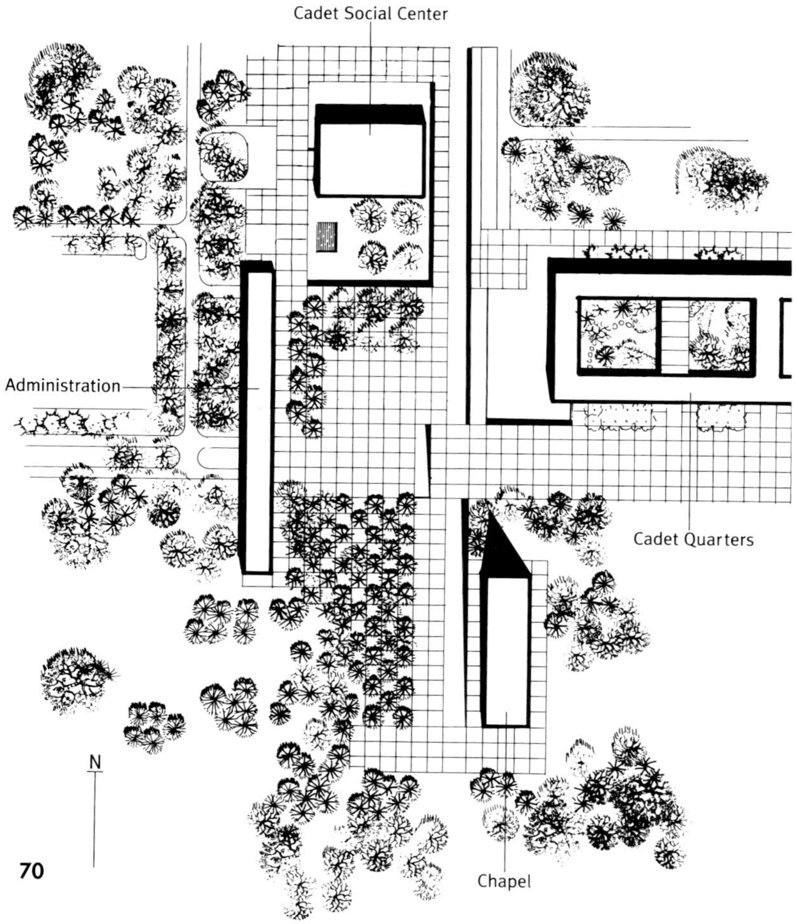

70

landscape. Because they were protected by the dormitories, Kiley proposed lush plantings and small pools that would seem to flow underneath the dorms from one courtyard to the next. They were never developed beyond Kiley's preliminary sketches, but one would never guess that the wiggles, curves, and free forms came from Kiley's hand. They look more like the work of Thomas Church and other landscape architects of the period but they lack Church's precision and economy. Nor did they have the elegance of the courtyards at Connecticut General Life Insurance designed by the sculptor Isamu Noguchi for Skidmore, Owings & Merrill just before the Air Force Academy design. "Aren't these wild?" Kiley exclaimed thirty-five years later as he unfolded a drawing of the courtyards. "I would never do this now. There should be a contrast, but this is a little much. Needs more spatial structure (fig. 69)." [43]

The Air Garden Kiley stresses that design should respond to life and to need. "It needs to release the spirit and achieve a spiritual fulfillment of a particular place and how people live there."[44] The 700-foot-long Air Garden responded to the need to break the straight lines of the rest of the Terrazzo Level. Kiley winks as he explains that this was where "the cadets could take their girlfriends. Instead of walking like this [marching motion] they would have to walk like this [Kiley pantomimes a flirtatious side-step around the pools]. It was special, just for the cadets" (fig. 71).[45]

Ed Mast, a former engineering professor at the Academy, remembers that the faculty wanted the cadets to be disciplined but also to develop the edge and risk-taking ability they would need in battle. "There were a lot of pranks with the water garden. Once, after a couple of Cadets had been disciplined for putting a 'submarine' in the pools. I asked them if they would do it again. 'No Sir!' But was it worth it? 'Yes Sir'."[46]

72. Axonometric projection of Air Garden at maturity in 1970. Drawn by Brad Conover after drawings by Dan Kiley Associates, dated June 16, 1956, and evidence of later photographs. The Air Garden's trees, large shrubs, and water offered a playful, fully three-dimensional experience to the cadets. In 1975, the pools were filled in and the shrubbery was removed.

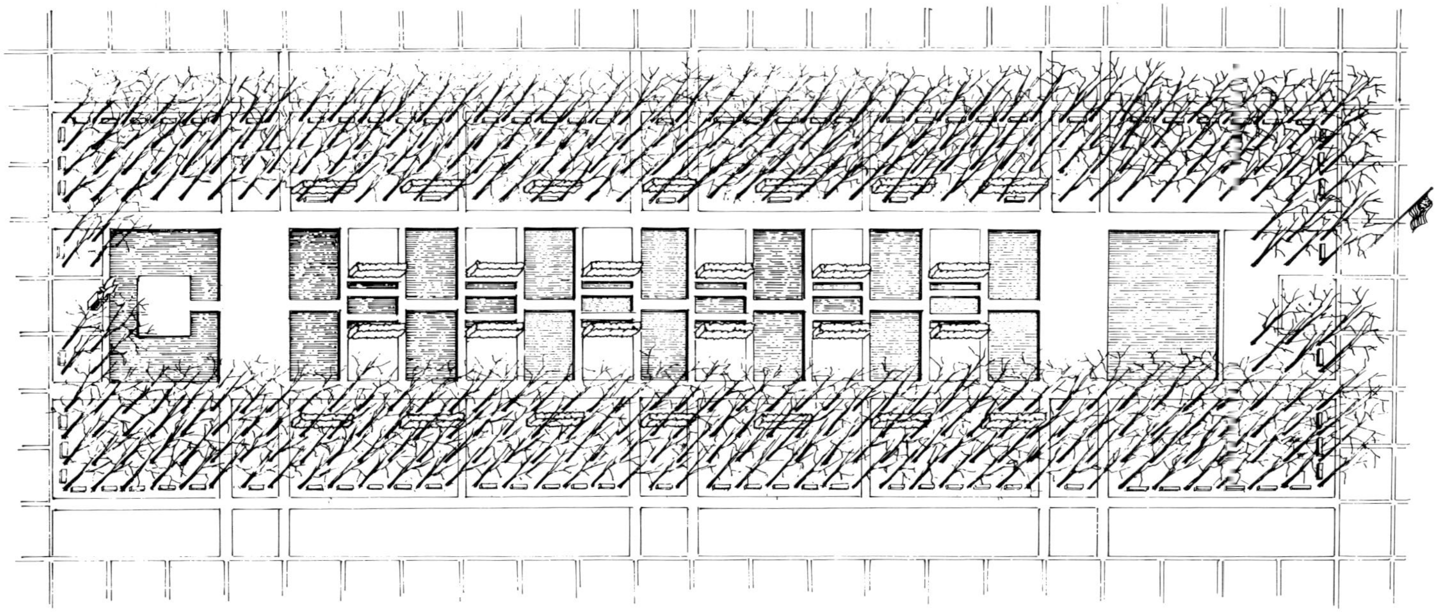

As Kiley explains, the Air Garden is not intended to have the same sense of dominion as Versailles or other grand French gardens: "We have to look at where we are today. I use geometry and Le Nôtre used geometry, but we have different understandings of the universe." Instead of extending the prominence of a particular building or institution—the gardens of Versailles radiate from the Chateau—the Air Garden extends the life of the cadets. Reflected in the all-glass dining hall, it is, as Walter Netsch asserts, "A gift back to man and nature."[47]

The Air Garden at its short-lived maturity was fully three-dimensional (fig. 72).[48] Solid, inconvertible five-foot-high holly hedges stood alongside the pools and provided a visual rhythm as cadets appeared and disappeared behind the segments. It is what Kiley calls

> **A walk in nature. . . . Movement is ever-continuous and elusive, like a maze. . . . Every time you walk in nature it is a fresh experience. You might squeeze through some small maple trees, pick your way across a rushing stream and climb up a hill into an open meadow. It's always moving and changing spatially. . . .What I did with the Air Garden was create a man-made scene having those spatial qualities.**[49]

It is, above all, a landscape of intelligence and purpose conceived at a time when confident designers were rethinking the way we live and the spaces in which we order our lives. If we paid enough attention to what we were doing and how we do it instead of debating self-conscious symbols or styles, they believed, then beauty would emerge. "It is just like skiing," Kiley explains. "As soon as you try to look like you're skiing, you're not skiing. It's the same thing with design. Emerson said something like if you seek beauty, you get a bunch of junk, but if you seek truth, you might get beauty."[50]

Most of the ideas Kiley developed at the Academy would find their way into important projects throughout his career, but never again would he have the opportunity to realize a complete integration of people, architecture, and landscape on a scale commensurate with his ambitions and idealism.

Major Vegetation

SOUTH-FACING SLOPES

juniper (*juniperus sp.*)

mountain mahogany (*Cercocarpus montanus*)

ponderosa pine (*Pinus ponderosa*)

scrub oak (*Quercus gambelii*)

NORTH-FACING SLOPES

Douglas fir (*Pseudotsuga mentziesii*)

VALLEYS

Colorado blue spruce (*Picea pungens*)

quaking aspen (*Populus tremuloides*)

FLOWERS AND GRASSES

anemones (*Anemone patens*)

blue gamma (*Bouteloua gracilis*)

blue mist (*Eriogonum flavum*)

buffalo grass (*Buchloe dactyloides*)

fringed sagebrush (*Artemisa frigida*)

Indian paintbrush (*Castilleja sp.*)

prickly pears (*Opuntia erinacea*)

rattlesnake master (*Eryngium yuccifolium sp.*)

tickseed (*Coreopsis sp.*)

Yucca (*Yucca filamentosa*)

Notes

1. "Bring Me Men," inscribed on one of the primary overpasses leading up to the Terrazzo Level.

2. Good overviews of Colorado's natural history are found in Mel Griffiths and Lynnell Rubright, *Colorado: A Geography* (Boulder: Westview Press, 1983), and Cornelia Fleischer Mutel and John Emerick, *From Grassland to Glacier: The Natural History of Colorado* (Boulder: Johnson Books, 1984). Excellent state maps are found in Kenneth A. Erickson and Albert W. Smith, *Atlas of Colorado* (Boulder: Colorado Associated University Press, 1985). The best general survey of the cultural geography of Colorado is Kenneth I. Helphand, *Colorado, Visions of an American Landscape* (Niwot, Colo.: Rinehart Roberts, 1991).

3. Interview with Walter Netsch, 9 July 1993.

4. Interview with Dan Kiley, Chicago, 8 December 1992.

5. The use of "man" as a synecdoche for human beings is characteristic of both the 1950s and Dan Kiley's speech. It should also be noted in this particular context that there were only male cadets in 1955 so the use of "man" by the designers is intended to be taken literally.

6. After the completion of Sijan Hall, the only remnant of the natural landscape within the Terrazzo Level was a large mound covered with trees and shrubs, all of which were removed. The smooth, grass knoll was dubbed "Marilyn Monroe Hill" by the cadets.

7. A venturi effect is the turbulence and updrafts created when wind passes over a tall, vertical barrier, a phenomenon well known to anyone who walks near high-rise buildings in windy cities.

8. Netsch interview, 9 July 1993.

9. A biotic community of plants and animals that exist within a specific habitat. The grasslands of the Colorado plains, with bison, deer, and other grazing animals living off the tall prairie grasses, constitute a temperate grassland biome. Biomes may be very large or, as at the Academy site, they may be small "pockets" in which certain plants and animals encounter favorable conditions created by extreme topography or hydrology. Thus, one set of plants can exist on the south-facing slopes and

another on the north-facing slopes. In less extreme topography or altitude, the difference in temperature would not be enough to enable all different biomes to exist within the same general region.

10. Not to be confused with the type of Douglas fir found in the Pacific northwest that can reach 300 feet. The variety present found in Colorado matures between 40 and 80 feet.

11. Helphand, Colorado, 64.

12. George V. Fagan, *The Air Force Academy: An Illustrated History* (Boulder: Johnson Books, 1988), 49.

13. David J. Varnes and Glenn R. Scott, *General and Engineering Geology of the United States Air Force Academy Site,* Colorado. (Washington, D.C.: Government Printing Office, 1967).

14. Nathaniel Alexander Owings, *The Spaces in Between: An Architect's Journey* (Boston: Houghton Mifflin, 1973), 153.

15. Varnes and Scott, *Geology,* 2.

16. Actually, the United States government is exempt from some environmental regulations and building codes. Nevertheless, for anyone who has shepherded large projects through hundreds of reviews and statements, the planning and construction of the Academy takes one back to a much simpler time. Peter Walker, a landscape architect then a partner with Sasaki Walker Associates, estimates that by the 1970s his office was spending as much as 50 percent of its time on environmental issues compared with perhaps 20 percent in the 1950s. It is probably conservative to estimate that, in the 1990s, a project of this magnitude would be stretched out by two to five years by the necessary permits, environmental impact statements, and the myriad review boards, commissions, and citizen groups.

17. Since the suitability of a site for construction or other land uses is dependent on the complex interaction of many different factors—e.g., vegetative cover might mitigate the adverse effect of another factor such as a steep slope—hand-drawn maps are limited in that they can consider only a few factors at a time. In 1990, far more site analysis information would be digested and analyzed by Geographical Information Systems (GIS)

18. Golf's ancestral home in Scotland resembles the rough, windy ridges of the Academy more than the South Lehman Valley location. But in the 1950s, for President Eisenhower and most average golfers, the game was inseparably linked to the lush greens of Augusta, Georgia, rather than the windswept dunes of Scotland.

19. From interview with Walter Netsch, 12 December 1993. This motto was posted on a wall in an Skidmore, Owings & Merrill conference room.

20. Technically, a mesa is a flat-topped hill with steep slopes and a hard, almost horizontal table of resistant rock. Though the term is applied colloquially to the ridges of the Academy site, a true mesa would have presented severe structural constraints for buildings as large as those in the Cadet Area. The romantic associations of mesas are clearly alluded to in the hard Terrazzo Level and the projecting architectural structures and buildings.

21. See Vincent Scully, *Pueblo: Mountain, Village, Dance* (Chicago: University of Chicago Press, 1989). For a contemporary interpretation of this landscape/architecture relationship, see the work of Antoine Predock.

22. Fagan, *Academy,* 84.

23. Allan Temko "The Air Academy Chapel—A Critical Appraisal," *Architectural Forum* (December 1962): 75–78.

24. Ibid., 75.

25. John Dixon Hunt, *Gardens and the Picturesque: Studies in the History of Landscape Architecture* (Cambridge: MIT, 1992), 299.

26. Kiley interview, 8 December 1992.

27. Stephen Jay Gould, "Form and Scale in Nature and Culture: Modern Landscape as Necessary Integration," in *Between Home and Heaven: Contemporary American Landscape Photography* (Washington, D.C.: Smithsonian Institution, 1992), 77.

28. Skidmore, Owings & Merrill had landscape architects in their own office but frequently hired famous landscape architects or artists on important projects. They made preliminary inquiries of the famous and flamboyant Brazilian landscape architect and artist Roberto Burle Marx and, at the other end of the spectrum, the California landscape architect Thomas Church. Kiley was such an obvious choice that the others were never seriously considered. Kiley first visited the site in December 1955 and began refining the landscape plan in the spring of 1956.

29. Kiley interview, 8 December 1992.

30. As related by Walter Netsch, 8 December, 1992. Unlike Kiley, many landscape architects thought that straight lines were "unnatural" and modeled their designs after the eighteenth-century British picturesque gardens or the modernist forms of Noguchi, Miro, or other modern sculptors or painters.
31. A French term for a rectangular manicured lawn in a formal garden or plaza; literally a "green carpet."
32. Interview with Kiley, Chicago, 12 December 1992.
33. Kiley interview, 8 December 1992.
34. "ASLA Notes," *Landscape Architecture* (Fall, 1962): 47.
35. Warren T. Byrd and Reuben M. Rainey, eds. *The Work of Dan Kiley: A Dialogue on Design Theory* (Charlottesville: University of Virginia School of Architecture, 1983), 10.
36. Netsch interview, 9 July 1993.
37. Kiley interview, 8 December 1992.
38. Ibid.
39. Letter to Walter Netsch, 28 January 1957.
40. Kiley Interview, 8 December 1992.
41. Ibid.
42. Dan Kiley, "Nature: The Source of All Design," *Landscape Architecture* (January 1963): 127.
43. Kiley interview, 8 December 1992.
44. Ibid.
45. Ibid.
46. Interview with Edward Mast, retired professor of mechanical engineering. 14 January 1993.
47. Conversation with Walter Netsch, 23 February 1994.
48. It was removed in 1976 to save energy costs and because some persistent leaking was creating problems.
49. Kiley interview, 8 December 1992.
50. Warren and Rainey, *The Work of Dan Kiley,* 19. Given Frank Lloyd Wright's opposition to the Academy, it is hard to resist adding his pronouncement that "Truth is more important than the facts."

73. View of Terrazzo Level with Cadet Quarters to the right and Administration Building in distance. Photograph by Hedrich-Blessing, 1959. This juxtaposition of natural and man-made forms is defined by the geometric grid. Presided over by its human occupants, it is a landscape of technological timelessness. Chicago Historical Society: Hedrich-Blessing #22362 I.

Robert Nauman

Presenting the Academy

No image better captures the spirit of Skidmore, Owings & Merrill's United States Air Force Academy than a photograph taken by Hedrich-Blessing's Bill Hedrich in 1959 (fig. 73). In this image, taken from a vantage point in front of the Cadet Quarters looking west, Hedrich's purpose was not to simulate an actual architectural experience, but to capture instead the intention of the work. In photographing contemporary architecture, he cited its defining characteristics as being "clean and disciplined."[1] This photograph of the Academy captures that essence.

The Air Force, newest branch of the service, lacked the time-honored tradition of the Army and Navy, and the Academy architecture, unlike that at West Point or Annapolis, sought not to evoke historical precedent but the technological capabilities of the present. To that end, the architects described their work as "timeless," and avoided references to fashionable architectural "fads." Within the carefully cropped frame of this image, specific references to time are nonexistent. Even seasonal indicators are lacking, as a sense of timelessness pervades the image. The three uniformed figures in the photograph, set within a stark architectural environment, display no sense of "fashion" in their dress, and are as architectonic as they are human. The center figure, like an architectural span, is bracketed by the two columnar figures flanking him. Appearing as a continuation of the architectural grid behind them, they reinforce the sense of disciplined order inherent in this military institution. Closer analysis reveals that the image itself is as geometrically rigid as the architecture it frames. The slightly off-center trio of figures offers the eye relief from the sweeping perspective that dominates the left part of the photograph, creating a composition that splits the image in half vertically. The zones of earth and sky further divide that half into dualities of mass and void. The lower left area is again divided into a hierarchical pattern of grids, complementing and emphasizing the architectural organization. A sense of discipline informs the regulating lines of both photograph and architecture; a sense of control unites the two-dimensional image with the three-dimensional architectural experience and the Academy program. There is no room for random willfulness within this precise environment, as even nature has been photographically separated from the site by the architecture.

In employing Hedrich-Blessing to photograph the Academy, Skidmore, Owings & Merrill chose a firm whose photographic style would complement their architecture. Hedrich often emphasized that his role as architectural photographer was to work in alliance with the architects.[2] Both he and Skidmore, Owings & Merrill were very aware of the role of photography in disseminating an image to the public that would operate both as a document of the architecture and as a carrier of meanings that transcended their physical reality.

The Colorado Springs Exhibition On 1 April 1954, President Dwight D. Eisenhower signed the bill establishing a United States Air Force Academy. Historians have noted that this act took place during a period of relative tranquility and prosperity, ushered in by Joseph Stalin's death in March 1953 and the signing of the armistice ending the Korean War on 26 July 1953. It was a period during which Eisenhower's popularity continued to grow.[3] In the summer of 1955, political commentator James Reston of the *New York Times* remarked that "the popularity of President Eisenhower has got beyond the bounds of reasonable calculation and will have to be put down as national phenomenon, like baseball. The thing is no longer a remarkable political fact but a kind of national love affair."[4] This period would last until the launching in October 1957 of Sputnik, which catapulted the Russians and Americans into the space race. While this optimistic view of the years between 1953 and 1957 might gloss over some of its contradictions—the public's continued fear of nuclear warfare, the inconclusive nature of the Korean War settlement, and the erosion of faith in technology—it does reflect the mood that the firm of Skidmore, Owings & Merrill sought to convey to the public in its initial Academy design presentation.[5]

Well-known for its Modernist architectural works, Skidmore, Owings & Merrill had been awarded the contract to design the Academy on 23 July 1954. For the initial design presentation at the Colorado Springs Fine Arts Center on 14–15 May 1955, the architects enlisted the respected Bauhaus graphic artist and exhibition designer Herbert Bayer; the renowned landscape photographer Ansel Adams; the aerial photographer William Garnett; and the architectural delineator George Cooper Rudolph. The exhibition not only served the purpose of introducing their architectural style to a targeted audience—members of Congress, the armed forces, and the press, who were flown to the exhibition aboard Air Force jets—but was also intended to underscore the appropriateness of that particular style for an American military academy.

The presentation was designed by Herbert Bayer, at that time a resident of Aspen, Colorado. Bayer had been a student and teacher of design at the famous Bauhaus school instituted by Walter Gropius in Dessau, Germany. After leaving the Bauhaus in 1928, Bayer pursued a career in graphic design as art director for the German *Vogue* in Berlin. Immediately after immigrating to the United States in 1938, he began working on a Bauhaus exhibit at New York's Museum of Modern Art, and followed it with exhibitions at the museum in 1942 and 1943. Titled "Road to Victory," the 1942 exhibition integrated photography by Edward Steichen with a text by poet Carl Sandburg.[6] A propaganda effort to boost wartime morale, that exhibition chronicled the growth of the United States and the country's ideological war against Fascism. It employed ramps, dramatic juxtapositions, and vistas to lead the spectator through a carefully choreographed sequence of spaces in which aesthetic devices reinforced the political message. In 1945 Bayer designed an exhibition for the Container Corporation of America which opened at the Art Institute of Chicago, an event not likely to have escaped the attention of Skidmore, Owings & Merrill, whose headquarters were located in the same city.[7] The other participants in the initial presentation were equally experienced.

Ansel Adams's career was already well launched. With Beaumont Newhall, the famous American photographic historian, he had curated the first exhibition of the newly formed Photographic Department at the Museum of Modern Art in late 1940. Included in that exhibition were some of Adams's own images.[8] His epic photographs of that decade made him famous, and magazines like *Life* and *Fortune* sought his work. As a publicist, he produced numerous photographic books (three in 1954 alone) and contributed in 1952 to the founding of the magazine *Aperture*. An outspoken environmentalist, he also served on the board of directors of the Sierra Club for thirty-seven years, writing extensively on environmental issues and often using his photographs to argue those issues before Congress.[9] One week prior to the Colorado Springs exhibition of the Academy design, Adams's work had appeared at the San Francisco Academy of Sciences in an exhibition titled "This is the American Earth." The exhibition, with a text by Nancy Newhall, encouraged guardianship of the country's resources. In that exhibition, Adams's images of unspoiled nature contrasted with aerial photographs by William Garnett depicting the urban chaos of Los Angeles.[10] It was Adams who recommended that Garnett's aerial photography be used to complement his own photographs in the Academy presentation.

Garnett, although less well-known as a photographer than Adams, was one of America's first aerial photographers. Prior to

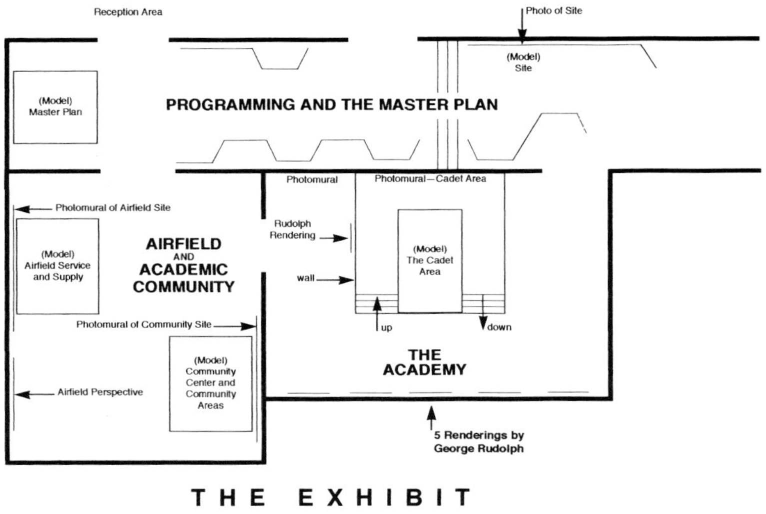

74. Plan of the 14–15 May 1955 exhibition at the Colorado Springs Fine Arts Center. From the reception area, visitors proceeded in a counterclockwise direction across the corridor and through several rooms, eventually reentering the corridor at its far end. Redrawn from original plans by Robert Nauman.

World War II he worked as an architectural photographer, but it was his aerial photography from the postwar period that was sought by magazines such as *Fortune*. In 1955, Beaumont Newhall gave him his initial one-man exhibition, the first ever devoted to aerial photography, at the George Eastman House in Rochester, New York.[11] That same year, Edward Steichen included Garnett's photographs in his famous "Family of Man" exhibition at the Museum of Modern Art.[12]

Adams's and Garnett's landscape photography was supplemented by the illustrations of George Cooper Rudolph, an accomplished free-lance delineator living in New York. He received a contract from Skidmore, Owings & Merrill to produce eight 40-x-60-inch illustrations of the proposed academy design.[13] Rudolph used an opaque water-based paint in these illustrations, which provided scenes of human interaction in the architectural surroundings.[14] His colorful renderings not only provided a contrast to the black and white photographs and models, but were easily accessible and understood by a viewing public that, for the most part, lacked architectural training.

The site of the exhibition was the Colorado Springs Fine Arts Center.[15] The Air Force Academy exhibition took place primarily in the Southwest Museum and Indian Museum rooms, the walls of which were covered by draperies and murals. Within this transformed atmosphere, a carefully choreographed sequence of spaces greeted the visitors (fig. 74). After leaving the reception area, visitors went through a doorway, crossed a corridor, and began a counterclockwise journey through several rooms. As they crossed the corridor, they passed an alcove to their right which contained a model of the entire Academy design. Behind it, against a solid blue wall flanked by curtains, were the words, "THE MASTER PLAN" (fig. 75). This was the only model in the exhibit that was not backed by a photomural. The model, elevated to waist height, served to introduce the complex Academy program, and the uppercase letters, against their celestial background, set the mood for the rest of the exhibition.

The first room past the corridor was devoted to the airfield and academic community areas. Models of those areas, backed by gigantic black and white photomurals of Adams and Garnett, were accompanied by explanatory texts (fig. 76).[16] The panoramic photographs and architectural models created a dramatic mood—a mood that was heightened as the visitors ascended several steps to enter the next room.

In that second room, they first confronted a Rudolph illustration and a title plaque. Forced by the wall to continue their counterclockwise progression, they proceeded around the corner to reach the exhibition centerpiece, a large model of the central Cadet Area mounted on a platform (fig. 77). After climbing four steps, visitors circled the model before descending a set of stairs at the opposite side. A spectacular photomural of the area by Ansel Adams covered the back wall. Five more of George Rudolph's renderings hung opposite the photomural.

On leaving this room, the visitors reentered the corridor they originally had crossed. Along the corridor's perimeter, panels, designed by Bayer, projected obliquely from the walls. Text,

75. View of exhibition. SOM photograph. An intoductory corridor contained a site model and informational panels designed by Herbert Bayer explaining climatic conditions, water supply, and the airfield. SOM Archives, Chicago.

76. View of exhibition. SOM photograph. The first room the visitors entered at the 1955 exhibition displayed models and enormous photomurals of the airfield and academic community areas by Ansel Adams and William Garnett. The explanatory text at the right is divided into two parts: "The Airfield" and "The Base Service and Supply Area." SOM Archives, Chicago.

75

76

77. View of exhibition. SOM photograph. The centerpiece of the May 1955 exhibition was an enormous model of the Central Cadet area backed by an Ansel Adams photomural. On the wall opposite the Adams mural hung five George Cooper Rudolph illustrations. SOM Archives, Chicago.

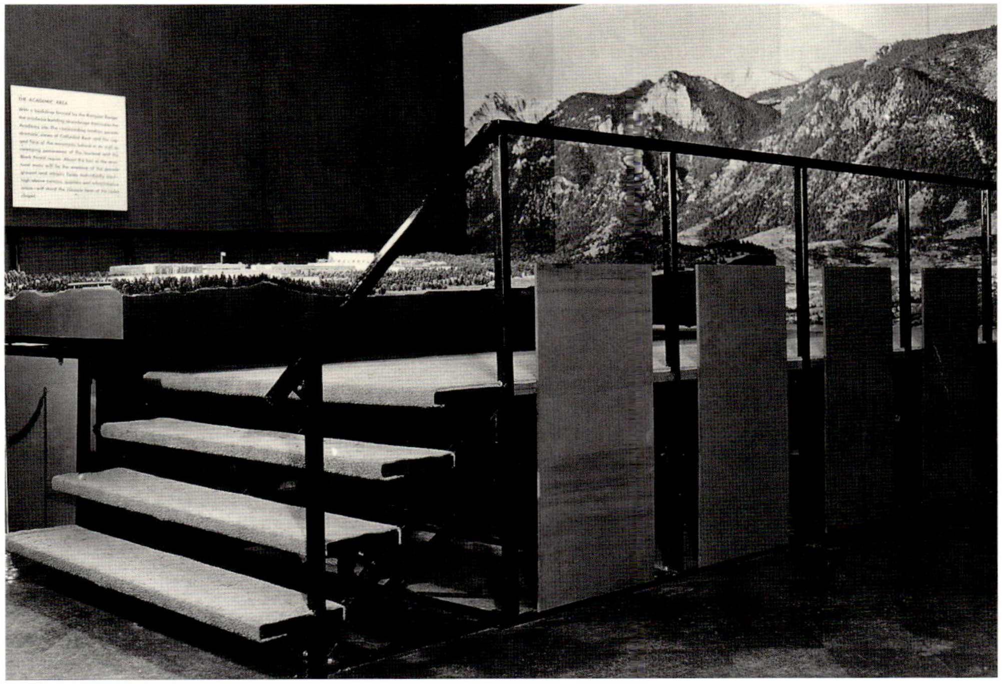

graphics, and photomontage combined to explain regional zoning regulations, transportation, climate, water supply, airfield and aviation conditions, and the cadet educational program. At the far end of the hallway, where the tour had begun, the perspective converged on the alcove with its model and text, “THE MASTER PLAN,” reminding the viewers that all they had seen and were about to see was part of that grand plan.

This exhibition, which Nathaniel Owings would later refer to as “great theater,”[17] created a vision of an Air Force Academy based on the notion of a heroic past progressing toward a utopian and technologically determinate future. Particularly revealing is the manner in which the mythic historical nature of this site in the West was integrated with the aspirations of modern architecture.

Despite the programmatic requirements that the new Academy be situated near a cultural center, accessible by highway, with available utilities and a water supply, the photomurals of Adams and Garnett conveyed little evidence of human presence. Instead, they depicted a pristine environment of mountains, foothills, mesas, valleys, and plain, recalling the vast “uninhabited” tracts of the frontier West. The Academy models, and by implication the Academy itself, were situated in the midst of the uninhabited “wilderness” of the photographs. The Academy functioned metaphorically as a frontier city, defining the boundary between education, order, and civilization and its untamed, uncivilized counterpart.[18] This allowed the viewer to engage in a psychological dialogue in which the development and conquest of the West by heroic pioneers could be metaphorically linked to the heroic achievements of a country emerging triumphant from a world war. Because moral and political imperatives are often simplified through myth,[19] the link between heroic cavalrymen battling the savage red man to protect and advance civilization in the West, and between Air Force pilots protecting the civilized Western world from fascism and the "Red Menace" was easily made. Mediating between the myth of the pioneer civilizing the West and the pilot insuring the sanctity of the free world, was the concept of Manifest Destiny, another aspect of American mythology.[20]

As defined by John O'Sullivan and others in the 1840s, the United States had a "manifest destiny" mandated by God—a national destiny—to expand across the continent. This notion implied an opportunity for populated territories to join the republic, freeing themselves from the constraints of tyrannical or totalitarian political systems.[21] During the Spanish-American War, this concept of continental expansion shifted from one of incorporation and inclusion of neighboring peoples in the republic to a policy of guardianship that expanded beyond national boundaries. During the Cold War, the term gained new import: "making the world safe for democracy," as well as extending United States influence through investment abroad, were among the objectives of the Eisenhower administration. These mythic associations to Manifest Destiny and the Western frontier were evoked within the context of wilderness as a zone of confrontation. But wilderness also served as metaphor for another uniquely American experience—that of the individual within a democratic society.

In declaring the frontier closed as of the 1890s, Frederick Jackson Turner launched a reassessment of the idea and nature of wilderness. In his writings he compared the American and European experiences, stating of the American: "Out of the wilderness experience, out of the freedom of his opportunities, he fashioned a formula for social regeneration—the freedom of the individual to seek his own."[22] Wilderness was recast by Turner, not as a counter to civilization, but as a beneficent influence upon civilization. As he noted, "the very fact of wilderness appealed to men as a fair, blank page on which to write a new chapter in the story of man's struggle for a higher type of society."[23] This association of wilderness with a utopian and democratic society was a theme reinforced by Theodore Roosevelt, who perceived wilderness as a means to recapture that which made us uniquely American.[24] It was this "cult of wilderness," the return to the mythic domain of the pioneer as metaphor for individual and cultural freedom, which Ansel Adams addressed. As his biographer Mary Street Alinder noted: "he believed in . . . the deeply romantic idea that the great vistas and microscopic details of the wilderness could be seen as metaphor for freedom and heroic aspiration. Adams's photographs seem to demonstrate that the world is what we wish it was—a place with room in it for fresh beginnings."[25]

Proponents of the wilderness never intended those "fresh beginnings" to occur within a technological void. It was, after all, through the development of transportation and communication systems that the wilderness had been opened to civilization.[26] Indeed, the concept of wilderness has, since ancient times, only existed within the context of civilization. The ancient Greeks contrasted the Dionysian spirits which inhabited the wilderness with the Apollonian rationalism of civilized man. Early settlers of this country had a similar outlook, but their solution was to subjugate rather than integrate those forces. As railroads opened this continent, wilderness experience entered into a new relationship with civilization. Nineteenth-century photographers such as William Henry Jackson and Carleton Watkins accompanied geological survey teams into the West and produced photographs of natural wonders that were used to secure congressional funding for both the preservation and future development of those areas.[27] Jackson's 1871 photographs of Yellowstone, for example, were used to secure its designation as a national park, but they also became the subject of interest to the Northern Pacific Railroad, which envisioned the park's potential as a tourist mecca, similar to Niagara Falls.[28]

The photographs of Garnett and Adams, also marked by the absence of man, paradoxically conveyed the potential of a technological state to preserve and maintain the environment. The belief that progress resulted from the application of science and technology to harness the raw forces of nature was not incompatible with Adams's or Garnett's attitudes. Nature, as re-presented in Adams's photographs, is not so much wilderness as nature tamed. A sense of disciplined structure informs his images, as he carefully orders the landscape through his camera lens.[29] Garnett's use of aerial technology in procuring his imagery is obvious. His photographs have been described as having "a kind of god's-eye awareness," but that too is an awareness ordered by man.[30] His photographs often reveal patterns of design either imposed by man or, if imposed by nature, framed and structured by man.

Bayer's graphics reinforced that notion of technology in the service of mankind. Facing the small site-model on the right side of the corridor was a panel that displayed a large figure of a man—a classical nude—with a jet plane superimposed across his

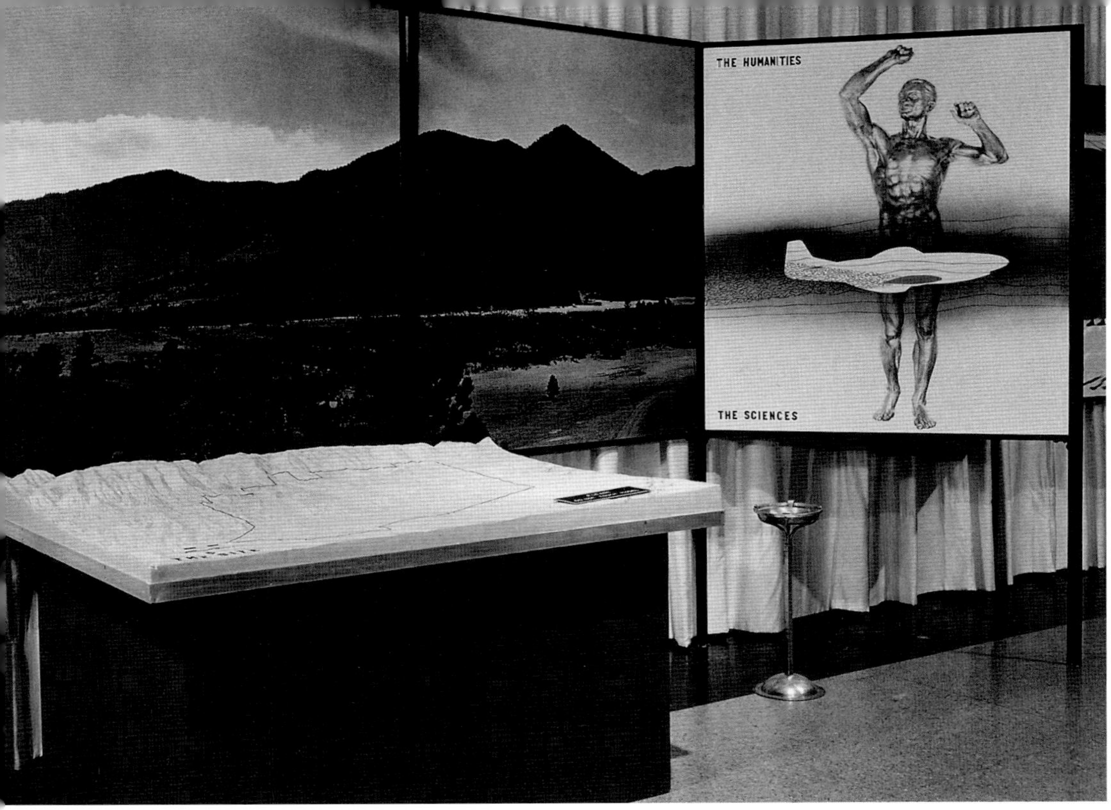

78. View of exhibition. SOM photograph. This display in the corridor included a site model, backed by a William Garnett photomural, and a supergraphic by Herbert Bayer. SOM Archives, Chicago.

midsection (fig. 78). To the upper left were the words "The Humanities," at the bottom left "The Sciences." Technology here, quite literally, inscribed itself across the geography of human existence. Along with survey charts and data analysis of the region, the panels were interspersed with photographs of men and aircraft. The ordering of the site, and of the world, was placed in the capable hands of "humane science"—the "master plan" was a plan for insuring world peace and prosperity.[31]

This ordering structure was made apparent to the exhibition visitors as they viewed the models. Seen from an aerial vantage point—one reinforced by the vast panoramic murals—they reestablished the belief that rational man presided over the random and irrational forces of nature. The effect of circling the primary model, raised approximately a foot off the platform floor, was akin to the experience of flying over the site. From that perspective, the grid plan of the central cadet area, superimposed on the natural terrain, was easily perceived, reinforcing a belief and faith in technological mandates. That was a belief that perfectly reflected United States military policy in the Cold War era.

It had become apparent during World War II that the future of defense systems would be aerial technology. Eisenhower's "New Look" defense policy, unveiled in 1955, concentrated on nuclear deployment systems that deemphasized conventional strike forces in favor of aerial delivery capabilities.[32] The enhanced role of the Air Force in protecting and watching over the world was quite literally alluded to by the placement of the models at the Colorado Springs exhibition. As the mythic hero, the Air Force pilot could assume the omnipotent power and vantage point of God. It was a position voiced by the legendary pilot Charles Lindbergh. Lindbergh, who had been a member of the Site Selection Committee that had chosen the Colorado Springs site the previous year, wrote, "I began to feel that I had lived on a higher plane than the skeptics on the ground. In flying, I tasted a wine of the gods of which they could know nothing."[33]

If all these mythic connotations were active at the exhibition, the architecture participated in a myth of its own invention. Since the early part of the century, modern architecture defined itself as an avant-garde movement which, in reflecting the technological developments of its age, selectively edited historical precedent with mythic references to the past.[34] The Swiss Modernist architect Le Corbusier, for example, illustrated his 1923 treatise, *Vers une Architecture,* with photographs comparing architectural and technological forms, such as the Parthenon and airplanes. His implication was that the airplane had become the classical expression of its own age—an aesthetic form generated through the precision and standardization of a technological world, as the repetitive rhythm of the airplane struts created a structural analogy to classical temples. As he stated, "We may then affirm that the airplane mobilized invention, intelligence and daring: imagination and cold reason. It is the same spirit that built the Parthenon."[35]

This approach, of using an edited architectural past to evoke the technological present, was shared by the partners of Skidmore, Owings & Merrill, who often compared their architecture to that of

79. View of Cadet Area. Rendering by George Cooper Rudolph, c. 1955. This rendering by Rudolph, shown at the May 1955 exhibition, depicts (from left to right) the Library, Chapel (in background), and Cadet Quarters. Adverse reaction to the Chapel design led to a series of design revisions.

classical edifices and Gothic cathedrals, as technological expressions of their eras. The classical comparison alluded to the clear expression of both the structural skeleton and the organizing grid which informed the architecture, an aspect of structural expression that was a characteristic of the International Style of Modern architecture as it had been codified in the 1931 exhibition at the Museum of Modern Art.[36] In the case of the Air Force Academy, the analogy to a classical past linked the modernist architectural myth to others which had specifically American implications.

Early in the design process, the architects made it common knowledge that the central Cadet Area was to be located atop one of the site's mesas, and referred to that aspect of the design as "Acropolis-like."[37] The primary model at the exhibition metaphorically recalled that association, with the elements of dramatic approach, disclosure and enclosure, ascent and descent, and backdrop of mythical landscape evoking that site. What better analogue for a military and educational institution than the Acropolis, precinct of Athena, classical goddess of defense and wisdom? Those connotations were also within an American architectural tradition that associated classical architecture with the classical ideals of virtue and democracy, a tradition which extended from the eighteenth century to the present in an unbroken series of public buildings. The metaphorical references linked the Academy architecture to that tradition, while allowing Skidmore, Owings & Merrill to avoid the revivalist style that some of their detractors sought.

Finally, evocation of a heroic classical past complemented the myth of the frontier at the level of heroic personal achievement. In his autobiography, Nathaniel Owings twice referred to the "Olympian" efforts of the architects in realizing the Academy design, once in describing their Colorado Springs exhibition and again in describing their struggle in the face of the skepticism of members of the armed forces, Congress, the public, and certain members of the architectural community.[38] Owings created an analogy between past and present: the architect as "civilized" hero, who has insight into the meaning of his contemporary situation and leads an "avant-garde" against the "uncivilized Philistines."

Skidmore, Owings & Merrill were fully aware of the subtle implications of Adams's and Garnett's photomurals and the siting of the Academy in the context of both the Cold War and architectural history. And certainly Herbert Bayer, who had used photography as a propaganda tool in his wartime exhibitions, was well acquainted with the medium's psychological power. His dramatic union of murals and models drew on that power, while his text and graphics explained programmatic requirements.

Mediating between these dramatic and informational elements were the illustrations of George Cooper Rudolph. Five of those renderings were organized in a sequence along the far wall of the second room, opposite the centerpiece model, and led the viewer back into the corridor. They represented the Library Court, the Dining Hall, the Court of Honor, the Physical Education Building, and an aerial of the entire Cadet Area.

The first image, showing the Library Court, represented rows of cadets in formation (fig. 79). They march from the distant right background seeming to emerge from the mountainous backdrop, to the left foreground, past the Chapel and Library. The image at once united the natural world of God, the man-made temple of God, and the temple of technological learning, while also uniting the present to a heroic classical past, as phalanxes of warriors march against a backdrop of classical architecture.

If that image represented the disciplined military activities of the cadets, the three images that followed showed concern for their physical, social, and religious well-being, while the final aerial rendering reiterated rational man's role in creating order out of chaos. Natural forms were minimized, while architectural forms predominated and framed the views. As surrounding nature entered the site, it was thinned and regularized to conform to the architectural grid. In this precinct, reason and technology ruled. Together these renderings illustrated the structured world of the cadet, while still drawing on the mythic content of the rest of the exhibition.

Within this carefully choreographed exhibition, designer Herbert Bayer created a vision of the Academy that mirrored the country's hopes for a future of opportunity and tranquility. It simultaneously recalled the country's past history while underscoring the appropriateness of the chosen architectural style. Notions of the glory of the United States during the nineteenth century were evoked by the photographs of Ansel Adams and William Garnett, while the political agenda of the United States in the mid-twentieth century—one of overseeing a peaceful and harmonious world order through a position of technological superiority—was maintained. These readings were not intended exclusively for the cadets attending the Academy but for a public facing the threat of nuclear disaster. The presentation, and subsequent architecture, provided a realm of security in a world that was becoming increasingly complex.

Photography and Modernism As the architectural plans for the Academy became architectural reality, Skidmore, Owings & Merrill sought the services of a photographic firm whose images could document the physical reality of their design and at the same time illustrate the rhetoric and reality of a specific architectural point of view and provide positive images compatible with American Cold War ideology. For images that would be disseminated to the public through both architectural journals and the popular press, it was important for the architects to do more than simply provide "pictures of buildings." Skidmore, Owings & Merrill turned to Hedrich-Blessing, also based in Chicago.[39]

Founded in 1929 by Ken Hedrich and Hank Blessing, the firm retained the hyphenated name even though Blessing left the partnership in 1930. Ken Hedrich quickly added to the firm's roster by hiring, among others, his brothers Ed and Bill. Their team approach to architectural photography was similar to the design approach of Skidmore, Owings & Merrill, in that each member of the firm had a particular area of specialty, such as the photography of interior or exterior spaces, or of architectural models.[40] For the Air Force Academy projects, it was Hube Henry who, in April 1955, photographed the earliest models, while Bill Engdahl photographed the model of the Dining Hall in October 1955. But it was Bill Hedrich's 1959 photographs of the realized architecture that came to be best known.

Hedrich-Blessing first achieved renown with its dramatic architectural photographs of the 1933 Chicago World's Fair, the "Century of Progress."[41] Ken Hedrich's black and white photographs of the fair made use of theatrical lighting effects in capturing the excitement of its dominant Art Deco architectural style. Although Adolf Hitler had proclaimed himself dictator of Germany in spring of the same year and the storm clouds preceding World War II had begun to gather, these images offered a utopian view of the future. As one critic noted, "What is most striking about Hedrich-Blessing's photographs of the exposition is the visual exuberance, the flair for the dramatic, and the essential spirit of futurism that is shared by both image and building."[42] Upon their surfaces, architectural imagery became symbolic of technology and standardization, and of the rationally ordered universe of the future.

The members of the firm continued to refine their photographic techniques during the following decades. No longer content to use wide-angle lenses to frame entire buildings in symmetrical

80

80. View of Library Staircase. Photograph by Hedrich-Blessing, 1959. Bill Hedrich's photograph of the helical staircase of the Library is quite similar in composition to his brother Ken's 1942 photograph of the spiral staircase in the May Residence in Ladue Missouri. Staircases were a favorite subject of the Hedrich-Blessing firm, perhaps due to their inherent biomorphic formal quality, which was often contrasted to the rectilinear planes of architectural designs. Chicago Historical Society: Hedrich-Blessing #22362 I2.
81. View of Dining Hall at night. Photograph by Hedrich-Blessing, 1959. The Dining Hall, its geometric gridded patterns contrasting with pools of light outside, displays the transparent quality of the Academy architecture. This photographic angle, with a clear view of the twenty-two-foot cantilevered roof, also conveys the essence of the structural capabilities of the steel frame. Chicago Historical Society: Hedrich-Blessing #22362 O.

81

compositions, they selectively framed their subject, often letting a portion take the place of the whole.[43] Their aesthetic concerns focused on the relationship of those parts, as arranged within the confines of the photographic frame. In other words, rather than depicting how architectural spaces actually functioned, Hedrich-Blessing began concentrating more on purely formal issues: the relationship between a curved staircase and the photographic frame that contained it; the contrast between the solid planes of a building's facade, captured from an oblique angle, and the spatial void that surrounded it; the juxtaposition of geometric forms in space (figs. 80, 81).[44]

Nature is noticeably absent in these photographs. It is a world created by man and his technology, as the geometric units create their own aesthetic language that is encased within, and determined by, the photographic frame. That frame, in turn, creates a transparent window through which the ordering structure of the universe is revealed. It was a similar ordering structure that the architects sought to reveal beneath the transparent planes of glass that defined their architecture.[45]

The Academy architecture recalled the tenets of the International Style, as defined by Henry-Russell Hitchcock and Philip Johnson in *The International Style: Architecture Since 1922*. In that manifesto of architectural Modernism, the authors emphasized the importance of expression of volume, rather than mass, as an essential characteristic of Modernist design. They declared that "the surfaces shall be unbroken in effect, like a skin tightly stretched over the supporting skeleton."[46] They further stated that windows "constitute a more important element in modern architecture than they have in any architecture since that of the Gothic cathedrals."[47] It was the use of transparent planes that allowed the structural elements to be revealed—not the massive bearing walls of earlier design, but the piers of steel or reinforced concrete that reflected the technological developments of the modern era, permitting an architecture of volume.

Bill Hedrich's photographs of the completed Academy illustrated those defining characteristics of Modernist architecture. Many of his photographs were exterior shots and clearly captured the structural grid of steel and glass (fig. 83). His intent was not to frame the architecture in a static symmetrical image, but to convey the regularity of its organizing grid while producing a dynamic composition, a technique analogous to that used by Modernist designers. Hitchcock and Johnson had urged architects to adopt a Modern style that would avoid axially symmetrical compositions; they encouraged, instead, compositions based on a sense of regularity and balance defined by the application of standardized units.[48]

If the Academy architecture revealed the logic of its three-dimensional nature by exposing its own internal structure, Hedrich's Academy photographs revealed their two-dimensional reality through similar structural concerns. It becomes difficult to distinguish a dormitory from a dining hall, as the functional realities of the architectural space become less an issue than does the production of eloquent patterns of forms on the two-dimensional photographic surface. If human figures or fragments of the landscape appear, they are used as a counterpoint and balance to the rigid architectural forms, much as Hedrich-Blessing's earlier photographs had juxtaposed various geometric shapes for contrast

82. View of Cadet Quarters. Photograph by Hedrich-Blessing, 1959. The geometric grid of the architecture, defined by the light, contrasts with the fine network of railing and human figure, creating a dynamic composition and exquisite interplay between the parts. Chicago Historical Society: Hedrich-Blessing #22362 J.

83. View of Cadet Quarters. Photograph by Hedrick-Blessing, 1959. A composition of geometric parts, this photograph juxtaposes the natural and man-made environments while capturing the literal transparency of the architecture. Chicago Historical Society: Hedrich-Blessing #22362 G.

82

(figs. 73, 82). The various components of Bill Hedrich's black and white images are clearly delineated by contrasting dark tones against light, creating abstract patterns that divide the page into zones dictated by formal concerns. That abstract quality contributed to a feeling of timelessness. Existing as they do in a world in which activities, or even seasons, are seldom indicated, these images simply are. And in that regard they also reinforced the theoretical intent of the architecture they recorded.

Hedrich's Academy photographs expressed and reinforced the technological metaphor of efficiency and modernity that proponents of the Academy employed. As Harold Talbott, former Secretary of the Air Force, stated, "We want the Academy to be a living embodiment of the modernity of flying and to represent in its architectural concepts the national character of the Academy. . . . We want our structures to be as efficient and as flexible in their design as the most modern projected aircraft."[49] It was an environment that Hedrich often photographed at an oblique angle, creating a visual analogy to the dynamic quality of supersonic flight, with the lines of the facades rushing into the distance. That technological metaphor was sometimes underscored by the inclusion of automobiles, or cropped fragments of them, in the foregrounds of the images (fig. 84).

The automobile had been a favorite symbol for "new world" technology since the Italian poet and editor F. T. Marinetti had used it as a metaphor for progress in his 1908 Futurist manifesto.[50] It was further associated with architectural Modernism in Le Corbusier's seminal *Vers une Architecture* of 1923. There he referred to the automobile's standardized construction as an argument for the potential efficiency of architectural standardization.[51] Ken Hedrich's images from the 1933 World's Fair, as well as his images of the following decade, abounded with depictions of the architectural creations of the automotive industry. In those photographs, the automobiles themselves were often depicted in the foreground, where they served as indicators of the advanced technological status of the United States. By the mid-1950s, the automobile had become a distinctly American icon, embracing notions of freedom and serving as a barometer for "taste" and "style." The purpose for Bill Hedrich's inclusion of its image in some of his Academy photographs was twofold. Its sleek aerodynamic lines perfectly complemented the geometric purity of the architecture, while it metaphorically evoked the promises of aerospace technology.

In addition to the technological metaphors they conveyed, Hedrich's photographs functioned as optimistic images of a democratic society. The underlying structure that ordered the architectural

83

84. View of Academic Building and retaining wall for Terrazzo Level. Photograph by Hedrich-Blessing, 1959. The automobile, symbol of American technology and mobility, provides a perfect contrast and complement to the architecture of an air academy. The composition of this photograph, by Bill Hedrich, is very similar to his brother Ken's 1943 photograph of Mies van der Rohe's Metallurgy Building at the Illinois Institute of Technology in Chicago. The quotation of the earlier photograph, symbolically linking Mies to the Academy design, may be more than coincidental. Chicago Historical Society: Hedrich-Blessing #22362 A2.

and photographic spaces corresponded to the optimistic notion that harmony and order could be maintained in the world through the judicious use of technology. There was, as well, a "truth" to this architecture, an honest expression of materials revealed through glass: "The architect who builds in the international style seeks to display the true character of his construction."[52] Glass, like the photographic image, is a surface through which one sees the world "as it really is." What better material for a military academy of the free world? Our Cold War adversaries were associated with deception and betrayal—concealment. Glass reveals and discloses the activities it contains.

Of course, photography has its own "truth." Although it is a medium that by its very nature is assumed to record in an objective fashion, it is a record framed and ordered by the eye behind the viewfinder. In a photograph, the image reveals whatever the photographer decides to emphasize; in that regard its truth is only partial. Its audience must decide whose truth it reveals, and whose purpose it serves. It was not the purpose of the Hedrich-Blessing photographs to reveal the contradictions and complexities of a decade. They did not attempt to document specific instances of cadet life, nor did they try to provide insight into the United States military establishment. In fact, they did not even attempt to re-create an actual architectural experience—how the buildings were approached, entered, and used. As eloquent images which emphasized certain formal relationships, they were meant to be serene and beautiful depictions of an architectural environment; their tone was optimistic, their message relatively uncomplicated. They presented an environment where discipline and rationality were valued, and where the world and history were still domains that, at least hypothetically, could be presided over and ordered by "the men behind the viewfinder"—be they airmen or architects.

Notes

1. Akiko Busch, *The Photography of Architecture* (New York: Van Nostrand Reinhold, 1987), 124.
2. Ibid., 123.
3. For more background on the period, see J. Ronald Oakley, *God's Country: America in the Fifties* (New York: Dembner Books, 1986), 147–327.
4. Ibid., 219.
5. For a discussion of some of the issues of nuclear technology in the Cold War period, see Paul Boyer, *By the Bomb's Early Light: American Thought and Culture at the Dawn of the Atomic Age* (New York: Pantheon, 1985). For a critical view of post-war technology, see Michael L. Smith's " 'Planetary Engineering': The Strange Career of Progress in Nuclear America," in *Possible Dreams,* a series of essays edited by John L. Wright (Dearborn: Henry Ford Museum and Greenfield Village, 1992), 111–23. And for issues of Cold War ideology and the Air Force Academy, see Richard Gid Powers, "The Cold War in the Rockies: American Ideology and the Air Force Academy Design," *Art Journal* 32, no. 4 (Summer 1974): 304–13.
6. For information on Bayer's background in exhibition design, see Gwen Finkel Chanzit, *Herbert Bayer and Modernist Design in America* (Ann Arbor: UMI Research Press, 1987), 111–50. Dr. Chanzit is currently curator of the Bayer Archives at the Denver Art Museum.
7. Ibid., 132. Also see James Sloan Allen, *The Romance of Commerce and Culture* (Chicago: University of Chicago Press, 1983), for Bayer's alliance with the Container Corporation of America, its director, Walter Paepke, and the Aspen Institute in Colorado. Interestingly, Bayer was selected to design the Air Force Museum at Dayton, Ohio, in 1959, but his project was unrealized.
8. Ansel Adams and Mary Street Alinder, *Ansel Adams: An Autobiography* (Boston: Little, Brown, 1985), 203. The Adams bibliography is extensive, but two canonical writings are this autobiography and Nancy Newhall, *Ansel Adams: The Eloquent Light* (New York: Harper and Row, 1980). A more critical series of essays dealing with the man and his myth is *Ansel Adams: New Light* (San Francisco: Friends of Photography, 1993).
9. Charles Hagen, "Land and Landscape," *Aperture,* no. 120 (Summer 1990): 16.
10. See the exhibition catalogue: Ansel Adams and Nancy Newhall, *This Is the American Earth* (San Francisco: Sierra Club, 1960).
11. Natalie Canavor, "William Garnett: Flying a 37-year Mission," *Popular Photography* 89, no. 12 (December 1982): 133.
12. Eric Lax, "William A. Garnett," *American Photographer* 4, no. 2 (February 1980): 50–60. For more biographical background on Garnett, also see the following: Edward Park, "Part Picasso and Part Red Baron," *Smithsonian* 8, no. 2 (May 1977): 74–81; and the special section on aerial photography in *American Photographer* 2, no. 5 (May 1979): 31–3 and 48–52. Mr. Garnett is still actively pursuing his photographic interests. In 1969 he collaborated with Nathaniel Owings on *The American Aesthetic* (New York: Harper and Row), and in 1982 his book *The Extraordinary Landscape* was published, with an introduction by Ansel Adams (Boston: Little, Brown). His latest collection of photographs is scheduled to be published by the University of California Press in late 1994.
13. This information was provided by George Cooper Rudolph in a telephone conversation of 22 June 1993.
14. In 1955, photographs of Rudolph's renderings of the Academy appeared in the following publications: the May 15 editions of the *New York Times,* the *Denver Post,* and the *Colorado Springs Gazette Telegraph*; the June issues of *Architectural Record* and *Architectural Forum,* as well as the August issue of *Architecture Forum;* the May 27 issue of *U.S. News;* the August issue of *Flying*; the August 1 issue of *Newsweek;* and the summer issue of *Art News.*
15. The Colorado Springs Fine Arts Center was itself a noted work by the New Mexico architect John Gaw Meem. Meem's style of regionalism marked an attempt to merge traditional Pueblo and Spanish Colonial styles with a modern language of unadorned geometric volumes. The Colorado Springs Fine Arts Center suggested that style in the massing and simplicity of its forms, but the expression of the monolithic poured-concrete structure, in which the marks of the wooden forms remained exposed, was more thoroughly modern. To record his own architectural achievements, Meem himself had at times retained Ansel Adams. For more on the Fine Arts

Center architecture, see Bainbridge Bunting, *John Gaw Meem* (Albuquerque: University of New Mexico Press, 1983), 145–54.

16. In telephone conversations on 18 March 1993, and 3 June 1993, William Garnett provided the following information on the process of constructing these murals: Adams and Garnett were flown to Denver the previous month by Skidmore, Owings & Merrill, transported to the site, and given the weekend to photograph. The negatives were then rushed to Bayer in Aspen, where they were enlarged and meticulously pieced together to form the gigantic photomurals hung at the exhibition.

17. Nathaniel Owings, *The Spaces in Between* (Boston: Houghton Mifflin, 1973), 156.

18. For a discussion of myth, and its application to the American Frontier and current events, see Richard Slotkin, *The Fatal Environment: The Myth of the Frontier in the Age of Industrialization* (New York: Atheneum, 1985), 3–47.

19. Ibid., 19. Slotkin terms this the "either/or" aspect of myth, which he identifies as an archetypal response rooted in collective and personal memory.

20. The issue of Manifest Destiny and its resonance and recurrence as a theme in the history of the Western United States has been well documented by Western historians. See for example, Gerald D. Nash, *Creating the West: Historical Interpretations,* 1890–1990 (Albuquerque: University of New Mexico Press, 1991), 225–30. Nash relates that in an acceptance speech for a civil rights award in 1953, Eisenhower mentioned his birthplace of Abilene, and the fact that its marshall had been Wild Bill Hickok. Like that mythic hero, Eisenhower urged Americans to face their foes in the Cold War period of which they were part. Citing the increased interest in the cowboy symbol as a cultural image in the postwar era, Nash notes "[the cowboy] is heir to an imposing body of emotions associated with the Manifest Destiny of the United States in the Far West." Also see Patricia Nelson Limerick, *The Legacy of Conquest: The Unbroken Past of the American West* (New York: W. W. Norton, 1987). Deborah Bright addresses the issue of Manifest Destiny and postwar landscape photography (including that of Ansel Adams) in her essay "Victory Gardens: The Public Landscape of Postwar America", in *Multiple Views,* Daniel Younger, ed. (Albuquerque: University of New Mexico Press, 1991), 329–61.

21. The concept of Manifest Destiny and its relationship to nineteenth-century expansionist policies in the United States is the focus of Frederick Merk's text, *Manifest Destiny and Mission in American History* (New York: Vintage Books, 1963).

22. Roderick Nash, *Wilderness and the American Mind* (New Haven: Yale University Press, 1967), 146.

23. Ibid., 146.

24. For a discussion of the development of this "wilderness cult," see ibid., 141–60.

25. Alinder, *Ansel Adams: Classic Images* (Boston: Little, Brown, 1986) 6.

26. Merk, *Manifest Destiny,* 50–51.

27. Two texts that provide an overview of the history of nineteenth-century landscape photography history are Beaumont Newhall, *The History of Photography* (New York: Museum of Modern Art, 1964), and Naomi Rosenblum, *A World History of Photography* (New York: Abbeville Press, 1984).

28. Nash, *Wilderness*, 111.

29. A source that deals with contemporary issues of American photography is Jonathan Green, *American Photography: A Critical History, 1945 to the Present* (New York: Harry Abrams, 1984). Pages 27–35 are especially useful in explaining the zone system, which Ansel Adams employed as a means of controlling image contrast and tone before the shutter was even released. Also see Bruce Nixon, "Saint Ansel of Yosemite," *Artweek* 22, no. 21 (6 June 1991): 12.

30. Lax, "Garnett," 50.

31. A fascinating collection of essays dealing with utopian views of technology is the previously mentioned *Possible Dreams,* edited by John L. Wright.

32. Oakley, *God's Country,* 211–12. Oakley notes the effect this had on the budget of the armed forces: in 1955, the Army's budget was cut by $4 billion and the Navy's was cut by $1.5 billion, while the Air Force's budget increased in the amount of $800 million.

33. Quoted in Judith Hicks Stiehm, *Bring Me Men and Women* (Berkeley: University of California Press, 1981), 52.

34. Two seminal texts that offered this view of Modernism were Le Corbusier, *Vers une Architecture*, first published in 1923 in French, and translated into English in 1927 as *Towards a New Architecture,* by Frederick Etchells (New York: Dover Press,

1986), and Sigfried Giedion, *Space, Time, and Architecture*, written as an outgrowth of lectures and seminars delivered at Harvard University and translated in 1940 by W. J. Callagan and Erwart Matthews (Cambridge: Harvard University Press, 1956).

35. Le Corbusier, *Vers une Architecture*, 109.

36. The text published concurrently with that exhibition was *The International Style: Architecture Since 1922*, co-authored by the exhibition's organizers, Henry-Russell Hitchcock and Philip Johnson (New York: Norton, 1966).

37. Owings, *The Spaces in Between,* 155.

38. Owings at one point actually compared the firm's partners with Ictinus, Callicrates, and Phidias, the designers and patron of the Parthenon. Ibid., 156 and 153.

39. This is not to imply that Hedrich-Blessing adjusted its photographic style to fit the demands of Skidmore, Owings & Merrill, but rather that their photographic style was sympathetic to the firm's architectural agenda. Of the firms employed by Skidmore, Owings & Merrill to photograph the Academy, Hedrich-Blessing was the one whose images were most often published. For the relationship of Hedrich-Blessing's photography to other photography of the time, see Cervin Robinson and Joel Herschman, *Architecture Transformed* (Cambridge: MIT Press, 1987). Robinson specifically addresses the firm's work in "Part III: 1930 to 1970" (pages 107, 123, and 143).

40. Robert Sobieszek, *The Architectural Photography of Hedrich-Blessing* (New York: Holt, Rinehart and Winston, 1984), 4. For more insight into Hedrich-Blessing's approach to architectural photography, see Busch, *The Photography of Architecture,* 121–55; and David Lowe, "Hedrich-Blessing," *Interior Design* 51, no. 10 (October 1980): 265–81. The Chicago Historical Society has the collection of Hedrich-Blessing negatives taken prior to 1969.

41. At that fair, Louis Skidmore worked as chief of design. He, in turn, offered Nathaniel Owings the job as development supervisor. Three years later the two formed the partnership that would soon become the architectural firm of Skidmore, Owings & Merrill.

42. Sobieszek, *Photography of Hedrich-Blessing,* 9.

43. Ibid., 7.

44. Ken Hedrich's series of architectural photographs from the years 1942–43 offer interesting comparisons, in terms of similar subjects and compositions, to Bill Hedrich's 1959 Air Force Academy work.

45. The issue of transparency in modern architecture was analyzed by Colin Rowe in his essay "Transparency: Literal and Phenomenal," in *The Mathematics of the Ideal Villa and Other Essays* (Cambridge: MIT Press, 1976), 159–83.

46. Hitchcock and Johnson, *The International Style*, 45.

47. Ibid., 46.

48. Ibid., 59.

49. Hearings before the Subcommittee of the Committee on Appropriations, House of Representatives, 84th Congress, 1st Session, 30 June 1955, 224.

50. For the entire text of the Futurist Manifesto, see Herschel B. Chipp, *Theories of Modern Art* (Berkeley: University of California Press, 1968), 284–89.

51. Le Corbusier, *Towards a New Architecture,* 135.

52. Hitchcock and Johnson, 44.

85. Color sketch of uniform design, rendered by John Jensen, c. 1956. Cecil B. DeMille reassigned his best costume designers from the film *The Ten Commandments* to work on the new uniforms for the Air Force Academy. John Jensen's sketches bear DeMille's final "OK" in red in the lower right corner. Shown is the winter parade dress uniform. U.S. Air Force Academy Collections.

Sheri Olson

A Comprehensive Design Vision

In their plans the designers of the Air Force Academy tried to take every element into consideration, from the mass of color presented by the uniforms of the 2,600 cadets in formation on the Terrazzo to the salt and pepper shakers on the Dining Hall tables. Experts with varying specialties from across the country came together under the direction of Skidmore, Owings & Merrill to produce a total design environment. Two of the most successful contributions came from remarkably different sources; Hollywood director Cecil B. DeMille created the striking cadet uniforms and New York industrial design firm Walter Dorwin Teague Associates designed the elegant yet durable furnishings.

Cecil B. DeMille and the Design of the Cadet Uniforms The problem of the cadet uniforms preceded the existence of the Academy. Discussions were held as early as 1952 as to whether the cadets should have a unique uniform or wear a modified Air Force uniform.[1] No decision was made and the issue continued to plague the Material and Supply Office over the next few years. In 1954 a definitive step was taken with the appointment of an Air Force Cadet Uniform Board. It developed an interim uniform to be worn by the incoming cadets while the search for a distinctive uniform continued. Up to that time, military tailors had produced unsatisfactory and often outlandish samples featuring clouds and lightning bolts.[2] After another review of more unacceptable proposals, Air Force Secretary Harold E. Talbott reportedly told the Superintendent and Commandant, "You two don't know a damn thing about uniforms. I know even less than both of you. What we need is some real imagination. Some of those men in Hollywood should be able to give it to us—men like Cecil DeMille and Walt Disney and Louis Mayer. I'm going to get some outside help."[3]

Talbott contacted his old friend Cecil B. DeMille, who was engaged in making *The Ten Commandments*. Associates urged him to turn down an assignment that might prove impossible since so many different groups would need to be satisfied. But in his autobiography DeMille cites patriotism, definite ideas about uniform design ("attractive, but thoroughly masculine"), and his love of planes as factors in his decision to take on the challenge.[4] His interest in aviation dated back to 1919, when he had founded the Mercury Aviation Company, one of the first commercial and passenger services in the United States.[5]

DeMille formed a committee of four men from his staff to help him with suggestions and sketches. The final designs were primarily the work of John Jensen, an artist who had served in the Army, and Henry Wilcoxon, DeMille's associate producer and a former naval gunnery officer.[6] For inspiration, the committee's first step was to obtain photographs of uniforms from around the world, a process that took several months to complete. After preliminary sketches had been made, DeMille invited General H. R. Harmon and Colonel R. M. Stillman to come to Hollywood to review the designs. Once their approval had been given, DeMille engaged the Western Costume Company to produce prototypes to be modeled by Air Training Officers. After a series of reviews and modifications, a uniform design was approved by the new Secretary of the Air Force Donald A. Quarles in September 1956.[7] The contract for the production of the uniforms was awarded to the Globe Tailoring Company, which was to deliver winter dress uniforms and overcoats by October 1957.[8]

The approved family of distinctive uniforms included five different ensembles: winter and summer service dress, winter and summer parade dress, and evening dress (figs. 85-88). The workhorse of the wardrobe was the winter service dress, which resembled the standard Air Force uniform and was to be worn to classes, meals, athletic events, and for travel. The winter parade dress featured a high-necked jacket with rows of buttons that formed a "V" down the front to emphasize the width of the cadets' shoulders. The evening dress uniform had a jacket with rolled lapels and was to be worn with a white pleated shirt, bow tie, and cummerbund to formal dances and social functions. The summer uniforms varied from the winter in the type of fabric used—cotton instead of wool.

The press had a field day with the collaboration between the military and Hollywood. A typical comment was, "Don't be surprised if the cadets of the Air Force Academy appear in Egyptian helmets and Roman breastplates and bear crusader shields and oriental swords. Their uniforms are going to be designed by Cecil B. DeMille."[9] One columnist joked that "foreign agents are trying to find out how many straps Cecil will put on his puttees."[10] Finally, Secretary Talbott sent out a memo suggesting that all hands play down the Hollywood angle: "It's getting out of hand; people better understand that we're still making the final decision, not Hollywood."[11] Overall, the Academy was pleased with the work of DeMille; he understood better than anyone how to produce a sensational image in an appropriately theatrical style. After the job was completed, DeMille was invited to a luncheon at the Pentagon and was presented with the Defense Department's Exceptional Service Award.

When slides of the new uniforms were first shown to the cadets the response was overwhelming approval; the cadets not only applauded but actually cheered. DeMille predicted "these are uniforms that the cadets themselves will want to wear. If the man in the uniform is happy with them, that is the main thing. If his girl admires them, that is even more important."[12] Little did he imagine that fifteen years later the Air Force would be struggling to modify his design to include an appropriate uniform for the new female cadets.[13]

Walter Dorwin Teague Associates' Furnishings for the Academy In February 1956 the Air Force Academy retained one of the country's oldest and largest industrial design firms to handle the interior arrangements, equipment, and furnishings for all of the Academy buildings. At first glance the choice of an industrial design firm to furnish interiors services on an architectural project may appear to have been unusual, but as far as breadth of experience, technical ability, and established capacity were concerned, Walter Dorwin Teague Associates was a logical choice, since the firm could provide for all of the Academy's needs under one roof.

The firm came to the project after having maintained an unusual number of long-term accounts with some of the country's largest corporations, including Eastman Kodak, Proctor and

86–88. Color sketches of uniform designs, John Jensen, c. 1956. "These are uniforms that the cadets themselves will want to wear. If the man in the uniform is happy with them, that is the main thing. If his girl admires them, that is even more important," stated Cecil B. DeMille. Left: Evening dress uniform. Center: Summer parade dress uniform. Right: Winter service dress uniform. U.S. Air Force Academy Collections.

89. Coffee service, c. 1958, Walter Dorwin Teague Associates. This stainless steel coffee service is part of the 1,500 items Walter Dorwin Teague Associates designed for the Air Force Academy. Walter Dorwin Teague Associates Archives.

90. Interior of Arnold Hall, c. 1958, Walter Dorwin Teague Associates. The lounge area in Arnold Hall shows Walter Dorwin Teague's use of color to establish the character of an area and gain variety throughout the Academy while reusing a basic design for the table and chairs. Walter Dorwin Teague Associates Archives.

89

Gamble, and Boeing. The interiors that the firm designed for the Boeing 707 Jet Stratoliner in 1955 set the standard for the commercial airline industry.[14] Teague's office had also done research and development work for the armed services since 1942, and had devised the standard materials inspection system for the Navy's Bureau of Ordnance.[15] "If not the most spectacular industrial designer . . . one of the most practical," was a commonly heard maxim about the firm.[16] Teague himself would not have taken offense at this comment since he valued functionalism and efficiency in design. This made the firm and the military eminently compatible.

For the Air Force Academy, Teague Associates was responsible for the installation and arrangement of 3.5 million square feet of interiors with 60,000 kinds of equipment and fittings, 1,500 of which would be specially designed.[17] The original budget for almost 80 acres of furnishings and equipment was $15 million, making it the largest industrial design project of its time.[18] The Air Force stipulated four basic requirements; economy, standardization, compatibility with Skidmore, Owings & Merrill's architecture, and furnishings with a durability span of fifty years.

Due to the scope of the project, Teague Associates performed the dual roles of interior designer and equipment engineer. As interior designer, the firm chose or designed all the furnishings and selected the colors, fabrics, and floor coverings. In the role of equipment engineer, its members had to write specifications on tens of thousands of items, some needing 20 pages of specifications. For many firms this would have been an organizational nightmare, but Teague Associates devised an automated data-processing procedure based on a 13-digit code to keep track of the huge quantities of equipment. The last 7 digits of the code provided complete identification of every item in all its variations,

including frame material, special designation, upholstery, and color. Code numbers were marked on each article and on each crate to make identification in the Air Force's warehouse fast and simple. Floor plans were keyed to this system for ease of placement and identification.

With huge numbers of items to be furnished, and working across several time zones without benefit of overnight delivery services or fax machines, the firm was able to accomplish the project successfully through sophisticated organizational systems. It produced four basic types of documents which together described the total project. Definitive floor plans were developed for each building, with each piece of equipment or furniture keyed to a code number. Facility Line Item Master Equipment Lists tracked all items in a given command area with codes and quantities. The Catalog of Equipment was organized by agency, and each page showed a separate item accompanied by a code. The Master Catalog was a comprehensive view of all items at the Academy. These documents accounted for everything from the soup ladles on the cadet dining tables to the shoeshine stands in their rooms to the barber chairs at the commissary (fig. 89).

From the signing of the contract in 1956 to the completion of the job in 1958 Teague's staff put in a total of 94,075 hours on the project.[19] The firm organized the project team into two groups, one in Colorado and the other in New York, with Teague and Robert Harper coordinating both operations. In Denver Carl Conrad worked with a team of twelve designers in close collaboration with Skidmore, Owings & Merrill and the Academy to get approval on preliminary designs. Twenty designers in New York, under the supervision of John Lee, executed finished or definitive plans from the Denver group's preliminary designs. The New York team also researched the availability of commercial items and was responsible for follow-through on equipment, including the preparation of procurement documents. For each stock piece of equipment Teague Associates recommended at least three bidders, but specially designed pieces had to be open to general bidding. The firm worked closely with manufacturers to insure high standards even to the extent of suggesting new methods of manufacture.

One of the key pieces of equipment that Teague Associates designed was a chair that, in addition to meeting the need for economy and durability, had to meet the Academy's peculiar requirement that freshmen sit on the edge of their seats in order to develop good posture and remain alert. To address this need

91

91. Interior of cadet quarters in Vandenberg Hall, c. 1958, Walter Dorwin Teague Associates. The cadet rooms were studied in full-scale mock-ups to determine everything from the arrangement of furniture and durability of materials, to sound and light control. Two second lieutenants lived and worked in the mock-up under conditions approximating those of the cadets. Walter Dorwin Teague Associates Archives.

92. Shoeshine stand, c. 1958, Walter Dorwin Teague Associates. This elegant cadet shoeshine stand displays the functional efficiency of the Teague designs. Walter Dorwin Teague Associates Archives.

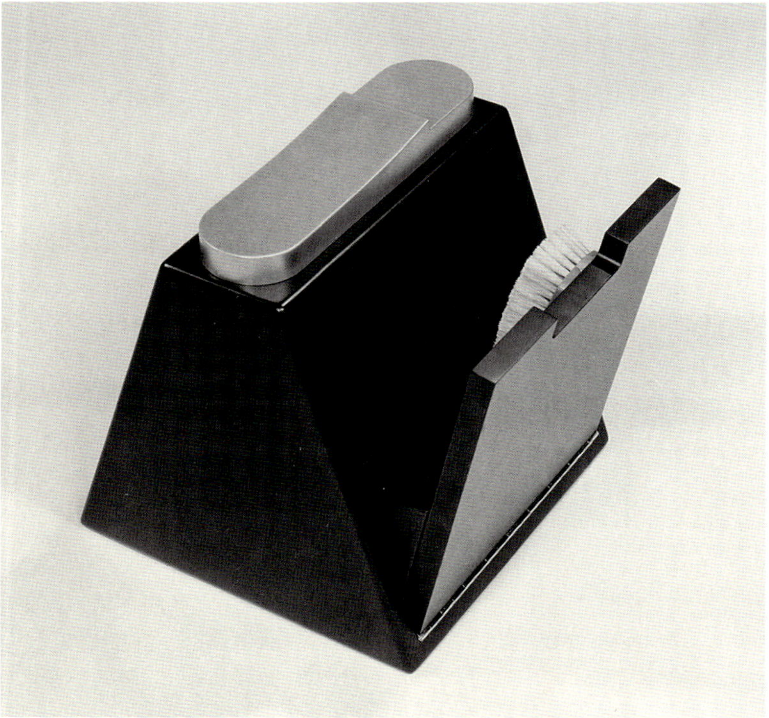

92

93. Interior of Fairchild Hall, c. 1958, Walter Dorwin Teague Associates. A typical classroom showing a portion of the miles of blackboard at the Academy. The luminous ceiling and color of the chairs represented an attempt to relieve the austerity of windowless rooms. Walter Dorwin Teague Associates Archives.

93

Teague Associates designed a chair whose seat was tolerable for the first four inches as well as forward-balanced for stability. To gain variety in an item to be repeated 13,000 times, the firm devised three versions: a basic plastic upholstered armchair for the cadet rooms, an armless version to be used as an occasional chair, and an armless chair with molded plastic seat and back for the classroom. One version featured an under-the-seat hat rack. Color—red, yellow, black, or blue—was used to facilitate and coordinate the character of an area (fig. 90). Thonet Industries won the contract to manufacture this chair and was still offering it in its Air Force line ten years later. To achieve a durable and maintenance-free finish, Teague Associates worked with the Aluminum Company of America to develop a special welding technique that allowed the aluminum frame to be anodized and heat-treated after welding. Previously, welds had been made after anodizing, leading to dark and unsightly joints. This development was another example of the firm's technical ingenuity and persistence in the search for quality.

The design of the cadet room had to serve the double function of accommodating both students and military men (fig. 91). One of the military requirements was that cadets change their uniforms several times a day. This necessitated careful study of storage arrangements and organization of floor space to facilitate a quick change. Dresser drawers were designed with compartmentalized sections for fast selection of accessories. The valet unit featured a pull-out laundry hamper, towel racks, and a section for a specially designed shoeshine stand (fig. 92). To obtain objective and precise data on everything from the arrangement of the furniture to sound and light control, a full-scale mock-up of two cadet rooms was built on the site. Two Air Force second lieutenants lived and worked in these rooms under conditions approximating those of the cadets.[20] Few personal items were allowed the cadets, only a record player and one photograph, so that visual relief was an important consideration. To accomplish this, the designers used color on blankets, bathrobes, and nameplates. Color also helped build esprit de corps as each class was assigned either red, blue, gold, or blue-gray.

Classrooms were designed to complement the advanced teaching techniques being developed at the Academy. These

94. Interior of Officers' Club, c. 1958, Walter Dorwin Teague Associates. Walter Dorwin Teague's designs for the nonacademic area—shown is a lounge in the Officers' Club—featured the same family of furniture, equipment, and materials as in the rest of the Academy. Walter Dorwin Teague Associates Archives.

windowless rooms featured extensive blackboard space, enough for sixteen cadets to work on problems simultaneously (fig. 93). The ceiling, which appears to float above the classroom, is a fine, half-inch square, egg crate of aluminum with fluorescent lights and sound-absorbing material above. Desk tops were of light gray melamine to reduce reflectivity and also resist scratches and stains.[21] Color was used in the molded plastic book-box under the desk, in the molded plastic seats of the chairs, and on the classroom door. The instructor's desk was aluminum and walnut, echoing, as did all the furnishings, the use of these materials in the architecture of the Academy.

The desks at the Academy were all derived from a modular system of seven major components. Of all the thousands of desks, only three were custom-designed, one for each of the three general officers. The furnishings for the generals' suites were all reiterations of the design theme established in the classrooms and the cadet quarters. To establish variation between the suites, color was used in the carpet, the upholstery, and the wood paneling. Changes in materials, from melamine table tops to marble, were also used to differentiate the general officers' furnishings from those of the cadets. Teague Associates also designed and selected furnishings for the nonacademic areas, including housing, recreation, and public areas (fig. 94). As a result of standardization throughout the project, the model of desk lamp specified for the cadets' quarters was also specified for the faculty housing.

During the late 1970s the furniture by Teague Associates was removed from the cadet quarters and replaced with furnishings considered more compatible with the new computers in each room. This replacement furniture was not very durable and in the early 1990s the Academy was faced with the proposition of having to remove it. Since the Teague Associates' furnishings were both durable and well liked by the cadets (two rooms that had managed to retain the Teague furniture were highly sought), Academy architect Duane A. Boyle suggested that new designs be developed based on the originals, but modified to address current requirements.[22] In preparation for its eventual manufacture, the Civil Engineering Department worked with the Academy's furniture maintenance shop to produce mock-ups that share Teague Associates' material choices and design aesthetic, but are updated to provide built-in computer screens and disk drives. In the classrooms of Fairchild Hall almost 90 percent of the original furniture remains and is in excellent condition, proof that Teague Associates did indeed met the military's requirement to design furnishings to last 50 years.

Notes

1. *History of the United States Air Force Academy: 27 July 1954 to 12 June 1956,* prepared by Lt. Col. Edgar A. Holt, Dr. M. Hamlin Cannon, and Dr. Carlos R. Allen, Jr. (Colorado Springs: U.S. Air Force Academy, 1 August 1957), vol. 2, 862. I would like to thank Duane Reed, Archivist and Chief, Special Collections and Directorate of Academy Libraries, for providing me with copies of this material.
2. George V. Fagan, *The Air Force Academy: An Illustrated History* (Boulder: Johnson Books, 1988), 78.
3. *Time,* 28 March 1955, 70.
4. Donald Hayne, ed., *The Autobiography of Cecil B. DeMille* (Englewood Cliffs: Prentice-Hall, 1959), 204.
5. Gabe Essoe and Raymond Lee, *DeMille: The Man and His Pictures* (New York: A. S. Barnes, 1970), 238.
6. Hayne, *The Autobiography of Cecil B. DeMille,* 205.
7. *History of the United States Air Force Academy: 13 June 1956 to 9 June 1957,* prepared by Lt. Col. Edgar A. Holt, Dr. M. Hamlin Cannon, Dr. Victor H. Cohen, and Dr. Emory H. Dixon (Colorado Springs: U.S. Air Force Academy, 1 November 1958), vol. 1, 414.
8. Ibid.
9. Hayne, *The Autobiography of Cecil B. DeMille,* 204.
10. Ibid. Puttees are leather leggings secured by a strap.
11. *Time,* 28 March 1955, 70.
12. *Hist. USAFA,* 1956-57, vol. 1, 415.
13. Fagan, *The Air Force Academy,* 191.
14. "The Great American Design Machine," *Industrial Design* (July/August 1976): 40.
15. Ibid.
16. Ibid., 35.
17. "Teague wins U.S.A.F. contract," *Industrial Design* (April 1956): 10.
18. "Half-Century Life is Goal of A.F. Chairs," reprint from *Contract,* June 1969.
19. "Furnishing for Fifty Years," *Industrial Design* (April 1958); 30.
20. "Mock-up tests comfort, work conditions of Air Academy," *Architectural Forum* (June 1956):17.
21. Melamine, which resembles plastic laminate, is a synthetic resin used for surfacing plywood, chipboard, etc. to create a durable surface.
22. Interview with Duane A. Boyle, Academy architect, 2 September 1993.

95. Detail of aluminum cladding on Academic Building. Photograph by Elizabeth Gill Lui, 1986. To make what appears to be a simple, smooth surface of aluminum and glass requires complicated hidden architectural hardware to keep the aluminum skin and glass in place, to keep the weather out, and to allow for different rates of expansion and contraction. The architects used mosaic walls to add color to the ensemble. Walter Netsch originally wanted greens and blues to harmonize with the landscape, but the primary colors finally chosen derive instead from the palette used by Bauhaus architects. According to cadet lore, the red, yellow and blue walls, plus the silver of the aluminum, represent class colors.

James S. Russell

Learning from Industry:
Architectural Technology at the U. S. Air Force Academy

The huge scale of the Air Force Academy commission provided Skidmore, Owings & Merrill a unique opportunity to move into the building industry many technological advances that had been developed in the preceding years—specifically by the military during World War II. This transfer of technology from manufacturing to architecture had long been a dream of modern architects, but it took a large firm, managed along the lines of successful American corporations, to make the dream real.

SOM hired Robertson Ward to set up a separate technical and materials research group.[1] "We wanted to be sure that we used the magnitude of the project to bring into being those kinds of technical advances that were going to be of help to us," says Ward. The architects were keenly aware that their refined aesthetic of flush metal-and-glass walls was ahead of the building industry's ability. Most of the research effort went to support the design of the Academic Building, Cadet Dining Hall and the Cadet Quarters, both because they came earlier than the Chapel and because the architects could more readily apply achievements on these structures to future corporate and institutional work. The Chapel, though extremely demanding technologically, was a "one-off" design, where research would not have a long-term payoff.

Aluminum In common construction practice for large buildings the use of exterior walls to carry a building's weight and other applied loads had long since given way to column-and-beam frames, from which were hung "curtain walls"—weather barriers that supported only themselves. SOM led the way in developing extremely thin, membranelike metal, stone, and glass claddings. Contrary to their simple, technologically sophisticated appearance, the thin curtain walls used on buildings erected prior to the Academy were extremely complicated, using off-the-shelf steel and glass components in little-tested ways. Such curtain walls often had significant problems with leakage and long-term structural integrity.[2]

Aluminum, however, could be extruded, i.e., forced, in molten form, through a mold, which permitted fabrication of single components that had flush exterior profiles and complex interior legs, extensions, and penetrations to accept glass, shed water, and be fastened to the building structure. To the mid-1950s, aluminum's use as cladding was limited. Ward and his team saw that the limitations were surmountable.[3] With SOM's encouragement, manufacturers doubled the width of standard extrusions to make the column covers and horizontal frame covers. SOM also pushed anodizing, a then-emerging finish process for aluminum (which does not take paint well). Anodizing overcame the metal's susceptibility to pitting and discoloration from airborne salts and pollution (fig. 95).[4]

Glass SOM's house style—not to mention the drama of the landscape—virtually mandated using large areas of glass. The problem of conventional clear glass was that the transmittance of the extraordinarily powerful sunlight would have created unacceptable glare inside the building. Also, the sun's heat transmitted by the glass would have required a very large and costly air-conditioning system. Even if the glass walls had been operable—which they weren't, except in the Cadet Quarters—the sheer amount of glass would likely have made summer heat intolerable. The team pushed manufacturers who were developing new glass tints and reflective coatings. Up to this time, glass tinted to reduce glare and absorb heat without compromising vision had only just been commercialized. By threatening to use a Belgian tinting process, says Ward, SOM convinced American glassmakers Libbey-Owens Ford and Pittsburgh Plate Glass to produce the types they were looking for. The gray tint ultimately chosen reduced transmittance to only 35 percent.[5] The firm considered specular reflective (mirrorlike) coatings for the "transparent" end walls of the chapel, but Ward says the quality control was not acceptable at the time of the Academy's design.[6]

Air-conditioning Though energy prices were low, most mid-1950s institutional owners weren't prepared to assume the large up-front costs of mechanical cooling. Also, the austerity of the cadets' lives would have mitigated against the use of what was then regarded as a luxury technology. On the other hand, programmatic and technological reasons made air conditioning virtually mandatory. The very large buildings with their deep floor plans came from specific Air Force directives, according to Ward. Such plans made the ductwork runs needed for air-conditioning much less expensive. A conventional layout would likely have required many wings so that each classroom could be exposed to outside light and air (a building-code requirement), but this would have spread the complex over a much larger area. Pedagogically, too, there was a gathering consensus that the more controlled the conditions, the better the learning environment. Removing windows was justified as key to focusing cadet concentration, and better suited to the anticipated use of then-new television for teaching.[7] Also, the Air Force thought cadets needed a great deal of blackboard work. Thus it approved an integrated HVAC (heating, ventilating, air-conditioning) system in the administrative and social areas, but not the Dining Hall.[8] Classrooms were also air-conditioned, permitting the replacement of windows with blackboards. Lighting, too, was carefully controlled within the classrooms. Fluorescent light was filtered through a suspended "eggcrate" diffuser.

Installing air-conditioning affected the design in other ways. If the architects had not succeeded in finding a glass that would absorb a great deal of solar heat, for example, they might have had to redesign the building, using far less glass, to avoid the huge costs associated with installing enough cooling capacity.

Precast Concrete The road and rail bridges that approach the project were an early use of precast/prestressed concrete beams (fig. 96).[9] Up to this time, steel was typically used because it could readily span large gaps (120-foot and 80-foot spans at the academy).[10] The combination of prestressing (the placing of reinforcing cables prior to casting) and post-tensioning (in which the cables were jacked to a predetermined stress and bolted at the ends to permanently maintain this tensile force) dramatically improved the

96. View showing placement of precast, prestressed concrete beams on Academy approach bridges. Photograph by Stewart's, 1957. The prestressing of the beams allowed for much longer, stronger spans than would have been possible with ordinary reinforced concrete. U.S. Air Force Academy Library, Special Collections Branch, Stewart's No. 1-21.

tension strength of concrete, permitting its economical use in spans such as those encountered at the Academy site. Indeed, the economies of precast/prestressed beams came to be essentially equal to that of steel. Concrete bridges also weren't as subject to rust nor did they need painting. Since then, they have become widely used in forms virtually identical to those chosen for the Academy.

Granite and Vinyl-Asbestos Tile Netsch credits Ward with not only technological sophistication but aesthetic understanding of how surface and pattern are perceived by people. These were played out in the way granite and vinyl-asbestos tiles were used at the Academy. Ward claims that research efforts for the Academy brought flame finishing for granite into wide use. In this technique, a series of high-temperature torches is run across what will become the finished surface of the granite. The high temperature irregularly fractures the stone's surface layer, which is readily removed. This roughened matte surface gives a larger-scale texture to the granite. (The typical honed or high-gloss polished finished would have looked patternless.)[11] The researchers also explored various means of prestressing and panelizing granite. These techniques were not perfected in time for the Academy project but were used later in important buildings.

Vinyl-asbestos floor tile was on the edge of commercialization at the time the Academy was in design. It offered a harder-wearing surface than linoleum at lower cost than tile or terrazzo. Vinyl tile went on to achieve very wide acceptance. By getting in on the ground floor, Ward says SOM was able to convince Armstrong, then a maker of cork and linoleum flooring, to create VAT flooring in colors and patterns the firm designed. Both Ward and Netsch worked to standardize use of a variety of patterns in the tile so they would not be too monotonous. Manufacturers, for example, were ordered to "randomize" patterned tile before packing it into boxes, so that the varation would be visible to users, yet consistent overall. According to Ward, some of the patterns SOM designed later became standard offerings.[12]

Computer-Aided Design The structural loads on the self-supporting circular stair in the library were analyzed with the use of a computer, which was among the very earliest applications of computing power for structural calculations. "Computers were pretty primitive," says Ward, "almost fancy calculators."

The Chapel The role of research at the Chapel was different. Here the expertise of Ward and his team was called upon to solve the extraordinary technical problems posed by Netsch's design. It represented structural technology used primarily for its expressionistic potential. It is hard to imagine Gordon Bunshaft, for example, doing a folded-plate structure that evoked the Gothic.[13] Netsch's tetrahedron scheme didn't derive from an innately efficient engineering rationale (the conveying of forces using the least material being the engineer's definition of structural purity). The three-dimensional tetrahedrons were themselves highly efficient structural elements. And nesting them together could have provided efficient resistance to loads imposed vertically by gravity and horizontally by both the outward thrust of the sloped roofs and the forces of high winds. At a conceptual level, though, Netsch's design undermined the innate efficiency of the idea by setting the tetrahedrons end to end (forming something akin to an hourglass-shaped column), and by placing strip glazing at the points where the tetrahedron surfaces meet. Because the tetrahedrons did not interlock and reinforce each other, thick structural members had to be introduced to bridge the gaps. Netsch's detailing method, however, *visually* emphasized a technological idea: The tetrahedrons' slightly grooved, reflective surfaces were expressed as membranelike skins; the glazed seams between the tetrahedrons, filled with colored glass, make the building seem nearly weightless.[14] The Chapel has been the most problem-plagued of Academy buildings, however, owing entirely to its daring forms.[15]

Though making the research arm of SOM permanent after the Academy project might have continued the innovative relationship between architects and industry, both Ward and Netsch felt the other partners were not truly committed to the research effort.[16] When the Academy project wound down, many team members went to the Chicago architectural and engineering firm of C. F. Murphy in similar capacities. That firm was doing a project equally gigantic and of arguably greater complexity: Chicago's O'Hare International Airport. Ward, however, stayed true to his commitment to "a more rationalized building industry." In 1960, he opened his own consulting practice and continued the kind of research he had done at SOM, consulting to stone, concrete, glass, and steel companies as well as to his former employer. Most prominently, he later worked with Ezra Ehrenkrantz and the School Construction Systems Development program, which was responsible for an integrated approach to the design of structure, walls, and mechanical systems for a series of schools in California. The results of that work form the basis of the integration of such systems in buildings that is still used today and that proved enormously influential in the design sensibilities of several architects who later became prominent. [17]

Notes

1. From the author's interviews with both Walter Netsch (WN) and Robertson Ward (RW). According to Ward, there were six senior designers under Netsch and himself. Ward describes a vertical arrangement in which teams worked on each of the primary structures: the academic complex, the dormitories, the support facilities. Ward saw his job as resolving problems common to the teams. Among those who worked with Ward were Douglas Ryhm, Bill Cureton, and Harry Shaxted. After receiving an undergraduate degree in electronic physics from Harvard, Ward served in the Navy, where he decided to become an architect. He received a master of architecture degree from Harvard's Graduate School of Design in 1951. Much of his work involved the transfer of technology from industry to architecture. He worked with Konrad Wachsmann, a pioneer in prefabrication, who emigrated from Germany to America. He also worked with Arnold Rossner, an engineer who did much to commercialize prestressed concrete. Rossner later worked with Ward, SOM, and Cold Spring Granite on the development of precast, prestressed granite panels. Ward worked with SOM on wartime prefabricated modular wood housing. He left SOM to work with Marcel Breuer on the Unesco complex in Paris, which had an elaborate sunshading system. SOM lured him back for the Academy project.

2. At SOM's Lever House, completed in 1952, the rectangular mullions and T-shaped vertical fins were stainless steel wrapping cold-rolled steel. Horizontal mullion supports were standard steel angles awkwardly overlapped and flashed to prevent corrosion. They corroded anyway. The opaque spandrel panels were wire glass, which improved strength. The panes, however, have not proved equal to thermal stresses, and many have cracked and been replaced. See James S. Russell, "Icons of Modernism or Machine-Age Dinosaurs?" *Architectural Record* (June 1989): 142–47. Ludwig Mies van der Rohe, SOM's spiritual mentor, liked to express the difference between structural frame and nonsupporting curtain wall by visually bringing the supporting frame to the exterior surface and showing the curtain wall as lightweight infill. Mies also preferred riblike verticals and complicated re-entrant corners. Netsch sought walls that looked ever thinner, prismatic, and crystalline, and is proud of the progress made at the Academy (WN-JSR interview).

3. Pietro Belluschi's Commonwealth Building, in Portland, Oregon (1948), was a successful use of aluminum panels and double-pane thermal insulating glass. (Belluschi had already recognized the technology-transfer potential of wartime production. The Pacific Northwest, with its cheap hydropower, had become a center of aluminum manufacturing for the airplane industry.) Aluminum is light, but not as strong as steel. Further, it has much lower thermal transfer, reducing interior condensation. See also "Air Force Academy," in Reynolds Aluminum Company, *Aluminum in Modern Architecture,* vol. 2 (1960), pp. 47–51. Another major use of aluminum was in the Alcoa Building in Pittsburgh finished in 1953. On this, see Victoria Newhouse, *Wallace K. Harrison, Architect* (1989), pp. 146–49.

4. The effect of pollution on mill-finish aluminum is vividly demonstrated at the Philadelphia Savings Fund Society headquarters in Philadelphia, a 1932 skyscraper glazed using aluminum bar stock. It is today pitted and black rather than shiny and smooth. See Russell, "Icons of Modernism or Machine-Age Dinosaurs?" Anodizing involves dipping the metal in an electrically charged solution. Colors were limited and some were subject to fading. The SOM research team at the Air Force Academy tested a number of colors on-site, before choosing the clear (metallic) tone ultimately used on the project. The color was a natural choice, referring to an aircraft's aluminum skin. It became more typical later to use the "bronze" tone, seen ubiquitously today on storefronts. The reveals—incisions around the windows—in the skin are emphasized through the use of dark brown or black anodizing. While the main color of the aluminum is virtually unchanged today, the dark reveals are significantly faded.

5. JSR interviews with WN and RW.

6. JSR interviews with WN and RW. Also, "Those Towering Spires," *Monsanto Magazine* (published by Monsanto, makers of laminated glass) (Summer 1962). The reflective coating held out the promise of rejecting more unwanted heat than tinted, heat-absorbing glass could. The team did select a nonspecular coating (which had a more diffuse reflecting appearance from the outside) within a laminated-glass light for use in the Chapel. The coating was applied to a polyvinyl butyral interlayer that "glued" two sheets of glass together. This technique reduced transmittance in the

chapel to only 5 percent. Eero Saarinen, one of the Air Force Secretary's design consultants, also expressed interest, which encouraged glassmakers to continue their research. Specular reflective glass products of consistent quality and in large volumes soon entered the market, and have been widely used. Quality control was still an issue when Saarinen used large volumes of reflective glass on his Bell Labs project in the early 1960s: "Bell Labs' Mirrored Superblock," *Architectural Record* (October 1962): 145–52. The laminated glass at the Chapel is today rather cloudy and is probably considerably more obscure than it once was.

7. "U. S. Air Force Academy," *Architectural Record* (June 1959): 151–62, confirmed in WN interview.

8. JSR interview with RW. "Mock-Up Tests Comfort, Work Conditions of Air Academy," *Architectural Forum* (June 1956): 17. Syska & Hennessy, the mechanical engineers, did not at the time describe the systems used as specifically new or cutting edge. They seem to be of "best" institutional quality for the time. According to a paper delivered to the American Society of Heating and Refrigeration Engineers (1957) by Sam Sachs that seems to be used as a basis for contemporary accounts, different systems were used in different buildings. Cadet areas: zoned, medium temperature hot-water system with perimeter finned-tube radiation heating; radiant-heating coils in floors above open levels; Academic Building: completely air-conditioned using an ethylene-glycol loop, and combined heating and cooling coils. The system used evaporative cooling at peak periods, in which water sprays absorbed heat from the dry Colorado air. External corridors were heated using direct radiation but not mechanically cooled. Dining Hall: The 22-ft-high glass walls were heated by air discharged up from base. A separate ceiling system forced heated air down. Administrative Building: Completely air-conditioned with a high-pressure, high-velocity system using perimeter induction units (these were an office-building standard for many years). Social Center: One air-conditioning system was designed to be shared by the auditorium and the ballroom. The assumption was that both would not be used at the same time. Physical Education: An ethylene glycol loop provided perimeter radiant heating. Heating coils were embedded in the deck around the pools. The structure was not air-conditioned. Further, the engineers embedded additional heating coils in exterior ramps for snow melting.

9. "Approach Bridges: U.S. Air Force Academy," *Architectural Record* (April 1958): 239–40.

10. Fazlur R. Khan and Andrew J. Brown, "Load Test of 120-ft Precast, Prestressed Bridge Girder," *Journal of the American Concrete Institute* (July 1958): 139. For prestressing, cables were draped in a predetermined downward curve in the concrete form, then post-tensioned, using jacks, after casting. (When loads are applied to a beam, it tends to bow downward, creating a tension or stretching force in the bottom of the beam and a compressing force in the top of the beam. Concrete is naturally efficient in resisting compressive forces but poor in resisting tension forces, except through the use of reinforcing steel.) SOM structural engineer Fazlur R. Khan, who led the effort at the Academy, later became famous for innovative wind-bracing schemes for SOM skyscrapers of the 1960s and 1970s.

11. JSR interviews with RW. Ward says the scale of the Academy effort encouraged the granite supplier, Cold Spring Granite, to bring techniques for prestressing granite to market, as well as innovative panelizing techniques, such as premounting granite on a steel framework for easy erection. These techniques were not, however, available in time for the Academy project. Working with Arnold Rossner (n. 1, above), Cold Spring mounted granite on precast concrete backing panels at the Municipal Services Building, in Philadelphia, designed by Vincent Kling.

12. Much of the tile has been replaced. What appears to be original tile is visible in some of the classrooms, however, and has much livelier variation in pattern than the less-inventive recent tiles. Today composition tiles are made without asbestos.

13. Saarinen, however, was thinking like Netsch. Consider his TWA Terminal, in New York (about 1958), and Stiles College, at Yale, which was designed contemporaneously with the Academy Chapel.

14. For structural efficiency, the tetrahedrons were fabricated of welded-steel pipe. Another architect might have left these structural members exposed on the interior as an expression of "how it was made." Characteristically, SOM clad them with plaster panels in aluminum surrounds, gracefully hiding insulation and electrical fittings. Exterior panels are embossed aluminum panels. "Gothic Tetra-Hedra: SOM's Chapel

at U. S. Air Force Academy," *Architectural Review* (April 1961): 222; "Tubular Tetrahedrons, Air Force's New Chapel," *Progressive Architecture* (September 1961): 182–87; "Air Force Academy Chapel," *Architectural Record* (December 1962): 85–92.

15. The structure persistently leaks. Double glazing at the colored glass seems to have been proposed, then deleted for cost reasons. It was added after completion and has solved the worst leaking problems. The complex shapes of the tetrahedrons and the large expansion coefficient of aluminum mean that the building is changing shape constantly on a sunny day as the panels expand or contract depending on the sun angle. (The visitor is virtually assured of hearing the creaking.) Today, a sophisticated computer program might have been able to analyze and accurately predict the movement of the panels. Advanced sealants, used as caulking, have no doubt helped, but neither of these were available when the chapel was designed. The complex has had other ongoing technological problems. Freezing and thawing cycles, along with de-icing chemicals, have wrought havoc with the huge plazas. According to Academy architect Duane Boyle, a long-term fix has yet to be found. The vast acreage of roofs must also be replaced frequently, according to Boyle. The combination of wide temperature swings and accelerated ultraviolet-light damage (exacerbated by the site's altitude) create problems that are common to similar roofs in the area.

16. In the partners' defense, the structure of American architectural practice at the time made sustaining such an experienced and talented group difficult. Government projects were usually awarded according to fixed fee schedules, and most private owners used schedules of fees recommended by the American Institute of Architects. A research group would have represented a significant fixed cost not readily covered by fees.

17. JSR interviews with RW. The "high-tech" architects of the 1970s trace their inspiration to the SCSD project. These include the British architects Norman Foster and Richard Rogers, and the Italian Renzo Piano. The most famous design of this school is the Centre Pompidou museum in Paris.

97. Sketch of Chapel interior. Drawn by SOM architect, probably Walter Netsch, c. 1955. In this early sketch the architects attempted to record the spatial experience of their folded plate Chapel design. This design was soon withdrawn in response to heated objections. SOM Archives, Chicago.

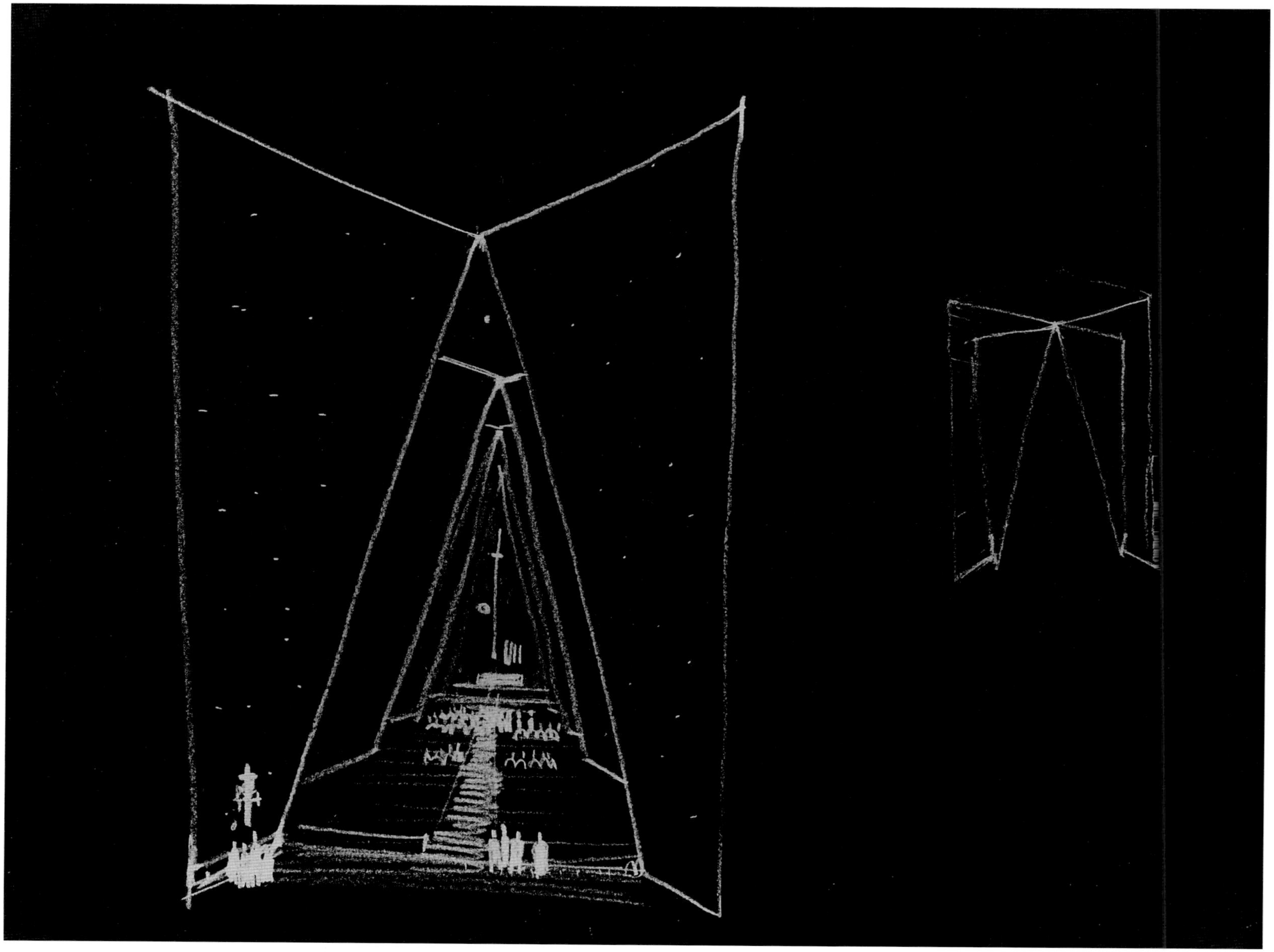

Sheri Olson

Lauded and Maligned: The Cadet Chapel

It is difficult to be indifferent to the design of the Air Force Academy Chapel; it has usually been either lauded or maligned. This polarization may perhaps be best understood in the context of the categories historian Henry-Russell Hitchcock predicted for postwar architecture—"the architecture of bureaucracy and the architecture of genius."[1] Hitchcock described the architecture of bureaucracy, without any negative connotation, as that produced by large-scale architectural firms organized to produce a "foolproof" system of rapid and complete plan production. This description of an anonymous architecture from which personal expression is largely absent is a fitting description of the majority of Skidmore, Owings & Merrill's work at the Air Force Academy. The architecture of genius, according to Hitchcock's definition, consists of works of architectural art, produced by an individual, which have an overall expressive impact. The Chapel manages to straddle both categories, eliciting vast differences of opinion.

The design of the Chapel was conceived in a moment of inspiration, typically a hallmark of the architecture of genius. According to the myth surrounding the project, a folded piece of paper resembling Japanese origami (but also folded plate architectural construction) was produced, under the pressure of a deadline, to symbolize a religious structure on the model of the Academy (figs. 20, 97).[2] When Skidmore, Owings & Merrill made its initial presentation of the master plan in May 1955, the Chapel became a lightening rod for criticism, described as everything from "paganistic" to "an assembly of wigwams." When controversy over the design threatened to throw the whole project off course, the Air Force directed that the chapel be removed from the model.[3] Nathaniel A. Owings backpedalled about the seriousness of the firm's intent regarding the initial design and suggested that it was only a symbol.[4] But a reporter for a Colorado Springs paper noted the intricacy of the model and questioned the explanation, stating that it "took more than a little folding to do."[5]

The journalist's claim may have been right on target about Skidmore, Owings & Merrill's commitment to the design. Even after Netsch had toured Europe to study religious architecture, the design retained its controversial elements. Upon viewing the revised plans, Congressional critics complained bitterly that "three years later they have come up with substantially the same appearing building that they had in the first instance."[6] Other critics claimed that they had been intentionally misled to believe that the revised Chapel would be more conservative, but instead found it

98

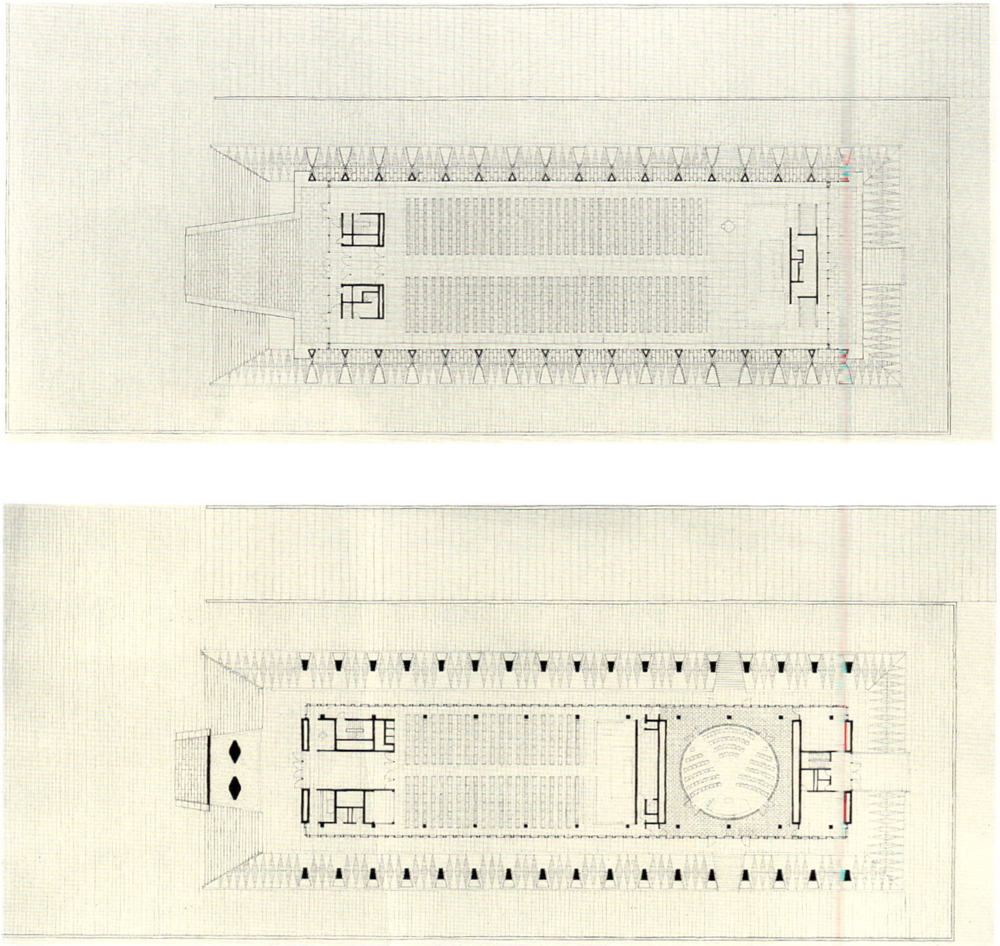

"worse than the old one."[7] Comparative photographs of the Chapel designs published by *U.S. News and World Report* were ironically labeled "old" and "new."[8]

Replacing the folded plate construction of the original design was a space frame of tetrahedrons made of tube steel and enclosed with aluminum panels.[9] The orientation of the tetrahedrons alternated from the base to the pinnacle to produce a complex effect with a simple form.[10] The tetrahedrons were spaced a foot apart to allow light to flow through a narrow band of stained glass, which marked their juncture (fig. 99).[11] From a series of granite abutments the Chapel's spires rose to a height of 150 feet.

The complex geometric nature of the original design was not one that could easily be adjusted to respond to criticism; any significant change would have been drastic. Although Skidmore, Owings & Merrill was ordered by the Air Force to produce four or five alternatives, it's not clear whether the firm ever had any intention of significantly departing from the original design proposal. At one point a group of architects within the firm lodged a protest against the Chapel with the partners, but Gordon Bunshaft put a stop to the outcry by supporting Netsch's design.[12] Unlike the rest of the Academy, which was presented as the work of an anonymous team, the Chapel design was publicly attributed to Netsch.[13] He became the "avenging angel" for the project, embarking on a campaign to garner grassroots support, displaying a large model of the Chapel's interior, complete with lights, before architectural and religious organizations across the country in an attempt to counter all of the negative publicity.[14]

Congress was besieged with mail regarding the design, most of it critical. The most heated controversy focused on the untraditional nature of the Chapel. Some complained that its modern design would make worshiping in the chapel no different

98. Chapel, upper-level (above) and lower-level plans. Drawing by SOM. As precedent for a multilevel chapel, the architects referred to the Sainte-Chapelle in Paris and the church of St. Francis in Assisi. A wide flight of steps leads to the 1,200-seat Protestant chapel on the upper level with a 100-seat choir loft and pipe organ. On the lower level, a 500-seat Catholic chapel with an 80-seat choir loft was designed to recall the crypt-like quality of early Christian places of worship. The circular form and transparent walls of the 100-seat Jewish chapel were used to suggest a tent-like structure. SOM Archives, Chicago.

99. Section through Chapel. Collage by SOM architects showing proposed treatment of altar area. SOM Archives, Chicago.

from worshiping in a "museum of modern art or a skating rink."[15] Architects all over the country faced a similar dilemma as they struggled to reconcile modern architecture and church design without losing the richness of meaning associated with traditional religious forms. This reflected the growing tension in the United States between the desire for adherence to tradition and a demand for a new conception of religion befitting the modern era.[16] This conflict was heightened for the Academy Chapel because it was perceived as a national monument. Given the large numbers of people to be accommodated, and the need to make the building proportionate to the immense scale of the academic area, it would have been difficult to use more traditional forms, if not absurd. As Owings commented, a "New England chapel to accommodate 1,500 persons would be like a 10-foot-high dog."[17]

99

The interdenominational nature of the Academy Chapel also precluded certain forms. Three faiths were housed under one roof with the Protestant Chapel on the upper level and the Catholic and Jewish chapels below (fig. 98). At one point, when General Harmon appeared insistent on a cruciform shape for the building, the Air Force chaplains protested that the "Jewish Welfare Board and other Jewish agencies would strenuously object to worshipping in a building which was deliberately constructed as a cruciform."[18] Some critics were amazed at how such essentially divergent religious viewpoints could be reconciled in one structure to begin with, especially since "Protestantism, by its very nature, is in contradiction to Catholicism, and Judaism is in contradiction to both."[19] Where optimists saw the Chapel as a "unifying symbol appropriate for our democracy in a world of conflict," others perceived a danger in the smoothing over of differences.[20] Whether it was possible to accommodate profound modes of variances within both Protestant and Jewish observance provoked similar concerns. Aware of the problems of meeting the unique requirements of the different Protestant denominations within one chapel, the chaplains requested early in the design process that they be closely involved in the development of liturgical furnishings and appointments.[21]

The decision to house three faiths in one chapel rather than build separate facilities, as originally considered, was the result of rising construction costs at the Academy, as well as limited space in the master plan.[22] The Air Force chaplains were unhappy with this compromise, but their overriding concern was with the possibility that the Academy might open without any provisions for worship at

100

100. Interior of Protestant chapel. Photograph by Balthazar Korab, c. 1963. Walter Netsch laid out by hand the design for the thousands of pieces of stained glass. The glass creates a subtly varied pattern that gradates from rich dark colors to gold over the altar.

101. Interior of Catholic chapel. Photograph by Elizabeth Gill Lui, 1986. All furnishings in the chapels were provided by private donations. The interior furnishings of the Protestant and Catholic chapels were designed by architect Harold E. Wagoner; the mosaic reredos was executed by painter-sculptor Luman Martin Winter.

101

all. Square footage was divided up among the religions in a democratic manner, with the largest space going to the Protestants, the most heavily represented religion among the cadets.[23] Theirs was also the most spectacular location—on the upper level under the full impact of the stained glass and soaring structure (fig. 100). Owings later joked that the Protestants "needed those extra seventeen-and-a-half feet for a head start to heaven."[24] The military chaplains were more concerned than Owings though, that the great disparity in ceiling heights between the chapels, in combination with the less than desirable location of the Catholic and the Jewish spaces on the lower level, would be unacceptable to the public. Amazingly, there was little or no protest.

One of the biggest battles the Chapel faced was waged in Congress over the budget. It began when increasing construction costs caused concern that if the Chapel was not included in the original $126 million appropriation for the Academy, funds for it might not ever be found. Funding was threatened again when the $4 million requested for the Chapel was slashed in half by the Secretary of Defense because the sum was considered out of line with the cost of chapels at other military bases. In the end, two of the original nineteen spires fell victim to budget constraints. This was done without significantly affecting the design, which suggests that the Chapel was like the accordion earlier critics had called it, "extensible as the student body increased."[25] Congress even debated the significance of the number of spires. "Why should there be 19 spires instead of 20 or 16 or 14?"[26] According to the standing Academy joke, the 17 spires represent the 12 apostles and the 5 members of the Appropriations Committee.[27] This arbitrariness was at odds with Skidmore, Owings & Merrill's attempt to link the Chapel design with modern scientific principles and rational planning.

Art News enthusiastically noted this association and praised the chapel design as the next step forward in Le Corbusier's "Machine for Living."[28] A mechanized image fit the regimentation of military life. An early design directive required that the cadets be able to march into the chapel three abreast, presumably to recite the Lord's Prayer.[29] But as architectural critic Allan Temko pointed out in his scathing review of the completed building, a truly rationalistic "technoscientific" project would not place a religious structure at its center. There was also the questionable intention of using public funds for sectarian purposes. To avoid this sticky issue, liturgical furnishings for the chapels were provided by private donations (fig. 101).[30] Some of these funds were actively solicited by the Air Force in an Easter Sunday campaign conducted at U.S. Air Force bases worldwide.[31]

Skidmore, Owings & Merrill was more successful borrowing on the cultural authority of technology through the use of experimental structural systems and materials developed by the military

102

103

102. Tetrahedrons en route to site. Photograph by Stewart's, c. 1961. The 75-foot-long tube-steel tetrahedrons that made up the Chapel's structural skeleton were fabricated in Missouri and then shipped by rail to Colorado. Local History Collection, Pikes Peak Library District.

103. Aerial view of Chapel under construction. Photograph by Stewart's, c. 1961. One of the biggest struggles in the design of the Chapel concerned its location. Many places were suggested for it—up on a small hill, outside the Academic area, on the Court of Honor—until the architects, with the help of Eero Saarinen, rotated it ninety degrees into its present location. Local History Collection, Pikes Peak Library District.

104. Installer holding stained-glass panel for Catholic chapel. Photograph by Stewart's, c. 1961. While working on the designs for the stained-glass windows, Walter Netsch discovered that hammer-striking thick dalle glass would produce subtle faceting and variation. The pattern for the Catholic chapel windows is more random and abstract than the rectilinear pattern found in the Protestant chapel. Local History Collection, Pikes Peak Library District. Stewart's No. 44-66.

during the war. A system similar to the tubular steel that made up the 100 tetrahedrons of the Chapel structure had been investigated earlier by the Air Force for airplane hangars. The Chapel's tetrahedrons were prefabricated and shipped by rail to the site, where they were hoisted into place by cranes (figs. 102, 103). This was a very unusual construction technique for a religious building, but not for the military, the leading developer of methods of prefabrication. The link with cutting-edge technology was strongest in the use of aluminum (which had been developed during the war for airplanes) as the main material for the Chapel enclosure. Although this choice of material brought outcries, it also had its supporters, who believed that if aluminum was good enough for the cadets to fight and die in, it was good enough for them to worship in.[32] This association also bordered on the ridiculous, as noted by the congressman who suggested that as an "emergency measure we might mount some jet engines on each of these spires, then if trouble comes just take off."[33] But the architectural applications of military technology proved problematic; the chapel leaked even before construction was completed.[34]

104

The juxtaposition of aluminum, prized for its advantages for aeronautics, with Gothic stained glass exposed the uneasy alliance between the military and religion inherent in the design of the Chapel (figs. 104, 105). Although the building was promoted as emblematic of "Air Age Gothic," it was the militaristic, rather than the architectural associations, that stood out. The sharp upward-thrusting spires, combined with the geometry of the tetrahedrons and metal skin, are more suggestive of upended fighter planes than Chartres Cathedral. In the Protestant chapel the design of the pews contributed to this image; their ends resembled airplane propellers and metal strips on the seatbacks suggested the leading edge of an airplane wing.[35] Linking military strength with religion took on an added significance in the climate of the Cold War where architecture was used as a weapon and to bolster claims for American cultural and technical superiority.[36] At the dedication ceremony in 1963 the Chapel was praised as "a symbol for the world to know that the U.S. is truly a nation under God."[37]

Skidmore, Owings & Merrill realized that the chapel design called for a touch of genius among the impressive but repetitive forms of the overall academic complex. The Chapel was to be the "daring architectural leader" of the Academy, acting as a catalyst to transform its disparate pieces into a whole.[38] Louis Kahn, an

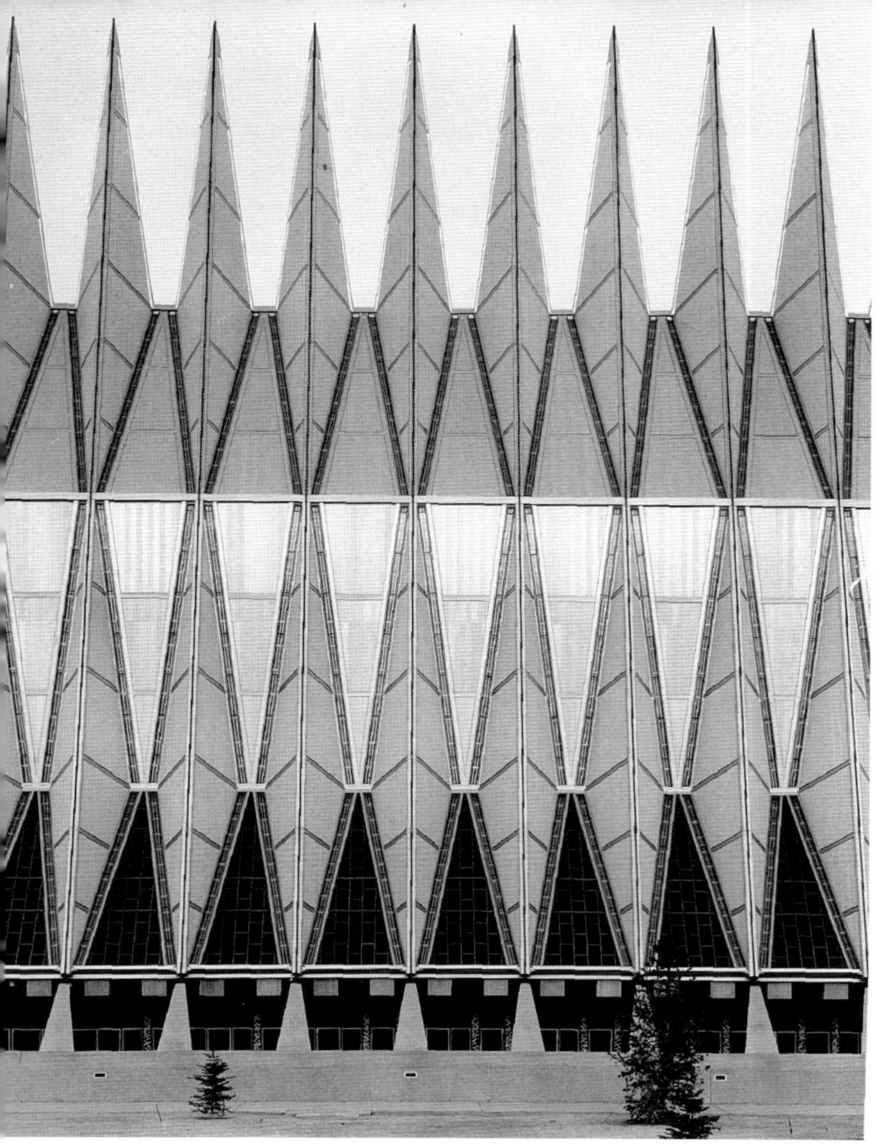

105

105. Side view of Chapel. Photograph by Stewart's, c. 1963. The one hundred tetrahedrons that form the faceted structure of the chapel are clad in aluminum with stained glass panels marking the multiple changes in plane. Local History Collection, Pikes Peak Library District. Stewart's No. 69-61.

106. Silhouette of chapel. Photograph by Balthazar Korab, c. 1962. When Hungarian-born architect Balthazar Korab arrived in the United States in 1955 he was transfixed by the gleaming new building ensembles he saw, particularly the General Motors Technical Center near Detroit and the Air Force Academy. Turning to photography, he created some of the most evocative images of postwar American design.

architect intensely interested in creating what Hitchcock would call an architecture of genius, referred to the Academy project as an "assignment worthy of a master architect."[39] But, he continued, it is "too difficult an assignment for a firm of architects, because we can assume that such a firm would not have an artist master at its head. It would have taken Corbusier many months more time than was apparently allowed the architects to conceive the Academy into the form of art."[40]

From under the combined burden of the extraordinarily high expectations of the public, politicians, and the architectural profession, the Chapel achieves a certain success as a finely articulated form outlined against the Rockies, and as a precise backdrop to the daily formation of the cadet corps. It is these images of the Chapel that continue to draw more than a million visitors every year to Colorado Springs (fig. 106). The controversy over the design may have faded, but the issues regarding tradition, symbolism, and cultural values persist. The Chapel remains a reminder of a time when architects were optimistic about proposing answers to these questions.

Notes

1. Henry-Russell Hitchcock, "The Architecture of Bureaucracy and the Architecture of Genius," *Architectural Review* (January–June 1947): 4. I would like to thank Joan Ockman for bringing this to my attention.

2. Walter Netsch, "The Air Force Academy Chapel—The Very Visible, Invisible Building," 13 November 1987, photocopied. Netsch credits Karl Kohler with having folded the piece of paper to form the controversial chapel model.

3. Memo, Mr. John M. Ferry, Spec. Asst. for Installations, to ACS/Insts, 24 June 1955, in Wiley, "The United States Air Force Academy Chapel" (1954), 8, photocopy, in Special Collections Branch of the Air Force Academy Library, Colorado Springs.

4. Owings did not represent all of his colleagues' feelings about the seriousness of Skidmore, Owings & Merrill's intent concerning the initial presentation of the design for the Chapel; Netsch was devastated when it drew heavy criticism. He recalls how Owings tried to comfort him with: "They approved all, except the chapel, and you can always do another." Interview of Netsch by Robert Bruegmann,

5. *Gazette-Telegraph* (Colorado Springs), 24 June 1955, in Wiley, "The United States Air Force Academy Chapel," 7.

6. U.S. Congress, House, *Supplemental Appropriations for 1958. Congressional Record*, vol. 103, pt. 10, 85th Cong., 1st Sess., 6 August 1957, 13790.

7. "Air Chapel Design Hit," *New York Times*, 17 January 1958.

8. "Controversy Over a Chapel," *U.S. News & World Report,* 17 January 1958, 14.

9. Netsch had considered using large diamond-shaped panels of Mexican onyx as a possible enclosure for the tube-steel tetrahedrons. This scheme would have produced a strikingly different building: translucent, with the frame of the tetrahedrons visible behind. Unfortunately, the difficulties of getting the necessary quantity, size, and quality of onyx (cracking was a problem) made this scheme unfeasible. By using marble, instead of onyx, Gordon Bunshaft overcame these problems and achieved translucent walls in one of his best-known projects, the Beinecke Library at Yale (1960-63).

10. The geometric manipulation of the Chapel's tetrahedrons marked the genesis of Netsch's field theory, culminating in his design for the Architecture and Art, Behavioral Sciences, and Science and Engineering buildings on the Chicago campus of the University of Illinois.

11. Netsch's original design for the stained glass was a Matisse-like rendition of portions of the Old and New Testaments. When this design was rejected by the chaplains, Netsch developed a simpler scheme composed of thick, rectangular pieces of stained glass. The task of laying out the thousands of pieces of glass (which totaled about a mile, with six pieces per foot) fell to Netsch, who spent winter evenings coloring by hand a subtly varied design which went from rich dark colors to gold over the altar. From Walter Netsch, "The Air Force Academy Chapel."

12. Ibid.

13. According to Netsch, this was probably to the relief of the Illinois Institute of Technology faction within Skidmore, Owings & Merrill, who did not approve of the Chapel design, and wanted to distance themselves from it. Because of this his name became linked with the Chapel and, he believes, this helped to break the firm's rule regarding the anonymity of team members. After this, other designers' names within the firm started appearing on projects. Although Netsch's name is the only one typically associated with the Chapel, other team members at Skidmore, Owings & Merrill credited with making significant contributions to the design and construction of the Chapel include: Kenneth Naslund, structural engineer; Ralph Youngren, Netsch's chief assistant; Albert DeLong, job captain; Andrew Brown, chief structural engineer; and Robertson Ward, architectural technology researcher.

14. Nathaniel A. Owings, *The Spaces in Between: An Architect's Journey* (Boston: Houghton Mifflin, 1973), 159.

15. U.S. Congress, Senate, "Approval of Design of U.S. Air Force Academy Chapel," *Congressional Record,* vol. 104, pt. 1, 85th Cong., 2nd Sess., 16 January 1958, 543.

16. Pietro Belluschi, who had considerable experience dealing with this issue, was one of the architectural consultants on the Chapel (the others being Eero Saarinen, Welton Beckett, and Roy Larson). Belluschi was considered one of the outstanding ecclesiastical architects in the United States at the time. See Meredith L. Clausen, *Spiritual Space: The Religious Architecture of Pietro Belluschi* (Seattle: University of Washington Press, 1992). Saarinen also brought outstanding experience in religious design to the project with the recently completed Kresge Chapel at MIT (1955).

17. "Radical design dropped for Air Academy Chapel," *New York Times,* 4 July 1955.

18. John S. Bennet, Chaplain (Colonel) USAF to Director, Academy Installations, Attention Major Witters, Subj: Plans for Academy Chapel at Colorado Springs, September 27, 1955. Transcript in Record Group 120, Series 22, Special Collections Branch of the Air Force Academy Library, Colorado Springs. I would like to thank

Kristen Schaffer for providing me with copies of this information.

19. Paul Thiry, architect, in a letter responding to a query by the editors in "Air Academy Chapel: Professional Opinion," *Architectural Record* (December 1957): 278.

20. "Air Force Academy Chapel," *Architectural Record* (December 1962): 86.

21. Memo for Secty, AF, from Chaplain (Maj Gen) Charles I. Carpenter, subj: Air Force Academy Religious facilities, 1 November 1955.

22. For an account of the development of the Air Force's programmatic requirement for the Chapel see Wiley, "The United States Air Force Academy Chapel."

23. The average percentages of military personnel among the three major faiths in 1955 was approximately 66% Protestant, 29% Catholic, and 5% Jewish. Memo for Secty, AF, from Chaplain (Maj Gen) Charles I. Carpenter, Subj: Air Force Academy Religious Facilities, 1 November 1955 in Wiley, "The United States Air Force Academy Chapel," 23. There is also a very small room on the Terrace Level to serve a variety of denominations.

24. Owings, *The Spaces in Between,* 160.

25. U.S. Congress, Senate, *Supplemental Appropriations Bill,* 1956, Full Committee hearings on H.R. 7278, 84th Cong., 1st Sess., 1955, 380.

26. U.S. Congress, House, *Supplemental Appropriations for 1958, Congressional Record,* vol. 103, pt. 10, 85th Cong., 1st Sess., 6 August 1957, 13789.

27. George V. Fagan, *The Air Force Academy: An Illustrated History* (Boulder: Johnson Books, 1988), 83.

28. "Grown up at last," *Art News* (Summer 1955): 14.

29. Design Directive FY 1955 No. 42, U.S. Air Force Academy, in Wiley, "The United States Air Force Academy Chapel," 11.

30. Fagan, *Air Force Academy,* 82.

31. This is how the 4,334-pipe concert organ in the Protestant Chapel and a smaller organ in the Catholic Chapel were funded. From "The Air Force Academy Chapel: From discord to eventual harmony, it finally took flight," *Colorado Springs Sun,* 11 May 1985. I would like to thank Robert Bruegmann for bringing this material to my attention.

32. U.S. Congress, House, *Supplemental Appropriations for 1958, Congressional Record,* vol. 103, pt. 10, 85th Cong., 1st Sess., 6 August 1957, 13789.

33. Ibid., 13926.

34. U.S. Congress, House, Committee on Appropriations, *Department of Defense Appropriations for 1965,* Hearings before a subcommittee. 88th Cong., 2nd Sess., 1964, 503. In fairness to Skidmore, Owings & Merrill, it should be noted that the firm's contract to provide continuing construction supervision and inspection of the Chapel was not extended past 1 June 1961, even though 17 March 1962 was the scheduled completion date. But it is questionable about how much difference this would have made. The complex geometry of the structure, the miles of joints on the chapel's exterior skin, the constant change in material from aluminum to stained glass, and the significant thermal swings of the Colorado climate (the building creaks loudly as it expands on a sunny day), all combine to produce a building that consistently leaks.

35. Netsch objected to Harold E. Wagoner's designs for the liturgical furnishings in the Protestant Chapel but was overruled by the Council of Churches which was financing this portion of the project. He found the dagger-like quality of the cross that hangs over the pulpit questionable and the references to propellors in the pew-ends romantic imagery in a jet age. The mosaic reredos in the both the Protestant and Catholic chapels were executed by painter-sculptor Lumen Martin Winter. The classical pipe organs in the Protestant and Catholic chapels were designed by Walter Holtkamp and built by M. P. Moller Company.

36. Serge Guilbaut discusses how American art was used during the Cold War to promote U.S. cultural superiority abroad, in *How New York Stole the Idea of Modern Art: Abstract Expressionism, Freedom, and the Cold War,* trans. Arthur Goldhammer (Chicago: University of Chicago Press, 1983).

37. "Chiefs See Cadet Chapel Dedication," *Air Force Times,* 2 October 1963, 24: 2. I would like to thank Duane Reed, archivist and chief, Special Collections and Directorate of Academy Libraries, for providing me with copies of articles from the Air Force Times.

38. "The air-age acropolis," *Architectural Forum* (June 1954): 161.

39. Louis Kahn, notebook, dated 1955, K12.22.55, Louis T. Kahn Collection, University of Pennsylvania, Pennsylvania Historical Museum Commission, Philadelphia. I would like to thank Sarah Ksiazek for this information.

40. Ibid.

107. Cadet Area, first phase, c. 1962. Most of the major buildings called for in the original master plan had been built by 1959 except for the Chapel, which was completed in 1962. Drawing by Skidmore, Owings & Merrill from 1985 *Cadet Area Master Plan* book.

108. Cadet Area, later construction, c. 1985. In the mid-1960s a major expansion of the Academy made necessary the construction of a new cadet dormitory building, located to the west of the Dining Hall, an extension of the Academic Building at its south, and construction of the Field House north of the Cadet Gym. In 1983 the Library was enlarged. Drawing by Skidmore, Owings & Merrill from 1985 *Cadet Area Master Plan* book.

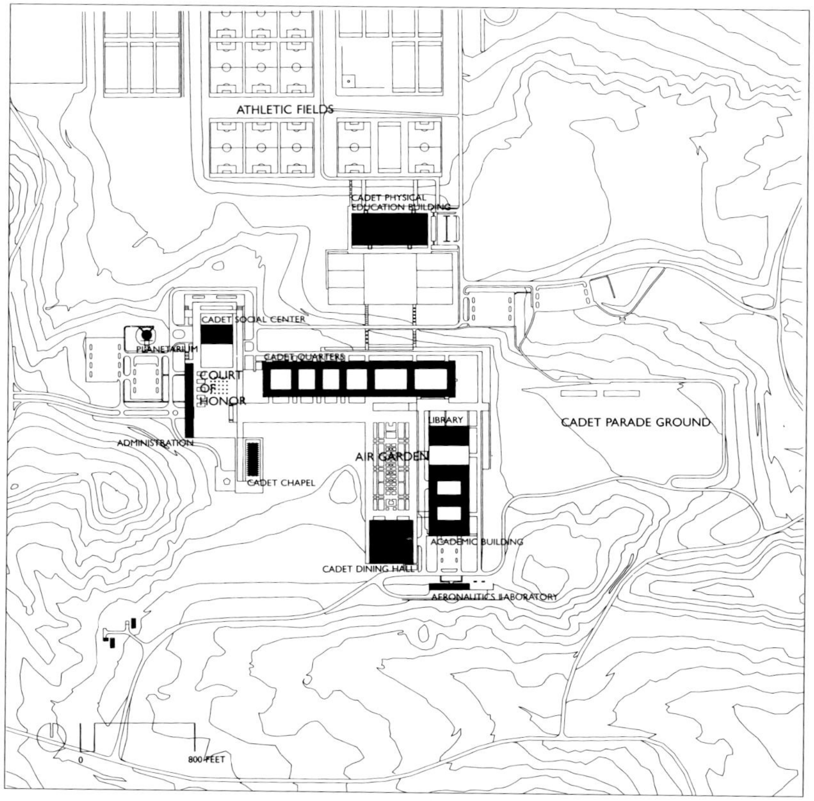

107

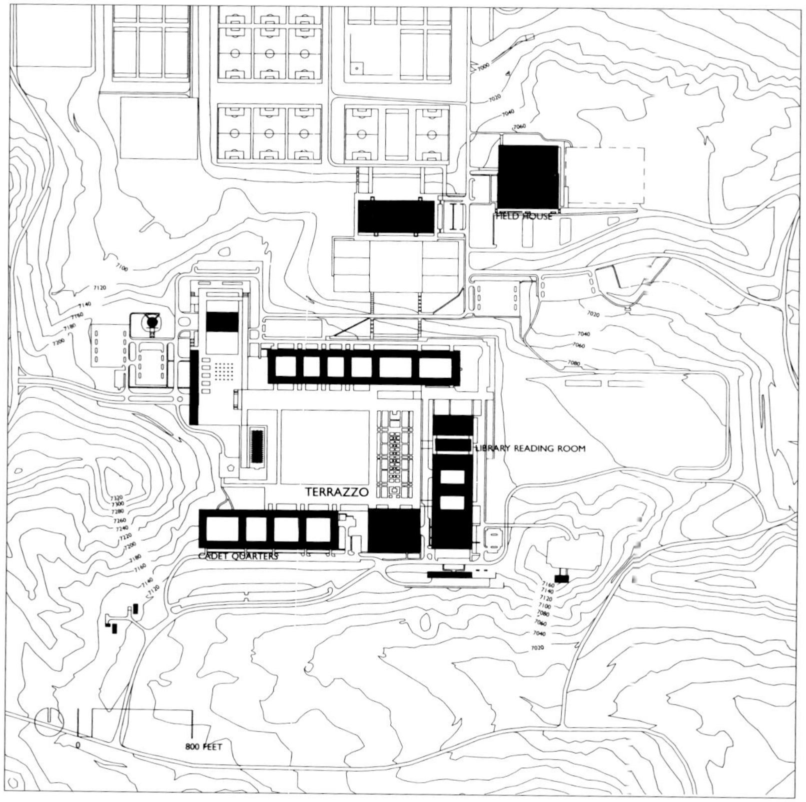

108

Robert Bruegmann

Epilogue

The essays in this volume have focused on the design and construction of buildings at the Air Force Academy and the critical reception they received through 1962 when the Chapel was completed. Of course there has been considerable construction at the Academy since that date and reactions to the buildings have inevitably changed. Because this tale would take us well beyond the scope of this book, what follows are a few comments on the fate of architecture at the Academy since 1962.

The record on new construction and remodeling has been mixed. In the Cadet Area, the most significant single event was a major expansion program initiated in 1964 (figs. 107, 108).[1] Prominent among these projects was the construction in 1965 of a new cadet dormitory, Sijan Hall, on the south side of the Cadet Chapel and Court of Honor. Although the architects, Leo Daley and HD&R, both of Omaha, chose materials and detailing that matched fairly closely those of the original Cadet Quarters, the site selected did not conform to the SOM master plan. It had the effect of blocking off the visual and physical connection between the central Cadet Area and the hills to the southwest that originally came directly into the formal paved area of the Terrazzo Level and Court of Honor. The placement of the new dormitory structure also turned what had been a dynamic L-shaped composition into a far more conventional quadrangle. At the same time the Academic Building was extended to the south and the Field House was constructed near the Cadet Gym.[2] The 1970s witnessed some of the most insensitive intrusions into the Cadet Area, notably a group of small buildings east of Fairchild Hall and the filling in of Dan Kiley's Air Gardens. The admission of women, starting in 1976, also necessitated some modifications, but they took place primarily within the interior of buildings. The Cadet Library was enlarged in 1982 and the Barry Goldwater Visitor Center, located just over the hill from the Cadet Area, opened in 1986.[3]

Outside the Cadet Area there has been a considerable amount of new construction. The largest project was the creation of the Air Field in the southeast corner of the Academy property in the 1970s. In the Community Area the Noncommissioned Officers (NCO) Club, Child Care Center, Base Exchange (BX), Youth Center, and Bowling Alley were all constructed in the 1960s and 1970s. Elsewhere a building for the Corps of Engineers (now the Communications Building) was put up in the 1960s, and offices for the Association of Graduate Alumni (AOG) were built in the 1990s. A great deal of the housing has also been substantially modified. Most of these changes have affected areas not usually seen by visitors. With the exception of the new Sijan Hall, very little has disturbed the integrity of the public areas of the Academy.

Although the physical environment of the Academy has

enjoyed a considerable stability, perceptions of it have changed significantly. It appears that by the time the Chapel was finished, the modernity of the buildings had ceased to shock much of the general public, and from all indications the Academy quickly took its place along with West Point and Annapolis as national symbols of the American military. These associations were, if anything, intensified during the years of the Vietnam War as the Academy, like all of the more public military installations, became the focus for anti-war sentiment. Because it was accessible to the public, because it provided striking film footage for the evening news, and because the mandatory attendance policy insured that there would be an audience, the Chapel became the scene of numerous demonstrations involving picketing, leafleting, and the disruption of services.[4]

After the Vietnam War, memories of these activities gradually faded, but not before they had fixed in the public consciousness an association of the Academy with stirring historic events in the national life. By the early 1990s the imagery of the Academy had become so recognizable that a view of the Chapel could serve as backdrop for a Colorado Springs television news show or a diagramatic sketch evoke Colorado on a U-Haul trailer. In the process of becoming an icon, the Academy has largely emerged from the controversies surrounding its design. This is suggested by the laconic entry under Colorado Springs in the AAA guidebook to Colorado and Utah:

> **U. S. Air Force Academy, 12 mi. n. on I-25, prepares students for careers in the Air Force. Grounds include a B-52 bomber display, scenic overlooks, chapel, planetarium and Falcon Stadium. The Noon Meal Formation can be seen from the Court of Honor Monday-Friday during the academic year. Allow 2 hours minimum.**

The Academy today is one of the most heavily visited man-made tourist sites in the nation, receiving over a million visitors each year. On a summer day the Chapel often accommodates 6,000 people.

In architectural circles, however, the reputation of the Academy seems to have followed a different path. As the essays in this book have demonstrated, there was considerable controversy in the architectural press at a number of key moments during the years it was being designed and built. Although many conservative architects would probably have preferred something more traditional in style, the magazines were dominated by advocates of the Modern Movement, and the Academy received mainly good press. As the 1960s wore on, opinions about the Academy became more negative. The nadir was reached in 1973, when architecture critic Charles Jencks implicated the Academy's architectural design in recent, well-publicized cheating scandals, and a writer in the scholarly magazine *Art Journal* described the Academy design process as an example of bureaucratic despotism.[6] After this, the Academy tended to disappear altogether from the literature of the architectural world. It is hardly even mentioned in any of the histories of American architecture published in the 1970s or 1980s.[7]

The reasons for this eclipse are complex. One explanation is that construction of the buildings, many of which had been designed in 1955, had taken so long that by the time they were finished in the late 1950s (or in the case of the Chapel, the early 1960s), they were no longer fashionable. Although the architect Nathaniel Owings had wanted to create a timeless design, within ten years it was already clear that architectural styles had changed, and the avant-garde had moved on. By the mid-1960s critical interest had already shifted from the sleek steel and glass prismatic solids of SOM toward the more personal and expressionistic late work of Eero Saarinen, for example, or to the heavier, more axial and symmetrical designs of Louis Kahn, or to the ironic, historically informed and more ornamented work of Robert Venturi. By the 1970s International Style modernism was under siege by younger architects who, under the banner of Postmodernism, claimed that Modernist architecture ignored history and local context and imposed cold, uncompromising forms and materials on a public that never really accepted it.

This explanation does not entirely account for the silence surrounding the Academy. Even in the years when the International Style was most under attack, many works by Mies and by SOM were still discussed and even admired. But it was conspicuously the commercial and residential work of these architects that was usually praised. Few of the histories of the 1970s and 1980s had much to say about Mies's Federal Center in Chicago, for example, which looked very much like a set of office buildings. The larger and more prominent the public building the more likely it was to be written out of history. Lincoln Center in New York, the Albany Mall in Albany, New York, the Kennedy Center in Washington, D.C., although they exhibited stylistic tendencies very different from those seen at the Academy, all came under attack.

It appears that the Academy, like an even more ambitious piece of high Modernist design, the new Brazilian capital city of Brasilia, further suffered from deflated expectations.[8] Because the aims of the Modernists had been so high (so unrealistic, its critics would say), and because so much of Modernism had been predicated on the ability of design to solve social problems, it was perhaps inevitable that when the design of Brasilia could not prevent the appearance there of the social inequities that had plagued the old capital city of Rio de Janeiro, or when the design of the Air Force Academy could not put an end to problems like cheating, there would be disappointment. In fact, what the Postmodern critics did brilliantly was to take the Modernists' own rhetoric about the ability of design to affect human behavior, and turn it on its head, blaming Modernism for many of the problems of the postwar era.

By the late 1980s, however, it had become clear that the attack on Modernism had, in turn, largely run its course in the architectural world. A flood of books and articles on many of the most important figures of the 1950s indicated a renewed interest in the buildings of the postwar years.[9] Along with this development went a growing concern with protecting the monuments of that era, many of which faced major maintenance problems, expansions or remodelings.

The Air Force Academy has certainly been affected by this change. In recent years there has been an increasingly strong desire on the part of Academy officials to maintain the integrity of the original master plan, particularly in the Cadet Area. The most significant change of the last decades was one that did not take place. A proposed enlargement of the Chapel in the 1970s that would have dramatically altered its appearance was not approved.[10] Commenting in 1981 on the failed expansion project and the appearance of a revised scheme by Walter Netsch, a writer in *Architectural Record* described the Chapel as "one of the most important works of modern American architecture built during the 1950s."[11] Architects from SOM were called back to the Academy in 1983 to update the original master plan, and they have been involved with planning work there ever since.[12] In recent years the Academy has put in place new guidelines that attempt to make all new construction more sympathetic to the style of the original buildings, and Academy officials point with pride at a Burger King restaurant in the Community Center area of the Academy designed in the International Style. Of minor functional importance, a partial restoration of the Air Gardens started in 1993 demonstrates what is apparently a new ethos grounded in conservation and restoration.[13]

It also appears that by the early 1990s a cycle had been completed. Buildings that once seemed ultramodern but then came to be seen as too conservative to individuals in the next generation, had reached an age when they were old enough to be considered historic monuments. Indeed, the entire Cadet Area is currently under study for possible inclusion on the National Register of Historic Places. In a story filled with paradoxes, it is perhaps the most delicious irony of all that a building complex that could arouse cries of outrage for its challenge to tradition in the 1950s could already by the end of the century function as a historic landmark, a bastion of continuity in an ever-changing world.

Notes

1. On the expansion program see *Architectural Record* (January 1966): 40.
2. The Fairchild Hall extension was designed by Leo A. Daly, the Field House by Sverdrup & Parcel.
3. The Visitors Center was designed by John James Wallace of Colorado Springs.
4. George Fagan, *The Air Force Academy: An Illustrated History*, 178–179. Mandatory chapel attendance was ruled unconstitutional by the U. S. Supreme Court in 1973.
5. *Colorado Springs Sun*, 11 May, 1985, 28.
6. Charles Jencks, *Modern Movements in Architecture*, 1973, 202. According to Jencks's hyperbolic analysis: "The Air Force Academy so over-asserts regimentation and impersonality that one can understand why there has been continual cheating among the cadets." Richard Gid Powers, "The Cold War in the Rockies: American Ideology and the Air Force Academy Design," *Art Journal* (Summer 1974): 304–17.
7. It was either not mentioned or dismissed curtly in William Jordy's *American Buildings and Their Architects* of 1976; in the two volumes of James Marston Fitch's *American Building*, the second edition of which was published 1966–72; in Leland Roth's *A Concise History of American Architecture* of 1979; in Marcus Whiffen and Frederick Koeper's *American Architecture 1607–1976*, published in 1981; in David Handlin's *American Architecture* of 1985; or in Alan Gowans's *Styles and Types of North American Architecture* of 1992.
8. On Brasilia, see Norma Evenson, *Two Brazilian Capitols,* published in 1973, and James Holston, *The Modernist City: An Anthropological Critique,* 1989.
9. Among these books were monographs on SOM designers Myron Goldsmith in 1987 and Gordon Bunshaft in 1988, and on Wallace K. Harrison of Harrison and Abramovitz in 1989.
10. Drawings for this addition had gone all the way through the Air Force and Corps of Engineers approval process before they were stopped. The Academy then hired Walter Netsch to design a new addition.
11. Bradford Perkins, "Preserving the Landmarks of the Modern Movement," *Architectural Record* (July 1981): 108. The Netsch design was not built either, but the need for the addition has not disappeared.
12. The most notable result of this work was the Cadet Area Master Plan, issued in 1985.
13. Interview with Academy architect Duane Boyle, December 1993.

PART 3

INTERVIEWS AND RECOLLECTIONS

A Conversation about the U. S. Air Force Academy between Walter Netsch and John Burchard

The conversation between architect Walter Netsch of Skidmore, Owings & Merrill and architectural historian John Burchard, from which the following excerpts have been taken, was held about 1958, shortly after the completion of the major academic area buildings but before the arrival of the first cadets and the start of construction of the Chapel. The typescript was apparently a draft manuscript for a publication that never materialized. Burchard, professor and Dean of the School of Social Sciences and Humanities at MIT, was a well-known figure in the architectural world, an influential magazine editor, and the author of several important books on architecture and history (fig. 109).

John Burchard: You and I have talked about the Air Force Academy almost from its beginning a long time ago. We have walked around the site from time to time and have just completed another such trip at the end of June 1958. There was another night not long ago when you littered the floor of your Chicago apartment with studies for the glass of the chapel and filled its air with studies of how to play Beethoven's Sonata no. 32. In two or three months now, the cadets will begin to march about their new academy grounds, to recite in the new academy class rooms, to eat in their new academy dining hall, to sleep in their new academy dormitories. Let's start at the beginning. Were you in on the site selection?

Netsch: No, we were not. But the Air Force did have professional assistance. Their own staff included such experienced people as General Lindbergh and General Spaatz. Their own technical planning groups and an outside architectural firm were competent to help them evaluate the proposals.

Burchard: I know you liked the site and I gather you think it was all right that you were not in on the first decisions. . . . But suppose you had been confronted with a site on the sand dunes or on the flanks of Mt. McKinley? Would you have declined the job?

Netsch: Perhaps not, but it is an iffy question. I suppose we might have accepted the commission if the conditions were not ludicrous, have worked hard to get the site changed, and then, if we failed, have done our best on the sand or in the snow. . . . These were national decisions, transcending architecture. As a citizen I can naturally have an opinion about this that might be quite unrelated to architecture. The population of the United States is now centered in Illinois, not in the East. The Naval and Military Academies were founded very early when the total confines of the United States hardly stretched to the Appalachians. As things came out, Annapolis was located in a southern environment, West Point in a northern. If only on the basis of national symmetry, the Western choice seems to me, as an American, to have been the right one.

Burchard: What then?

Netsch: One of the first jobs was to determine the boundaries. An architect does not often have the chance to come in as early as this. It is useful when he can. He is not thinking about specific buildings at this early stage, or anyway, should not be, but his training does prepare him to sense some things that are by no means obvious without the training.

For example, given the location north of Colorado Springs it was pretty apparent that the mountains and the Pike National Forest ought to form the western boundary. This would provide excellent protection by previously owned federal land or federally controlled land the Air Force would not have to acquire.

The other boundaries were less obvious. There were no major east-west roads in the area and consequently the problem at the north end and the south, beyond that of providing enough acreage, resolved itself into procuring northern and southern boundaries, over the brows of hills, so to speak, so that nonconforming or conflicting land use on the adjacent properties would not be visible.

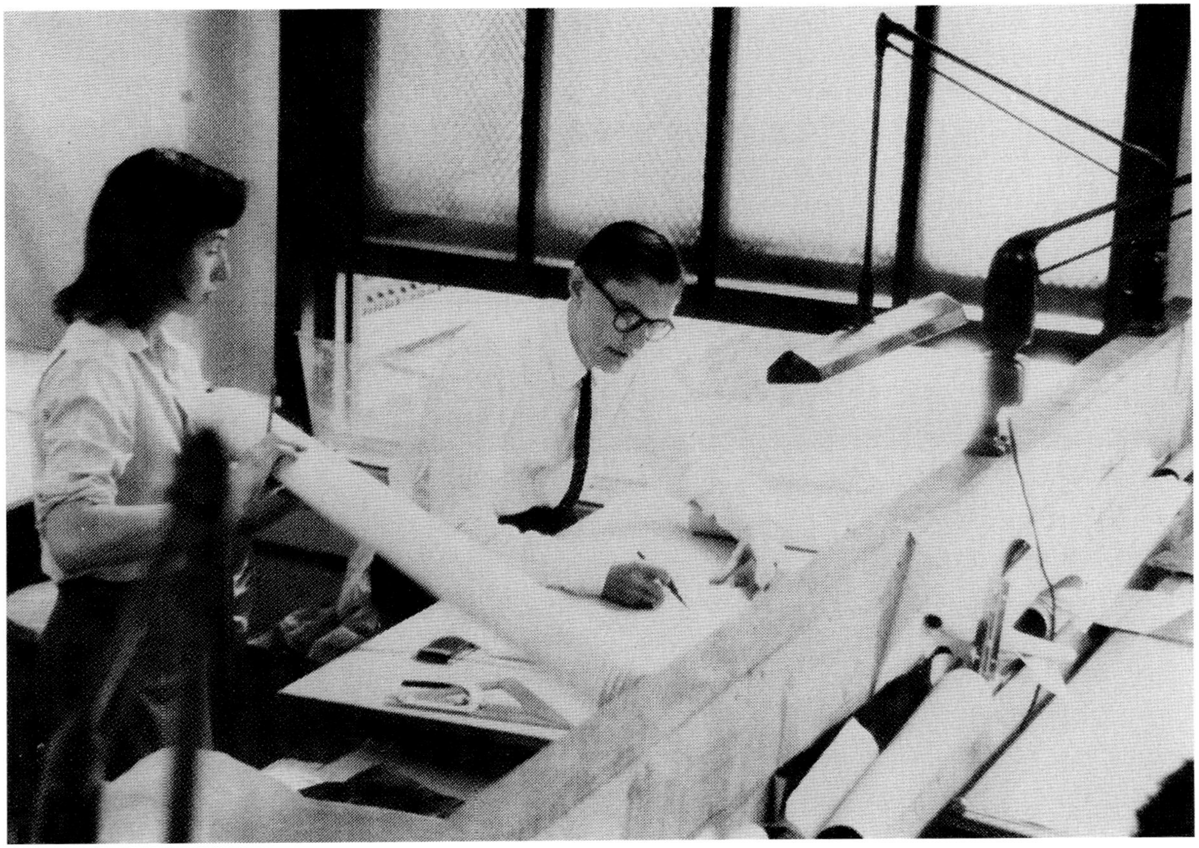

109. Photograph of Walter Netsch in drafting room at SOM offices, Chicago, c. 1955. Photo from *40, A Pictorial History of the Firm and Partners of SOM*. SOM Archives, Chicago.

The eastern problem was trickier. Here there was a main north-south highway and a busy one between Colorado Springs and Denver. This was bound to influence the Academy. It was important that the boundary be well east of the highway so that there could be no nonconforming or blighting development along the highway itself as it passed the Academy.

The airfield problem had to be faced at this stage. This was not to be a tactical field. It was to be only an operational field with provision so that it could accommodate aircraft anticipated later. It was essentially to be a laboratory for the cadets and an important means of arrival and departure for those who used military aircraft. A one-way airstrip was all that was required, and as it turned out this provided 93 percent wind coverage. But even this simplified, the airfield was ponderous to fit in and we had to find enough flat land. In the end there had to be some relocation of the main highway, U.S. 85/87.

Finally the area had to be big enough to allow for free and normal growth of the institution and to take account of the fact that the terrain is really hilly, hillier than it looks against the steep slopes of the mountains and that a lot of it cannot easily be built on. So it turned out to be a big site.

Burchard: And do I take it that there were also other decisions even before alternative master plans could be worked out?

Netsch: Oh, a good many. Let me give two or three examples.

For instance, we talked to the meteorologists to find out which of the valleys would be warm and which would be cool; we wanted to know whether there would be consistent differences in the snowfall and accumulation next to the mountains and out along the highway. We hoped there would be some physical answers. Every architectural study involves a search for all the limits of the program that may help to define it or at least give direction to it. To solve an architectural problem which has no limits is the hardest thing for an architect, not a freedom which he would covet. So we searched for these definers. The meteorology in the end declined to offer helpful controls.

Again we looked for estimates of the overburden on the mesas and in the valley. These might have been suggestive. But they too were neutral. The tree cover was more helpful. It was almost always on the northern slopes of the mesas and not on the southern. This was not surprising since in the winter snows melt much more rapidly on the unprotected southern sides. So the south slopes look over onto wonderful northern hillsides of pines. We picked a splendid overlook of this sort later on. True to life, the slope was burned over about a year after the project was started. It has been reseeded and will some day be what we originally intended.

Burchard: These are very interesting considerations. Were there larger ones?

Netsch: In the early stages we spent a great deal of time studying what the site and its development would do to its neighbors. We could perhaps protect the Academy against them. Could we protect them against the Academy, or could they protect themselves? How would the orientation of the airfield affect Colorado Springs? How would this great increment of federally owned land affect the development of the private areas? Were we going to add problems of schools, markets, transportation—burdens which the community might not be able to bear? How about water supply? We took all these things seriously. For example Colorado Springs, like much of the eastern slope, had water problems even without the Academy. We could not decently aggravate them. So part of the purchase agreement with the state of Colorado called for delivery of water, drawn from the western slopes, carried through tunnels to the eastern slopes. These conduits pass through the southern part of the site en route to Colorado Springs and five million gallons are, by this agreement, drawn off for the Academy.

Burchard: After this, you were ready to think about buildings?

Netsch: Not really. Of course once you see these beautiful mesas you will begin to dream of possible Xanadus but you must be careful not to dream the same dream too often. If you do think of the same Castilian castle every night and if you cover too much paper with the fruit of a single dream, it will finally become the architecture. Then if it meets the kind of considerat ons I have been talking about and if there is any kind of conflict, it may not be the architecture which will yield. This will lead to bad solutions.

In other words, once we had made the regional decisions and put together data on the technical problems of the site, we had to decide on a logical master plan.

The first stage of this could be quite abstract and determined by principles. This was more than a college campus; it really had several major components. One was the school itself, classrooms, dormitories, library, infirmary, dining halls, athletic facilities, drill ground; another was the airfield; another was the living community and its amenities for the academic staff; a fourth was the service and supply areas for maintenance, upkeep, warehousing, cold storage. We had to determine how to relate the academic community and the campus, the service area and the airfield and always the intangible condition that this was a national project and would be subject to public influence and inspection from the outset.

Burchard: Could the relation of these things end in one inexorable and logical answer?

Netsch: Certainly not down to the last P and Q. Each individual area was governed by its own inexorabilities. We thought railroads had to reach the supply area and it was then discovered that the valleys which had looked so flat had gradients of about 5 percent while railroad engines do not like anything much steeper than 1 1/4 percent. This naturally drove the supply area down to the flat just as the airfield had been driven there. Then we wanted to locate the airfield so that its inevitable noises would not disturb the educational and residential areas. Considerations and limitations like these helped to define a triangular relationship between the academic community, the airfield, and the housing. This led, logically enough, I think, to the internal net of roads that services the unit and the external net of roads that serves the inner net and also allows the public to see and to take part.

Burchard: How did you get this far without argument?

Netsch: Look, John, you know there are arguments all the time and that they go on inside an office as well as outside. Of course there were arguments. But up to this point we were dealing with abstract principles and these did not raise difficult objections. It was all vague enough in terms of planning criteria and there were no architectural details to fuss about. Laymen who want to influence architecture want to worry about the style of a building or its wall-materials or its cornices but do not often seem concerned with master planning. At this point we had no cornices for the critics to hang their objections on. But now some of these decisions had to be taken and there could no longer be ineluctable answers—consequently there could be legitimate, if friendly, differences of opinion.

Burchard: Did these focus around a few alternatives?

Netsch: Yes, there were certainly those who thought we ought to build in the valley. General Harmon, the superintendent, held this view for a while. He thought that the higher location might be overdramatic and might also unduly limit the room available for expansion. The latter practical apprehension we could show to be unfounded. The psychological position was an expression of a legitimate concern. In the end, and with the help of consultants, he was convinced that once you had a mountain site, it was foolish to cower down in the valley and that the development of the mountain area did not have, ipso facto, to be flamboyant. Then there were others who thought the Academy ought to be down on the highway as a kind of advertisement. But when these people stood on the road and looked at the mesa they realized that the visual experience would be much better when the Academy was closely related to the mountain rather than so far away that the mountain and the Academy would be like two distinct objects rather than the one they ought to be.

Burchard: Now Walter, this makes it all sound the way many people think an architect really works. In other words he makes up his own mind pretty early, according to the myth. He knows where the buildings belong and what they should be like. Then he argues and cajoles all the others and wears them down so that in the end those who want the campus in the valley and those who want the campus on the high road just lose an argument and might as well have saved their breath. Is that the way it really was?

Netsch: Not really, John. But we are human beings, not designing machines. While we were trying to get the programs together and to make logical decisions we were also putting our eyes and our senses to work. We made incessant trips to the site to become aware of its nooks and crannies. We had the use of a helicopter and we would go up and down, first looking at the edges of all the mesas and then, repeating the trip, would look out the other window, up and down all the valleys, and then we would stop at areas that seemed important and then do them on foot and by jeep. Thus we became familiar with every acre.

Burchard: And thus, intuitively, found the lovable, sensitive area which had to be?

Netsch: No, not at all. Feeding on the awareness of which I have spoken, we quit the site and worked up schemes for about five different areas. We did one in the valley, for example, to see what General Harmon's belief would lead to, trying to be reasonably objective. We found a fine little valley, hidden between two small peaks. This was a kind of Shangri-La, hidden away from the rest of society and we did a scheme for it. We did one on the mesa and we thought up a grandiose one, damming up one of the valleys, right up to the foothill of the mountain, putting one part of the school on one haunch of the mesa, another abruptly hitting the mountain. We tried a scheme on a different mesa and took a look also at the valley foreground next to the highway.

Developing these individual schemes, we discovered that there were certain practical problems that could not be resolved on every site. One of course was the question of providing enough area for future expansion. There was the parade ground whose thirty acres on a slope of not more than 2 1/2 percent could not be found everywhere. So some sites could not meet the minimal programmatic requirements.

Another question of this sort involved the marching men. Perhaps ten years from now it will not be necessary for men to march, as a way to discipline and esprit de corps. Other, better methods may be available. But at this time, anyway, it was essential to provide opportunity for men to fall out and to group and to march. A land situation that forced a scheme with lots of little stairs and small dormitories was not acceptable no matter how charming it might be for a different college. Here it was just too confusing. Then there was the question about how you feel about the West. I myself rate as an indigenous factor the sense of not being confined or pushed together in an artificial little community. Some schemes and sites were better than others at preserving this quality.

Burchard: Surely at this point some approach to buildings had to be made?

Netsch: Well, yes. For example, we began to wonder about the methods of construction and what special space characteristics they would demand, about whether they suggested a basic module. Now after we had been at this a while it became clear that the Cadet Quarters were the heart of the problem. The cadets, unlike ordinary college students, are isolated. They cannot go into town every night for movies or girls or beer. The cadet is so limited that his room is not only a place to sleep and a place to study; it is really his living space for four years. This made us realize that the dormitories were the heart, and that their relationships to the Dining Hall and the Headquarters and the Social Hall and ballrooms and the Administration Building, the Physical Education Building, the playing fields and the Library were fundamental, in a way they might not normally be.

Another question we were constantly aware of was "How can we bring the character of the land right in to the man-altered areas?" It was easier on some sites than on others. Sometimes the land was not very exciting, sometimes overexciting. This kind of melding of the land form into the total form was as important as the spaces between or in the buildings.

Burchard: I am particularly interested in the last remark. You know there are those who think you moved a lot of earth at Colorado Springs and who think you were genii of the great American bulldozer. How about that?

Netsch: Yes, we moved quite a lot of land but I think we did not aggrandize or diminish any part of the site with our equipment which looks so large to men but so small to mountains. We did take away a hill or two during construction and we built some so-called "Chinese" mountains around the dining hall. But we did not change the scale or the spirit of the terrain even on the "Chapel Hill" and it is true that the ultimate site was just more promising than the others for this natural marriage.

Burchard: Okay. Anyway, all this led you to some clear conclusions about which there was really no important dissent.

Netsch: That's right. Given all the conditions, we ended by putting the campus on the northwestern corner of the site and the airfield at the southeastern corner, and with the housing at the southwest. This was a happy outcome because I had come to think of the campus mesa as one of the most beautiful locations. Gordon [Bunshaft] and Eero [Saarinen] had the same feelings. As we walked around and even before we had really done anything we felt that here was a land that might permit layouts such as those of the California hillsides, making free use of the slopes. In the end we did not develop quite in this way, not like the slopes of Berkeley or Palo Alto. Instead we evolved what we call "the two up and two down" scheme for the Cadet Quarters so that from the campus plateau, at the vertical center, the amount of necessary rise or descent is minimized. The Physical Education Building down in the valley is certainly an exception and quite a hike back up, but the medics affirmed our defense that this much vertical coming and going was as therapeutic as anything else.

Burchard: Now let's talk in terms of the three Vitruvian postulates about architecture. Let's start with "firmness." What governed your decisions about structures? What decided the basic closure materials? Remembering the stone of West Point and Washington D.C., the brick and stone of Annapolis, was there a serious contention for more "conventional," more durable, more fortress-like, more "appropriate" materials than the pervasive metal and glass you have used at the Academy?

Netsch: Now you really start an argument. Are materials more durable if they are more conventional? I don't agree. Then what is conventional? In 1400 the conventional material was stone. But at the same time the conventional method of travel was by foot or by horse. Now the conventional method is to fly. Why then should we assume that a "conventional" material or a "basic" material necessarily comes ready to use out of the ground? In our society we must assume, I think, that any material that has passed reasonable tests of time and use can be conventional. Maybe for today glass is more conventional than stone.

We never thought of the closure materials as being conventional or unconventional. The program itself, the expression of the buildings influences the selection of the materials. If you have a dining hall that is to seat 3,000 people in non-obstructed space, you have a very large and unusual spatial problem that no "conventional" material could enclose.

We are not building for some land-bound group that has historical connections with a medieval fortress. The educational program of the new Academy is more far-reaching than that on which the older academies were built. These men are going to fly. The Western atmosphere is new and is not medieval. Why would anyone want a fortress? We are not protecting a past in the future. Don't think I press this to the point of suggesting that the materials we used are the only right ones aesthetically but also the right ones symbolically. The materials we used were fine and durable. There was no desire to use anything quick and shoddy. Early on we experimented with newer materials still and gave some of them up because we could not get adequate technical conviction that they would last or behave. We were really more concerned with trying to get the material suited for each element than with satisfying some preconceived old-fashioned notion of what everything ought to look like.

Burchard: You know that I have never had much truck with the nostalgia boys either. Leaving nostalgia out, the fact remains that we have buildings in a state that has fine stone all the way from sandstone and limestone to marble and granite. Do you think all these backyard riches really had nothing to say about the materials for the Academy?

Netsch: Once again we should remember one thing. Colorado is the site but the Academy is national, and it will bring students not only from every state but from many other nations, too. I see no reason in this day why the solution should be parochial. The idea never dawned on us that this was reasonable. The materials had to be presented to the consultants and the technical staff and approved by them and they never talked in these terms, either.

The choice of building materials varied with the possible cost, the use in the building and the function of the building itself. There is a lot of difference between a warehouse with a lot of precast concrete walls that can be expanded or rebuilt and permanent classrooms of the Academic Building with marble facings, where we wanted opacity, careful scale, and color. No, the materials, really evolved from the program. The structures themselves definitely resulted from the program but the final decision on the question of which structural system to use always involved properties of the materials and the problems of the particular program. It is just not so to say the structures are of one type. They are very different, although they are contained within one basic discipline, and surely no one but an architectural anarchist would want to eliminate a basic discipline. The Air Force Academy is no World's Fair, and the buildings cannot be as irresponsible to those next to them as the most brilliant artifices of the architectural world often are when they rise in our cities. The office building and the Academic Building are basically post and lintel. The Cadet Quarters is a bridge structure, rather hovering, sort of a connecting, hovering element between one end and the other. And the Dining Hall is a big sturdy structure, double trussed. Each of these can be defended on the most rigorous application of the Vitruvian principles. There are no a prioris, no tours de force unless the Chapel is. But I would not want to agree that even the Chapel is a tour de force.

Burchard: Let's turn to the second of the Vitruvian canons which SOM ignores. This is the question of "commodity." Let's put the question this way. What were the principal requirements of the Academy's instructional, recreational, and disciplinary program that you, as architects, thought you should challenge and how did you come out with the challenges?

Netsch: Of course we issued a lot of challenges. The architect ought to challenge the client at every point if only to force him to sharpen his understanding of what he really wants. But the architect will not always be right in his challenges and should not be so stubborn as never to admit he was wrong. Let me give some examples. Let's start with the classrooms. You know the system at the older academies and I know it still surprises you. Well, we were not fundamentally military men either and it surprised us, too. We were amazed, even appalled, by the thought that so much of the academic learning seemed to be by rote. That everyone should go to the blackboard every day seemed to us extraordinary in the mid-twentieth century in an institution of higher learning. Then as we visited West Point, at that time the interim school, we became aware of the kind of tension the cadets were under and began to understand that this tension might be a way of weeding out men who would be unable to work under stress. It was perhaps a psychological technique and not merely a vestige of Colonel Blimp turned professor. I might not still agree with it but it was a system that was going to continue for a while and that had in the past produced many fine officers and perhaps even its quota of highly educated men. It was not designed to produce creative artists, or poets, or great scientists.

Well, what do you do in such a situation? We are architects, not educators. Do you try to argue the client down on something as fundamental as this when you know you could be wrong? Obviously not. The most you can do is try to protect him if he should later change his mind. So we tried to provide classrooms that could be modified if the curriculum and the methods should change in time.

We went further than that, though. We were always worrying about the individual in the midst of discipline and trying wherever possible to provide changes of pace in the visual and other experiences of a regimented day. So we built the interior classrooms to give equal recitation opportunity to each man in accordance with the American military educational tradition. We put the classrooms in cluster patterns, though, so that if, some day, they are not needed then they can be thrown together. We set up interior classrooms to offer a closed and concentrated experience while the cadet was in it, because for the kind of instruction at the academy little is learned by gazing on the mountains and you had better concentrate on the blackboard. But then we made our corridors on one side only so that they all looked out to views or to interesting courts, so that between classes there was a real change of scene and environment. We were not going to bury the men in a single classroom environment. When they are in class they will be in class and no doubt about it, and when they are moving and talking between sessions they will have the enjoyment of being outside. This is certainly a lot more pleasant than the conventional double-loaded corridor. Of course we were a little lucky. The economics of this arrangement might not have stood up, had we not also had to provide extra storage space for coats, which worked into the plan in a way to make the economics feasible.

Burchard: Are there any other examples of how you learned?

Netsch: Oh, there are a good many. I think the most dramatic involved the problem of dining. As you know we were always struggling to preserve the cadet's individuality in a system which invariably imposed so many conformities. The dining arrangements seemed to us at first to offer a wonderful opportunity for this. We thought we would make a series of small dining rooms in the Cadet Quarters. This seemed to us to be a terrific idea. Everyone would be in his own little group, looking out over the mountains, enjoying himself at meals in a small, individually scaled element. Now this, we discovered later, was completely contrary to the real conditions, and weeks later we had to admit that our intuition had been wrong. Actually the cadet is part of a squadron from the very beginning and is identified closely with a small group of men from the outset and for four years. The problem then at the Academy was just the opposite. There were times when the Academy needed to get all the men together and they wanted these to be times of least tension. Eating was one of those times. Actually the large space where all the men can get together and feel themselves a homogeneous group was the logical thing. To provide for eating, one big space was more sensible even when you tried to understand the cadet as an individual related to a squadron and then to the whole community.

Burchard: One more question about commodity. Were there any situations where you were right and convinced the client?

Netsch: I wouldn't want to put it that strongly because even in the example I will cite here there were many officers who felt as we did, that after accepting the essential regimentations there had to be ways to give the cadet a sense of his own personality and individuality. Cadets cannot go in for fancy personalized decorations in their rooms; they can't play hi-fi records all night; they cannot have rooms that differ much in quality, one from the other. Yet if there were to be a preservation of individuality, much of the effort surely had to be made at the heart of the cadet's life, that is, in the dormitory. The cadet as we see him today is one kind of individual. Tomorrow he may be different. But the buildings will be there longer than the cadet. So we had to provide all the facilities in an environment which might expand or change, one which would allow as much freedom as possible for change, especially one that might in time release some of the limitations on the cadet as an individual. We were determined that the immediate solution should not seem limiting to the cadet, should not have the atmosphere of a caserne or barracks. And we had also to remember that the cadet as an individual, in a group, or in the mass was in a sense always on public display. These were the terms in which we had to design the quarters.

We have talked of the cadet rooms before and the ways we tried to provide spaces that would allow for a variety of treatments within one unit; and the use of color for the blankets that would vary with each class; red, say, for seniors and electric blue for juniors and golden yellow for sophomores and dark blue for freshmen. Thus you might have some variety within a regimented military space where all the quarters were masculine; and you could pick up accents through the special arrangements of the standardized furniture or through accent colors. We tried to do this wherever possible. We tried to imagine many ways of getting this to work.

We made the inner courts in different sizes, as you know. We abandoned the idea of imposing the standard great view on every cadet and provided different views but all good. We were conscious of the difference between living on the top deck and on the bottom floor and we tried to ameliorate their disadvantages. I think we succeeded.

Burchard: I think so too within the limits that finally had to be imposed by the system. Now, were there any arguments that you lost that you feel badly about?

Netsch: Well yes, many of course. This always happens. Most of them were minor and the disappointment is not serious or permanent. It is hard to know whether it is wise or foolish to air disappointments at all, as it may look like an effort to lay failures on the shoulders of the client. Clients do fail but so do architects. But perhaps it might be useful to those who participate in later ventures if I were to indicate the nature of one or two.

I suppose the most important one to me is that we are not achieving in the dining room quite what we had aimed at. We developed a fancy and quite technologically exciting system of putting all the kitchen services on the floor below and using elevators to carry heated service carts up. This produced a splendid amenity in that the men would eat in an unencumbered dining hall beautifully enclosed by glass *all around*. Well, of course, if there were a power failure it could happen that the elevators would not work and that the cadets might miss a meal or have to achieve it in some confusion. We thought the risks slight as against the gains and were not even sure that the chance to participate usefully in a crisis might not be a good experience for the cadets if the crisis arose. But we lost the argument. The final main heating and serving areas as well as the dishwashing will be on the main floor and so the cadets will not eat in a glass-enclosed pavilion. I think this concession sacrificed a great daily amenity to a minor contingency. A problem as fancy as this is not typical of architectural practice but there was another one that is more characteristic. One day the height of the cadet quarters was restricted in a rather arbitrary way. This was after we had gone to a lot of trouble to study the vertical and horizontal proportions. I am sure that a foot more to each room would have made the individual rooms much better and that the outside elevations would have been stronger. But we abided by this decision and no reevaluation was possible.

Burchard: Were there any more?

Netsch: No, these were the worst, and though they are disappointments they are not disasters. The debates we won far exceeded the ones we lost—and for most of the debates the terms "winning" and "losing" are really very inappropriate. Architecture should not be a war between the client and the architect. If the architect or the client really has to score a *victory* about a building, the victory is likely to be Pyrrhic. The development of the Academy was not such a war.

Burchard: Maybe now we ought to touch on the third Vitruvian ingredient: delight. Let's not try to dive into the deep and murky waters of aesthetic philosophy. I think the whole thing is swell and is going to be better still when the Chapel is set in the diadem. And I must assume you do. And I would not suppose that we would change the minds of those who don't buy anything we might say here. Let's talk about lesser but still important, if local, questions. Nobody would want mountain scenery to be urbanized less than I would want it. I think you have not urbanized the site. But many people say you have. How do you answer?

Netsch: I don't agree at all that we urbanized the site. I think that men coming to it a decade from now who know none of the history will feel that we have an indigenous solution in terms of its relationship to the land. I think that it will then seem to be, as I believe it now seems to be, nature embracing the scale of the terrain. We are not in a little New England community, we are not in Vermont. One of the constant problems of scale against the mountainous backdrop was to be certain that the forms of the buildings were large enough to be related to the mountains, which neither the Egyptians nor the Romans would have been able to overpower. The buildings themselves (and their materials) all reflect the temperature and the climate.

Burchard: Wait a minute. This is a very bright sky and land, bright in summer, blinding in winter; hot in the midsummer day, cool in a violent thunderstorm, bitter cold on a midwinter night. Generally men have met such conditions with small windows, thick walls. You meet them with glass and outdoor arcades.

Netsch: The glass is gray and heat-absorbent and will, I think, offer no problems. The classrooms have no disturbing outside light to accommodate to. There are plenty of areas of shade and plenty of shelters from the wind or rain. I can't imagine living in a cadet room without wanting to have a full eyeful of the country instead of peering through a porthole or a Pullman window. The windows can be cranked open and there should be no heat buildup. Now of course we were very conscious of these conditions and we would have been reckless and irresponsible if we had ignored them in favor of a scheme whose looks we liked.

It is very bright out there and I think the open arcades will be very pleasant to walk under. In thunderstorms or steady rains they will serve for cover. They give us another opportunity to alleviate the light with bright colors. These are in the recessed areas and will not be gaudy. But they will be interesting when you are close to them and their interest will be enhanced by the texture of the mosaic tile.

Burchard: Let's cling to the conditions for a moment more. You have talked of giving up the universal standard view as a way toward individuality. But is the multiple orientation really logical?

Netsch: Perhaps not perfectly. Nothing is perfect. It does emphasize the best exposures, which are north and south. The western exposure, which is so trying in many places, will not be bad here because the mountains are so near at the west that the late afternoon sun will not fall on the buildings. We got as close to the mountains as we could. Everyone will feel, I think, that he is on a foothill of the mountains, looking toward their heights or out on the plains. Situated close to the mountains, you can feel their grandeur; their very shadows will fall upon you towards dusk. Looking out over the expanse of the plain, you can feel its grandeur too and this is better than sitting out on the plain, looking at the mountains too far away and the plain too omnipresent and thus missing the grandeur of both. This is what we tried to provide.

Burchard: Earlier you have answered me about the Colorado materials. But was it equally reasonable to ignore Colorado architecture?

Netsch: Now John, you know that is a rhetorical question. Don't you remember the night you ridiculed the idea that there was a Colorado architecture? You asked whether it was Mesa Verde? The dismal shacks of the silver towns? The Victorian opera houses beloved by Lucius Beebe? The fire station in Georgetown, Colorado? The quaint wooden houses in Leadville that even have windows in their gables shaped like giant human eyes? You asked whether it was the imported Swiss chalets of the motels of Aspen, or the imported modern architecture of Herbert Bayer in the same town, or the brick of Klauder's university at Golden, or Meem's museum in Colorado Springs, or the Broadmoor Hotel, or Ieoh Ming Pei's Mile High Center in Denver. I agree with you when you insist that there is no such thing as Colorado architecture in the sense that there is New England architecture, or even Prairie architecture, à la Frank Lloyd Wright. No, in the narrow sense there is no Colorado material, no Colorado architecture. The mountains are the architecture of Colorado, not the Will Rogers Memorial. What is Coloradan is the land and the sky and the flora, and to these, I think, the Academy is true.

Burchard: Now for the landscaping itself. This is another thing that economizers believe to be extraneous to the building and thus permissible to eliminate or reduce when the money runs thin. But this is never really true for an important building is it, unless it was designed originally to repudiate planting, wanted none, and would be damaged by it? I felt in looking at your early schemes that the landscaping of the Academy was essential and not a bunch of sponge rubber pasted on a model as an afterthought. Yet I have heard recently and with some dismay that some of the landscaping will be left out. How about it?

Netsch: You are quite right. Most of the landscaping is absolutely essential to the Academy, but it has been a difficult struggle to keep it. We have been able to keep one of the major gardens and we have lost another. The main one we kept is the formal one leading to the dining hall [the Air Garden]. I think it is formal yet fanciful. It is exciting and important. It just had to be. And we have convinced enough people so that it will be. I wish we did not have to fight about these things, because they are as essential as the buildings. They are not landscaping in the sense of buying a new holly tree for your backyard. These open spaces and those of any serious architecture are integrated with the buildings and must be treated just as seriously as the building materials and techniques or the interior decoration and furnishings. I think it is utterly wrong to assume that they are extra. But most of the world does think of them as extras or at least as postponable. They aren't postponable. Landscaping is not something you stick on like postage stamps. It takes years to develop.

Burchard: Another question that has to be asked is perhaps the most elusive of all. I am one who thinks that symbols cannot be created by theorists or designers but grow out of the grass roots and through time. Yet they have grown in strong institutions. They needed some signs to cling to. The sally port, the parade, the overlook, offer West Pointers signs

of this sort. They have become an important part of the West Point experience. Do you sense any such signs in the Academy's architecture, or inherent in it? If so, did you seek consciously to provide them?

Netsch: Well certainly they were not consciously sought. At least not by the program writers and the architects. I would have argued against seeking them consciously had the question ever arisen. Now there are lesser symbols I am not happy about.

There is an almost frantic search for symbols in the modern world. The idea is force-fed. Up in Denver the cadets call the man who gives out coffee the "navigator," and the "pilot" does something else and I suppose the "runway" will be the open-floor area in the Cadet Quarters if it isn't called the "launching pad." Well, all this is harmless enough but it doesn't mean anything either. That is not what you are aiming at.

I think the symbolism you suggest may arise from the way the buildings relate to the expanse of the area; how they confine yet open out; how they contain and release and relax within an exhilarated space which is an earthbound version of the sky. That is what we would think about as architects, and if this should lead later to symbolic associations, that will be fine.

Burchard: There is another building at the Academy which is bound to be symbolic, though not necessarily of the Air Force alone. I mean the Chapel, of course. What shall we say of it? Certainly it offers a main contrapuntal note for the whole campus or will when it is done. Is it a good idea to try to discuss it before it has arisen?

Netsch: We can't exclude the Chapel. It is an integral part of the whole design. We took the responsibility for putting it up on top of Chapel Hill. In the beginning we took a sort of medieval approach to its location in the community and I think we were wrong. The Mont-Saint-Michel aspect would have been wrong. Cadets are not monks and there was no reason why they should be made to climb 125 feet to go to church. So I am glad the first proposal was rejected.

The final solution, which is integrated with the campus, still offers a much stronger and more integrated relation to the whole Academy. It becomes an active part of the cadet life. I think this is more logical.

Also I think the character of the building and its relation to the whole site is the thing to talk about here and not its details as an individual element. Think of it as part of the total group when you look again at the site plan. Here are the large spaces caring for the complicated needs of quarters, academic buildings, administration. Then there are the contrapuntal necessities, the little and round planetarium, the enormous Dining Hall and the dominating Chapel. This is the kind of counterpoint in spatial organization that provides the ultimate individual expression. For the rest, let's wait, John, until we do stand in the nave together. I hope we will then feel reverent. I think we will.

Recollections of Gordon Bunshaft

Gordon Bunshaft served as senior designer for Skidmore, Owings & Merrill in New York during the planning and design of the Air Force Academy and had ultimate responsibility for the design of the buildings. The following has been excerpted from the transcript of a taped session that was part of an oral history project conducted by SOM. (fig. 110).

The Air Force Academy, at the time the government was seeking the architects/engineers for the project, was perhaps the major project in the country. It was supposed to cost $125 million or something like that. It was a very large project, a whole new academy built at once for the Air Force. I was not involved in any of the seeking for that job. I don't know how it happened, but the firm made a presentation in Washington to the Secretary of Air, the final presentation. I believe there were five or six architects invited to that final presentation.

It was Saarinen who made the travel across the whole site and traveled around on the proposed site near Colorado Springs. I think there was Wally Harrison. I believe Nat visited the site, and Skidmore and Owings was represented by Nat and Skid, and I don't know who all else, but they were there in Washington. I guess Becket may have been one of the architects, but I'm not sure.

They all made their presentations to the future commandant of the Academy, Major General Harmon, and Secretary of Air Talbott and other officers. After the presentations, which must have been all done in one day, Talbott called Skidmore in and told him we had the job. I believe it happened that fast. After that, Talbott offered Skid a ride back to New York because Talbott lived in New York and was flying up in his plane. The reason I tell this is because, during the flight, Talbott said that there were two people who really influenced his decision in selecting us. He said it wasn't necessarily the presentation. He said to Skid, "Can you guess who they are?" Skid said, "I can guess one easily; it was Mrs. Talbott, because our firm did the New York Infirmary, a building for which she was the chairman of the board." Talbott said, "That's one that influenced me."

"The other one," he said, "was Frazar Wilde." Wilde was the head of Connecticut General when we did it. During the time when we were doing it, there was a great deal of talk about bombproof shelters for the future atomic world. Frazar asked us to do a study to see if we should provide bombproof shelters for his 2,000 people. After a careful study and research, we recommended against doing anything, because the instinct of most people would be to get home to their wife and children. Unbeknownst to us, Frazar checked with his old friend Talbott, the Secretary of Air, who ought to really be in the know. Talbott, I think, told him he thought SOM was right. But in the course of that conversation—this is Talbott telling it to Skidmore—he said that he was having a wonderful time and he had some

110. Gordon Bunshaft (center, with arm in the air) at a design meeting at the Academy in 1956. Photograph from *40, A Pictorial History of the Firm and Partners of SOM.* Among those pictured are (from left): Nathaniel Owings (in tweed jacket in foreground), L. W. Robert, Jr., Secretary of the Air Force Donald Quarles, General Hubert Harmon, Pietro Belluschi, Welton Becket, John Ferry, and Walter Netsch, the latter on crutches after he had broken his leg in a fall from a building the previous evening. SOM Archives, Chicago.

wonderful architects doing this great building for him. Talbott respected Frazar's judgment—in fact, many people respect Frazar's judgment because he's such a strong, honest, and bright person. That's why we got the Air Force Academy.

In starting this job, which was back in the early stages of SOM or relatively early, maybe the midpoint, SOM meant one firm nationally. The team that went to work on that job consisted of Nat and Skid as kind of supreme dealers at very high levels, John Merrill as the working administrative partner on the job, and myself as the overall old master designer overlooking and guiding, as best I could, the young Walter Netsch—I don't know whether he was a partner or not at the time—because the job was going to be based in Chicago. My impression is, and I may be wrong, Owings at that time was on the West Coast. Skid, of course, was in New York. Bill Hartmann was to look in every once in a while, but he used to attend major meetings and that's about all. That was essentially our team; in other words, five partners from all offices. It was a major project for the firm.

We had won out over the best architects that were around. Secretary Talbott, to protect himself from our influence, or to get professional advice other than ours, appointed an architectural advisory committee to report to the Secretary before he made a decision. It was a good idea. That committee changed a little bit from time to time, but the original one was Wally Harrison, Eero Saarinen, I think Pietro Belluschi, and Becket. I think Becket was a political appointment.

The first joint meeting to view the site and to set off the project was a huge gathering in Colorado Springs at the famous hotel there, the Broadmoor. It was quite a trip, with all the consulting architects, some of the Air Force, Secretary of Air, and all us partners from SOM. We all got into buses to view the site, which is fifteen thousand acres. One side of it was bounded by the main highway from Denver to

Colorado Springs, and the other long side of the project was defined by the prominent foothills of the Rockies. Those were the east and west sides. The north and south sides were guarded by an arbitrary line coming from the top of a knoll. There were five knolls that came out of the Rocky Mountains and in between them were four or five valleys. They had taken a little beyond the brow of two knolls, and that created the fifteen thousand acres. There were to be no airstrips or anything like that. This was to be a school, an academy for the training of officers, not pilots. We got into the buses with the Secretary and Harmon, especially, who was evidently a famous general whose brother was a famous football player, I think, at West Point, and we went to see one of these valleys that was sort of in the middle of the site that Secretary Talbott thought was the proper place for the project to be.

In the bus, Walter and I were talking with Eero Saarinen. Saarinen had really done some work when he was trying to get the job. He knew the site. He said it should be up on one of the top knolls towards the north. He said, "I've been there and it's a fabulous site." He thought we should get one of these buses and take a look at it. So when we arrived at Secretary Talbott's ravine, which was at an elevation of about 6,800 feet above sea level, we asked if we could take a bus and go see one of the other sites that Eero had seen. The Secretary said, "Do as you please." But Harmon smelled a rat, so he came along with us. We drove up to the site, and I must say you can't see much in wooded land of that size but we could see this knoll. It was beautiful. The view was unbelievable. Harmon said, "It can't be up here." He said, "This is two or three hundred feet higher than the ravine and the older people won't be able to stand it." Of course that was silly. If you could stand 6,800 you could stand 7,200. But we listened. Then the rest came straggling up there, including the Secretary.

We all went back to the hotel to have a cocktail party out on the big terrace. I will always remember Skidmore running up to me and saying, "We've got a problem." I said, "What is it?" and he said, "Harmon thinks this should be done in Spanish Colonial." He said, "I think we'll have to do it," and I said, "Like hell we will!"

So that's how it started. The next day, the Secretary let us all fly in helicopters. Some of us wanted to go in helicopters over the site, and that confirmed Eero's site location. We all had a free ride on that, and then we individually were taken on a jet flight. This was an early time for a supersonic, sort of trainer-fighter plane. We flew the site map, and that took about one-half second.

We were getting into serious final design of the basic concept. Until then I hadn't been in Chicago much. Walter had set up a team and was working his head off. In fact, I missed the first meeting where he presented an overall master plan, which Saarinen threw out, as well he should have. At that point, Nat thought I had better get out to Chicago, and Nina and I moved out there and stayed three or four months and worked on a basic placing of the major buildings. There was housing for the officers, their eating facilities, the school building, the Chapel, athletic facilities, then a commons building for visitors to meet the cadets, a library, etc., and access roads to this acropolis. That is what it really was, an acropolis.

At that time, Walter and I worked very well together, and the scheme which was developed I sort of sketched out and he developed. He came up with a beautiful idea of a stepping down the hill with the housing. It really was a six-story building; on the ground level of the high part, you looked right through the building. That acted as a walkway and garden for the upper three floors and was the roof of the lower three floors. It was a very nice scheme, and it was Walter's. That went over all right until we got around to the location of the Chapel.

Chapel requirements for the military world mean there are usually three separate buildings, as a rule; one for the Protestants, one for the Catholics, and one for the rest, which meant Jews and miscellaneous. I remembered that in the Church of St. Francis of Assisi, the upper church, you come in from the main approach and it is a very big church, very handsome, and down below is another church, sort of crypt-like, which is perhaps the most religious space I have ever been in. It has very low vaults with huge candles at the altar. I think it had marvelous frescoes. I got the idea for the Chapel of doing just that. It worked out well because the Protestant portion in an academy of 2,500 is about 1,200; about 600 are Catholics; then there is usually a chapel of one hundred or so for other faiths that can be adjusted. I guess there must be some that don't go. So we came up with this scheme that I have described. The appearance of the project and the structural concept of tetrahedrons, a favorite word of Walter's, were all Walter's. The basic idea of two levels, I guess, you might say was mine, or you might say, the architect who did St. Francis of Assisi. The military for a while had a problem, because the three chaplains of the three services weren't easy to convince to go into one building, especially where the Catholics would be below the Protestants! But,

I must say that they all were big enough, and that is the way it went ahead, with their blessings. It was a grand opportunity to do a grand project.

To give you an idea of how intense one can get about architecture, at one meeting in Chicago where Saarinen and all the others were there, and this latest Secretary of Air, Quarles, a very nice man, we presented the Chapel where we felt it should be. Everything else had been set. Saarinen disagreed. We had it partway up a smaller knoll within the project, and he thought it ought to be at the top. We didn't agree with that at all. This is not a little chapel you stroll up to; the men marched to chapel six abreast, which is not exactly a small, little clubby affair. We got so stubborn about not moving that chapel; Saarinen said it had to be moved; he insisted on it. But we excused ourselves, and Nat and I and all the others, and Walter, went and talked of quitting the job because we couldn't have our way. That was easy for me to do and for Walter to do, but, as I recall, even Nat wanted to do it. But we cooled off and came back and said we would explore Saarinen's idea and further explore ours for the next meeting. After some fussing, it became obvious that Eero was wrong in his location, and we were wrong in our location. Where we proposed putting it after study was the right place. When we showed it to the Secretary and Saarinen, they agreed, which showed that if you carry stubbornness too far, you can get into trouble. I like that story because it shows that both of us were so positive we were right and we were 100 percent wrong. I don't think we were wrong when we jointly agreed it was now in the right place.

The whole story of the Air Force Academy and its headaches of building can best be left to Walter, Nat, and John Merrill, of course, who was through it all in his quiet way, but who is dead, so he can't help. Bill Hartmann was involved in a superficial way. Of course, the man who was heavily involved was Gross Sampsell trying to collect money, which he eventually did. That is all I can honestly say about the Air Force Academy that has any semblance of correctness.

Interview with Lieutenant General Bradley Hosmer

General Hosmer (USAFA 1959) was in the first group of students to study at the new Air Force Academy campus at Colorado Springs in 1958 (fig 111). Later, he gained an entirely different perspective on the place when he returned as Superintendent, a position he held from 1991 through 1994. In August 1993 Academy architect Duane Boyle asked him about his impressions of the Academy as a cadet and as Superintendent.

Duane Boyle: Why did you want to go to the Air Force Academy?

General Hosmer: I guess a spirit of adventure is the best single answer. I had appointments to all three academies, and I could have chosen. My dad was a West Point graduate. I tried to get into West Point at one point but I was too young. You had to be 17 and I wasn't. That fell by the wayside, so I had a year to spend, and during that year the Air Force Academy was announced. So I competed like the devil to get into the Air Force Academy and was successful. The spirit of adventure was very high about aviation and the Air Force at that time. My dad [Clark Hosmer, West Point, 1936] was in the Air Force; I knew enough about it to know that it was worth a try. And I had kind of an active faith that, like West Point and Annapolis, the Air Force Academy would offer a very strong education.

Boyle: Did you ever think about going to another university other than a military academy?

Hosmer: I couldn't afford it. I could go to any school that I could afford, so I spent that year in between earning money just in case, but it was pretty obvious that if I wanted to graduate in four years an academy was the best bet.

Boyle: When did you actually first see the Air Force Academy?

Hosmer: Ah—that's a very good question. During the summer of '57, we were at Lowry [Lowry AFB, Denver], of course. I would often come down to the site, usually with a friend, as a weekend drive, an outing. Usually on weekends the site was deserted. You could just ramble around. So I saw the building foundations go up, and I saw the roof of Mitchell Hall. I didn't know what it was the first time I saw it. There was this big Tinkertoy structure of girders lying on ground. I saw the Academy in stages of developing but I didn't see the site in its finished form or any of the buildings finished until the famous hike in from North Gate. I'd been in Second Beast [BCT or Basic Cadet Training] cadre [the upper classmen responsible for the training]. We had come out of the field at Buckley [Buckley Air National Guard, Denver, used for training due to lack of space at Lowry]. We'd been out there 10 days or so, tired, whipped like dogs because in those days one cadre worked everything. We were the field instructors, the day- and nighttime trainers, the cadre command structure, everything. And I was a flight commander so I was doing that during the day and I was doing night E and E [Escape and Evasion] instruction at night. So we were all tired. Had a long hike with the packs to the get to the buses and nobody had told us that we weren't going to bus all the way back to the area. So we got out on the buses thinking, ah, the next stop is my room; somebody will have offloaded the gear that I left up at Lowry somewhere around my squadron area and we'll figure out where that is when we get there, and we all just sort of relaxed, my basic cadets and a couple of my elements leaders and me. So were heading down the old road from Denver to Colorado Springs and at one point, we think we're getting close to the area, the buses stop. And we figure, well they're waiting for the right time or something. Then an officer comes along and sticks his head in the bus and says, "Fall out." What do you mean fall out? "Fall out. You're going to march." We were somewhat upset, but we fell out, formed up, and the entire BCT marched in from the roadside through the North Gate up to the Academy. So the first time I physically laid my eyes on finished buildings was coming up what is now Parade Loop, having walked up from the North Gate, dog-tired, marching fast with my head high because I was in command of my troops, and not very pleased about the whole situation.

111. Bradley Hosmer, Class of 1959, with other Cadets at temporary Air Force Academy, Lowry AFB, Denver, c. 1957. Photograph taken for *Look* Magazine.

Boyle: I don't imagine so.

Hosmer: So I didn't probably appreciate the beauty as fully as I would have later and did later, but that's when I first saw it.

Boyle: You went up Parade Loop to the parade field and up on the south side of the parade field up by Fairchild then?

Hosmer: That's how I recall it. Came up the parade ground, up the Battle Ramp, up what is now the Bring Me Men Ramp, up onto the terrazzo. Halted in front of Vandenberg Hall.

Boyle: Were you impressed by the scale of everything at that time?

Hosmer: Yes, I was because I had not seen it with the terrazzo in. When I saw it earlier it was still rolling terrain, not flattened, construction debris around, very difficult to appreciate how the clean openness will grow out of that. So, yes, the scale was striking, especially after having spent three years at Lowry which is postage stamp by comparison. You could get the whole Lowry complex into the grass area in the terrazzo.

Boyle: When you first got here what were your first impressions?

Hosmer: Golly. They flood in. Size of the dormitory. Remember now, the whole Cadet Wing was under a thousand, so we were swallowed in Vandenberg Hall. Just the volume of space available for use was extremely impressive, especially after three years at Lowry. The second was the quality of the construction. I didn't have much of an eye for the quality at that time, but the way in which the whole complex had been finished didn't look new; it looked polished and cared for. Most new construction has so many rough edges. This didn't have any rough edges at all. There was still a lot of construction debris around but it was focused on the southwest corner and what soon became the foundation for the Chapel, which started during that year. And there was a lot of finishing work going on.

Boyle: What did you think of the rest of the base like the community center, hospital, those areas?

Hosmer: It's difficult to appreciate now but in those days no one had cars, therefore I didn't know anything about the rest of the base. We could not get cars until Easter of our senior year, our first class year. I actually bought an old car in San Antonio over Christmas and drove it back and kept it in Colorado Springs, where I worked on it. Didn't get to use it. I spent much of the time before graduation painting it. It was an old used Jag. But we could get in town on buses. They went straight down Stadium Boulevard and into town. Graduation week I think I was driving around and had a little time and I needed to go to the BX [Base Exchange]. That was the first time I ever went to the BX. So cadets didn't really appreciate the community center, the service area, the housing areas. I learned all about those two years ago when I came back to the Academy.

Boyle: Had you seen Annapolis? You obviously saw West Point before. How did you think what was here compared to those two?

Hosmer: Oh, I thought it was wonderful. An early saying that we thought we invented, but of course we didn't, was that the Army and West Point represented two hundred years of tradition untrammeled by progress. I've quoted it wrong but that was the gist of it. That really captured the sense that we had. I think my classmates and I had the sense that we were doing something new and different, unencumbered by tradition, unencumbered by old baggage, and that West Point and Annapolis represented the worst of all that. Of course we knew they had strengths too, but the extent to which they had fixed answers on how things should be done was something that we felt we didn't have to live with. We could figure out how to do things for the first time, because everything we did was for the first time. And that spirit of adventure was very strong.

Boyle: And was that reflected in the architecture?

Hosmer: Oh, very much. The architecture was absolutely consistent with our sense of what was core about the Air Force Academy.

Boyle: Does it work as well today as it did back then?

Hosmer: I think it works as well today. There were a lot of naysayers then and still are; some of my generation noted the modern-motel aspect of this architecture. Many similar buildings were put up about that time, not very good ones. I think that's given this style a bad reputation. Many people associate this style with a cheap mass-produced artifact. I think that impression's on the wane and in another decade it's going to be gone. Because most of that lousy stuff, the '50's and early '60's, has fallen of its own weight, and the quality construction remains. I think the enduring virtue of this architecture is really going to dawn on us in the next couple of decades. Especially if the Air Force is able to keep it in the condition that it deserves.

Boyle: What about some of the other cadets? Did they share your enthusiasm for it? What was the general feeling there?

Hosmer: I don't recall more than the most minor kind of critical comments. Maybe some good-natured typical cadet cynicism about it looks like a Howard Johnson motel, none of which was serious at all. I think most cadets appreciated the quality of the place that we'd been given to live in. I mean the wood paneling in the cadet dorms, obviously brand new at that time, was simply gorgeous. Of course, there were no carpets on the floor. We organized details to keep the place clean, and buffed. After Lowry, I think the average cadet felt that maybe some of that publicity about what a terrific group we were might be credible when you looked at the place they'd given us to live in. It tended to produce kind of big head on the part of the average cadet.

Boyle: How about the landscape? What did you think of that?

Hosmer: I can't say I was really sensitive to it, Duane. It was part of the whole picture. Today I would look at it and I would pick out things about the landscape because I just appreciate more about landscape. At that time it just seemed well integrated. I didn't notice things like deciduous versus fir or other evergreen. We did notice that the Academy command structure put an awful lot of effort into getting grass to grow around the roads. Sod was laid and it died. Sod was laid again and it died again, and we joked a lot about that. But aside from little events of that sort, I think the landscape was simply part of the bigger picture. There's something else important to realize here. Most of us never saw the original site in its raw form. Or if we did, we were not really focused on remembering or comparing. So the enormous amount of landscape work that took place here to shape the location and to control the drainage, and to put the roads in right, of all that we had no appreciation at all because we had no sense of what it was like before. Looking at the differences now I can appreciate what a huge amount of dirt got pushed around and put in the right place. But I didn't see it then.

Boyle: Were there any particular spaces here that you really liked, maybe to get away after classes were over?

Hosmer: Let's see. Cathedral Rock was a favorite hike. On the hill the library was terrific. Now remember we didn't have the recent addition, the insert between the two parts of Fairchild. But even without that, the library was, for the size of the Cadet Wing then, cavernous. It was huge. You could always find a quiet private corner to work in the library. There were spaces over in Fairchild Hall where one could set up shop, so to speak, depending on what you wanted to do. In those days we had a lot of clubs that were really designed around providing some authorization or authentication for one or another kind of activity. A couple of classmates put me up to sponsoring an engineering club my second class year, and I had a classmate who needed to rebuild an engine. He'd blown an engine out of a little Italian sports car that he had. So the engineering club "authorized" his use of a space. Actually he found it, down in the parking-garage level of Fairchild. I used to go over there at night. It was an official project to help rebuild his engine. Little things like that were going on all over the place. Arnold Hall was a favorite place. Remember again, there were no cars. There was a very active Cadet Wing hostess program at that time. So we spent a lot of time in Arnold Hall. Mostly dances, informal parties, gathering and yakking. Of course, there was no sports bar at that time. Alcohol was absolutely forbidden. Late that year we started drifting off more and more. We found ways into town somewhere after Christmas vacation. But during the fall semester we were really settling in and coming to know the place and we spent a lot of time in Arnold Hall.

Boyle: What kind of things did you do to make your environment more personal? I hear stories that you could only have one picture and a stereo or a record player.

Hosmer: That's right. You could have a record player—stereos didn't exist in those days. Rooms didn't get personalized. As a first classman, there were some variations, a picture and so on. It's really what you do with your books as much as anything to personalize it.

Boyle: How did you feel about the furniture that was in there?

Hosmer: It seemed suitable. It seemed good. Of course it was different than now. To me, for some reason, the furniture today makes the room seem more crowded. You've got the upper tier of the bed. We didn't have that. We had a low bed so visually you could sweep the room and you'd get the full room dimension at eye level. The floor space must have been more crowded then because you didn't have the double tiering of the bed and desk. But for some reason the room seemed more open.

Boyle: You may not want this in the book, but were there any kind of elements that made spirit missions [cadet activities that aren't supposed to happen but do] especially possible.

Hosmer: Oh, the tunnels. The tunnels. I'm not a good one to ask that question of because, of course, I was a firstie when we came down here. And most of us were fairly serious about being the guys who were supposed to be running the Wing. Which means that I was on the heavy side of what we now call spirit missions, and I was more interested in how you keep cadets out of the tunnels than how you get into them.

Boyle: That probably wasn't an easy job.

Hosmer: No, it was impossible. You couldn't keep cadets out of the tunnels.

Boyle: And the X-4 kept moving around.

Hosmer: Oh, yes. We started that up at Lowry. We moved everything. After I left, there was at least one case where the X-4 got moved away and it took the engineers and a crane to get it back.

Boyle: But the cadets got it without a crane?

Hosmer: Oh yeah, a lot of muscle. We had an F-86, a straight-wing F-84, a bent-wing F-84F, the X-4 , and at least one other at Lowry that we moved around. The F-100 went on a cement pedestal right from the outset so we never could push it.

Boyle: What did you think of the colors? There's always been a controversy about the red colors and the yellow colors and the blue colors.

Hosmer: We simply understood those to be class colors. They were representing our classes. And although that may be kind of a display of vanity on the part of cadets at that time, they seemed to us to be perfectly appropriate.

Boyle: The other things I wanted to talk about were the fountains. What did you think about them back then, and what do you think about the fact that we don't have them now?

Hosmer: I was very positive about the fountains. I liked them. Cadet squadron commanders worried about high spirits resulting in cadets getting pitched into the fountains. I worried about them bonking their head on the bottom or the side, getting hurt a little. But not much of that happened, in fact. Then I worried a little about the cadets doing that in the middle of winter and getting a bad chill. That didn't happen very much either. The practical aspects about leaks weren't really manifest during the time we were still here, not that I know of. The only physical problem here was the wind. And, of course, in those days we didn't have the shields around the doors. We lost a lot of doors, lost a lot of windows, lost a lot of hats on the lights.

Boyle: How much did you understand about how comprehensive the design was, that the same people who designed the furniture also designed the salt and pepper shakers?

Hosmer: I had no appreciation of that at all. I know periodically I would see something on a big scale that told me, oh, it's all one piece. For example, I remember the first time I saw the power plant. I thought, you know, wow, it's really part of the Academy. I had the same impression the first time I saw the Officer's Club, and then the Community Center. As my knowledge rippled out slowly across that year, I gradually became aware that the whole thing was an integrated design.

Boyle: I've been in meetings with you where you've talked a little bit about people versus objects. How do you feel about that?

Hosmer: I guess I'd say this. There is a natural tension in an air force between technology and people. Since so much of what drives the strength and the combat advantage of an air force depends on technology and equipment, that's our capital leverage, you might say. We tend to draw people who are intrigued by and adept at that. Unfortunately, while that is appropriate because it is air force specific, that orientation omits something which is as fundamental for an air force as it is for all forms of military, and that is the human component, the tightness and strength of units, the kind of leadership that develops that tightness and strength regardless of circumstances, stress, combat. In the end, for any form of military service, it is the leadership and the human component that determines who wins, how effective you are in combat. The technical aspect has a very heavy role, but while it is necessary, it is not sufficient. The human element is also necessary. Well, our mythologies, our focus, our language and our memorials tend to celebrate the technology and omit the human element. And those people who come to us because of their attraction for the power of leadership in the human element in the military miss it around Air Force installations because it is not advertised. This had led me to conclude that we need to reorient a bit how we display ourselves at the Air Force Academy and find better ways to focus also on the leadership component, not just the technical component.

"BRING ME